LOCAL COURT, PROVINCIAL SOCIETY AND JUSTICE IN THE OTTOMAN EMPIRE

STUDIES IN ISLAMIC LAW AND SOCIETY

EDITED BY

RUUD PETERS AND BERNARD WEISS

VOLUME 17

LOCAL COURT, PROVINCIAL SOCIETY AND JUSTICE IN THE OTTOMAN EMPIRE

Legal Practice and Dispute Resolution in Çankırı and Kastamonu (1652-1744)

BY

BOĞAÇ A. ERGENE

BRILL
LEIDEN · BOSTON
2003

This book is printed on acid-free paper.

Library of Congress Cataloging-in-Publication Data

Ergene, Boğaç A., 1971-
Local court, provincial society and justice in the Ottoman Empire : legal practice and dispute resolution in Çankırı and Kastamonu (1652-1744) / by Boğaç A. Ergene.
p. cm. — (Studies in Islamic law and society, ISSN 1384–1130; v. 17)
Includes bibliographical references and index.
ISBN 90-04-12609-0
1. Justice, Administration of—Turkey—History—17th century. 2. Justice, Administration of—Turkey—History—18th century. 3. Turkey—History—Ottoman Empire, 1288-1918. I. Title. II Series.

KKX283.E74 2003
347.561--dc21 2002043736

Die Deutsche Bibliothek - CIP-Einheitsaufnahme

Ergene, Boğaç A.:
Local court, provincial society and justice in the Ottoman Empire : legal practice and dispute resolution in Çankırı and Kastamonu (1652-1744) / by Boğaç A. Ergene – Leiden ; Boston
Brill, 2003
(Studies in Islamic law and society ; Vol. 17)
ISBN 90-04-12609-0

ISSN 1384–1130
ISBN 90 04 12609 0

PRINTED IN THE NETHERLANDS

To my parents, Yüksel and Cemil Ergene,
and my sister, Simay Ergene-Civelek

CONTENTS

LIST OF TABLES

LIST OF FIGURES

LIST OF MAPS

ACKNOWLEDGEMENTS

I would like to thank my mentor and friend, Carter V. Findley, for his intellectual support, encouragement, and enthusiasm, which made this book possible. Jane Hathaway, Margaret Mills, Ruud Peters, David Powers, and Sean Stilwell all read earlier versions of the manuscript and provided their much appreciated insights. Atabey Kaygun not only helped me prepare the maps in this book, but also offered his friendship in the process. I also owe gratitude to Elizabeth Lindsmith, who edited the manuscript and transformed it into readable English.

Brill Academic Publishers has invested a significant amount of time and effort in the publishing of this book. I would like to thank the production staff, and especially Trudy Kamperveen, for their assistance at various stages of production.

Finally, I would like to express my deepest love and gratitude to Febe Armanios. She proved that the distance that separated us in the last couple of years was not enough to keep her from being with me in every stage of the project. Without her emotional support and intellectual companionship, it would have been very difficult to write this book.

CHAPTER ONE

INTRODUCTION

This book studies the practice of law in Ottoman Anatolia during the late seventeenth and early eighteenth centuries. In particular, it focuses on the judicial operations of local Islamic courts (*mahkemes*) and the processes of dispute resolution as recorded in the court registers (*sicils*) of two northern Anatolian sub-provinces (*sancaks*), Çankırı and Kastamonu. It does not seek to explore the local histories of these two provincial centers or how people lived and died there, although this study does have much to do with such issues. Instead, it aims to examine the relationship between the courts and the people of these localities, and to understand the place of Islamic courts in Ottoman provincial life.

We have a great deal to learn about how provincial courts functioned in the Ottoman Empire. Although it is well established that these courts had important administrative and judicial responsibilities and constituted a crucial link between their localities and the central and provincial governments, we are not really sure how they dispensed justice and resolved disputes. Our ignorance of such issues is partly related to the fact that Ottoman history is a relatively young field, which is why a number of important topics have yet to receive adequate scholarly attention. Indeed, despite the abundance of judicial sources in our possession, the number of Ottomanists who specialize in judicial practice is still very limited.

Our ignorance is also partly a consequence of the state-centric character of the Ottoman studies. Although exceptions do exist, Ottomanists have been thus far more interested in examining state-society relations and the ability of the Ottoman imperial government to influence the social, economic, and political order in the provinces than, for example, investigating communal dynamics and institutions as relatively autonomous entities. Ironically, this tendency is particularly explicit in those studies, which surmise much about the place and the functions of the local courts in Ottoman Anatolia.[1] This is

[1] The most recent examples of this approach include, Huri İslamoğlu-İnan, *State and*

presumably because, in comparison to the Arab provinces of the empire, which were located far from the center, and to the Balkans, where a substantial portion of the population was non-Turkish and non-Muslim and, therefore, supposed to have enjoyed a significant degree of internal autonomy, Anatolia has been perceived as the Ottoman heartland where the state was in full control of the provincial affairs. I do not wish to challenge this perception here: It is undeniable that the Ottoman state was able to influence the provincial society and politics in Anatolia with relative ease even during the seventeenth and eighteenth centuries. Nonetheless, it is also unfortunate that this perception determines how and why local courts are examined by Ottomanists. Arguably, the preoccupation with Anatolian courts in many recent studies is related to the interest in documenting how the Ottoman state kept the countryside under control and how it legitimized its domination over the provinces. In other words, local courts seem to attract attention primarily because they are considered instrumental to the effectiveness of the Ottoman state in those locations far from the center.

The tendency to focus on state and its interaction with provincial society and then explore the courts from this perspective disregards the realm in which courts and the society interacted with relative independence from external forces. This may be why, in addition to the "underdeveloped" character of Ottoman legal history, many important issues that relate to this interaction have not been sufficiently explored. For example, it is not clear how local communities in Anatolia perceived their courts and their operations, or what the courts did in order to gain local support. It is often assumed that since the courts represented the holy law and the authority of the sultan, local communities acknowledged their authority,[2] though, as we will see later on, the relationship between the courts and their communities was not so unilateral.

Peasant in the Ottoman Empire: Agrarian Power Relations and Regional Economic Development in Ottoman Anatolia during the Sixteenth Century (Leiden; New York: E.J. Brill, 1994); Karen Barkey, *Bandits and Bureaucrats: the Ottoman Route to State Centralization* (Ithaca, N.Y.: Cornell University Press, 1994); Haim Gerber, *State, Society and Law in Islam* (Albany: State University of New York Press, 1994); and idem, *Islamic Law and Culture 1600–1840* (Leiden: E.J. Brill, 1999).

[2] Ronald C. Jennings, "*Kadı*, Court, and Legal Procedure in 17th C. Ottoman Kayseri," *Studia Islamica*, vol. 48 (1978), pp. 133–172; idem, "Limitations of the Judicial Powers of Qadi in 17th C. Ottoman Kayseri," *Studia Islamica*, vol. 50 (1979), pp. 151–184.

Likewise, we do not know how local courts shaped the balance of power among different social groups and classes, or how they reflected this balance in their decisions and operations. We need to take into consideration the fact that provincial courts were a part of the sociopolitical environment in which they operated; they not only influenced the local dynamics but were also influenced by them. One of my objectives in this book is to acknowledge this historical and context-based character of the courts and their operations, which is lacking in the literature. This lack is responsible for major interpretative shortfalls observed in some of the most recent contributions to the field. For example, scholars like Karen Barkey, Huri İslamoğlu-İnan, and Haim Gerber all seem to share the idea that one reason for the absence of major political and ideological challenges to the Ottoman center before the nineteenth century was the ability of the provincial courts to administer justice with relative fairness. According to these historians, the ability of the courts in Anatolia to correct the wrongs committed by the military-administrative officials must have contributed to the legitimacy of the Ottoman government. The main problem with this position is that it is a logical deduction and not a historical observation, and it will remain so until these historians accomplish the difficult tasks of not only demonstrating that the courts in Anatolia satisfied most of their clients by dispensing justice fairly, but also of proving that this satisfaction generated a continuous popular support for the regime. I will return to this topic later on.

At a different level, by not taking the local courts and their operations as the primary foci of analysis, the literature disregards individual litigants as legitimate topics of historical investigation. We do not know much about the issues that these people brought to local courts, the ways in which they presented their cases, and the judicial strategies that they employed against their opponents. This lack of attention on processes of litigation and dispute resolution denies us the chance to learn about the litigants' perceptions of the world in which they lived, the limits of their historical agency, the bases of their social mindset, as well as the nature of their political and legal consciousness. It is in the local courts that neighborhood relationships were negotiated, and it is only by studying the court processes that we can understand what it meant to be a part of the provincial society.

In this book I will focus my attention on local courts, their operations in their jurisdictions, and the ways provincial peoples used their services. In this context, my primary source of information will be the court records of Çankırı and Kastamonu from seventeenth and eighteenth centuries. This choice is not coincidental: As we know, seventeenth and eighteenth centuries constitute probably the least studied and one of the most controversial episodes of Ottoman history. What's more, our knowledge of Ottoman Anatolia in general, and Çankırı and Kastamonu—two provincial centers in northern Anatolia—in particular, is very limited in comparison to what we know about, for example, Arabic-speaking provinces of the empire. Although this book seeks to be first and foremost a contribution to Ottoman legal history, by studying the seventeenth- and eighteenth-century court records of Çankırı and Kastamonu, which contain a great number and variety of documents from all realms of life, I am also hoping to fill a void in the social, political, and economic history of Ottoman Anatolia.

It is impossible to exaggerate the importance of the court records for legal history: In addition to their widely recognized value for Ottoman social and economic history, these documents are particularly important for legal history since they supply rich and colorful information about the practice of Islamic law. Fortunately, the historical value of the court records has been recently recognized in the field; the number of monographs that benefit from these documents has been increasing since 1980s. Yet, the widespread recognition of the court records' value does not mean their potential has been fully explored. This fact is especially obvious in the few contributions made to Ottoman legal history, where much of the claims are based on selective evaluations of these documents. More often than not, individual cases and isolated examples are used to formulate broad assertions or to prove (or disprove) general conclusions.

There is nothing wrong with examining individual cases in detail and developing scholarly judgments based on a relatively few number of case studies. In fact, this form of inquiry has produced some of the most enlightening contributions by students of legal anthropology on dispute resolution in other societies.[3] Nevertheless, the Ottoman court records can offer us substantially more. Although

[3] Although, of course, the information available to anthropologists in their case studies is much greater than the information that we find in the individual accounts of the cases recorded in the court registers.

these documents present little information about individual cases, analyzing a large number of them as a whole allows trends to emerge that may not be too apparent in isolated examples.

I aim to utilize both "case-study-based" and "holistic" approaches in different chapters of this book. After a discussion in chapter two about the historical setting, chapters three, four, and five will provide a "macro-analysis" of the court records by focusing on those rhythms, movements, and generalities that become evident through quantification and statistical examination. Chapter three will examine the judicial and administrative operations of the courts of Çankırı and Kastamonu and will demonstrate that the functions and responsibilities of these two courts were quite different from each other. Chapter four will focus on the kinds of disputes that the inhabitants of Çankırı and Kastamonu brought to the courts and the ways in which such disputes were resolved. In this chapter I will also investigate the social and economic backgrounds of the disputants and see whether any correlation existed between the litigants' class affiliations and the results of the litigations that they were involved in. Finally, chapter five will study the monetary costs of court usage. Although thus far unexplored, this is an important issue since expenses for litigation and other court services must have had a significant impact on the ways in which local communities utilized their courts.

In chapters six, seven, and eight, I will change my approach and engage in a more traditional "micro-analysis" of the processes of litigation and dispute resolution. Chapters six and eight will focus on the ways the inhabitants of Çankırı and Kastamonu presented their problems, engaged their opponents in the courts, and devised various judicial strategies to ensure favorable resolutions. Chapter six will study these issues with some reference to the contemporary accounts of the Western observers of Ottoman justice; chapter eight will explore the court records in more detail. We will see in these two chapters that Western travelers to the Ottoman Empire portray the operations of the Ottoman courts very differently from how these processes are characterized in the court records. As will be demonstrated in chapter seven, this discrepancy illustrates both the limits and the shortfalls of the court records as sources of Ottoman legal history. I will argue in chapter seven that despite their great historical value, court records also restrict our ability to recognize certain aspects of the court process, and that is why we need alternative sources to complement our understanding of the Ottoman courts and their operations.

The next two chapters—nine and ten—will take us beyond courtrooms and processes of litigation. Chapter nine will shift our focus from the court to "alternative sites of dispute resolution," which existed independently of the provincial courts. My research has demonstrated that the inhabitants of Çankırı and Kastamonu had official and unofficial alternatives to provincial courts and did not hesitate to resolve specific kinds of disputes in these arenas. Finally, chapter ten will interpret what we know about the Ottoman courts and how they operated in light of the information available in the ethnographic and anthropological literature on conflict management. With the help of these ethnographic and anthropological contributions, I will attempt to construct an analytical framework that may enable us to interpret what we know about Ottoman court processes in a comparative perspective.

In this introduction, it is not my intention to disclose the conclusions that will be furnished in subsequent chapters. Yet, it should be emphasized that this book will challenge the common assumption in the literature that the Ottoman provincial courts and the practice of law in the seventeenth- and eighteenth-century Anatolia provided secure avenues for the weak to stand against the abuse that they occasionally encountered. I will demonstrate that the operations of the courts reflected the socioeconomic divisions of the localities where they operated and ensured the communal domination over the individual. It is time for us to consider the possibility that the Ottoman courts might not have been as independent from political and socioeconomic currents as has generally been assumed thus far.

It would be difficult to describe the nature of transformation that my work has endured since the time since I initiated my research. On one level, the general theme of this project and my fascination with the process of dispute resolution have remained constant. On another level, however, I feel that the questions that I wanted to ask and find answers for have changed considerably in the course of time. Now, when I look at my initial "notes for contemplation," I find many interesting and even important issues that I have not mentioned in this study. Walter Benjamin suggests that forgetting is never innocent or without a reason. In my situation, the reason to shift attention from particular issues to others must have something to do with the kind of interaction that I have had with "my" sources. Now I realize that the nature of these sources or the ways in which information was presented in them made some of my initial questions irrelevant or unanswerable. On the other hand, I also feel that "forgetting," at least in this particular context, may not necessarily be regrettable since it is a symptom of a dialogue that we seek to establish with the sources during our research. Like every dialogue, our interaction with the sources induces a redefinition of the basic issues, accentuation of specific questions, and, therefore, a neglect of, if not indifference to, other topics. In this sense, it is through this dialogue that our sources have an opportunity to transform our frames of thought and contribute to our understanding of historical issues. And for this reason "forgetting" keeps us honest, as Florencia Mallon argues, and probably modest, too: It makes us realize that not all of our supposedly important thoughts and questions may have any relevance to the people who produced our sources.[4]

Sources

In this book, I study twenty-five volumes of court records (*sicils*), which contain a total of about five-thousand individual entries. Thirteen of these twenty-five volumes belong to the court of Çankırı, and the remaining twelve volumes are from the Kastamonu court. At the beginning of my research I was not planning to examine the court records of Kastamonu. However, after about six months of intensive research in the National Library (Milli Kütüphane) in Ankara and reading the first ten volumes of the Çankırı court records, I realized that it was impossible to study the processes of dispute resolution by using these documents only. As we will see in chapter three, the court records of Çankırı (at least the ones that were prepared during the late seventeenth and early eighteenth centuries) contain relatively few documents that relate to local disputes and contentions. For this reason I decided to incorporate the court records of a neighboring town, Kastamonu, which embody a much greater number of such documents.

The thirteen volumes of Çankırı studied in this book span the years between 1652 and 1744. These volumes, however, do not

[4] Florencia Mallon, "The Promise and Dilemma of Subaltern Studies: Perspectives from Latin American History," *American Historical Review*, no. 5, vol. 99 (1994), p. 1506.

provide a continuous series since there are significantly lengthy gaps within this ninety-year period (see table 3.1); the court registers for these intervals are missing. On the other hand, the Kastamonu volumes begin at a later date (1684) and constitute a continuous series until 1743.[5] For Kastamonu, there are thirty-nine registers that cover this period without interruption. The twelve registers I examine here are concentrated at the beginning and the end of the sixty-year period (four registers for the period between 1684 and 1694, two for 1703–1713, and six for 1735–1743; see table 3.2).

I also conducted research in the Prime Ministry Archive (*Baş Bakanlık Devlet Arşivi*) in Istanbul and in the Old Records Archive of the Title Deeds and Land Surveys Office (*Tapu Kadastro Müdürlüğü, Kuyud-u Kadime Arşivi*) in Ankara. During my research in the Prime Ministry Archive, I had the opportunity to examine three major document collections—the *Cevdet Adliye*, *Cevdet Zabtiye*, and *Cevdet Dahiliye* collections—to complement my understanding of the judicial practices and institutions of the Ottoman Empire. As will be evident in subsequent chapters, materials from these compilations provide an opportunity to evaluate whether the conclusions drawn from the Çankırı and Kastamonu court records may be applied to other localities in Anatolia and Rumelia. My research in the archive of the Title Deeds Office produced four fiscal surveys (*tahrir defterleri*) of Çankırı and Kastamonu for the sixteenth century. I used these surveys to make projections for the social, economic, and demographic conditions of Çankırı and Kastamonu in the seventeenth and eighteenth centuries.

Finally, I have also benefited from several Western accounts that were composed between sixteenth and eighteenth centuries. As indicated above, these accounts are interesting for the purposes of this book because they provide the kind of information about Ottoman courts and judicial practices that we do not generally find in court records or other archival documents.

[5] According to the way they are categorized and numbered in the National Library, the "first" volume of the Kastamonu court records belongs to a later period than the "third" volume (see table 3.2).

CHAPTER TWO

TWO SUB-PROVINCES, TWO TOWNS, TWO COURTS

This chapter has two basic objectives. The first is to provide historical information about Çankırı and Kastamonu, whose court records I am going to study in this book. This is not an easy task to accomplish. As in the case of many other provincial centers in Ottoman Anatolia, local histories of Çankırı and Kastamonu are yet to be written. Hence, this chapter will combine the information found in the limited number of (and sometimes seriously problematic) secondary sources with my own observations in the court records. Nevertheless, and despite my best efforts, the following account is still an approximation at best.

The second objective of the chapter is to introduce the reader to the courts of Çankırı and Kastamonu. In order to do this, I will attempt to identify the court officials to the extent that the court records permit, define their roles and functions, and delineate the ways they participated in and contributed to the judicial and administrative processes that were conducted in the court. In this context, the emphasis will be on the strong ties that existed between the court and the local people, through which, as will be argued in subsequent chapters, the community was able to influence judicial processes.

Çankırı and Kastamonu: Historical Background

If asked for information about Çankırı, someone from Turkey would probably be able to give few specific answers. The most knowledgeable of these people might guess the approximate location of this town—"somewhere to the north of Ankara." This information, although imprecise, is indeed correct; Çankırı is located in north central Anatolia, at the intersection of the Tatlı ("Sweet") and Acı ("Bitter") rivers. But even those who may have an idea about the geographical location of Çankırı would not be able to say much about, for example, the historical, geographical, economic, or sociopolitical characteristics of the town and its surroundings. And who

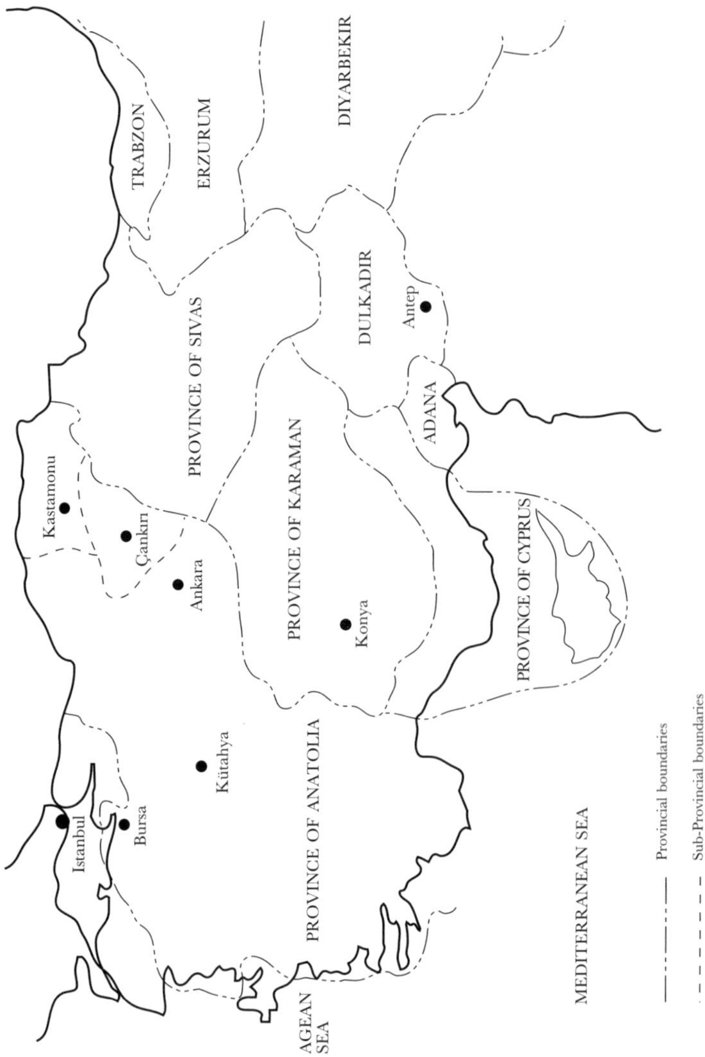

Map 2.1: Ottoman Anatolia in the Seventeenth Century: Administrative Divisions
Source: David E. Pitcher, *An Historical Geography of the Ottoman Empire* (Leiden: E.J. Brill, 1972), map 25.

can blame them? There are only a few specifics to be learned about the place: It is a small urban center (1990 population around 43,000) with no social, cultural, or economic characteristics of major interest. Indeed, the commentary on Çankırı constitutes one of the shortest articles in the *Yurt Ansiklopedisi* (Encyclopedia of the Homeland), which is devoted exclusively to providing information about the urban centers of modern Turkey and their environs.

Interest in the history and the socioeconomic characteristics of Kastamonu seems to be slightly greater. There are more books written about the history of Kastamonu, including one by a prominent Turkish historian.[1] There might be a number of reasons Kastamonu has been considered more worthy of study. This town was and still is a larger and more colorful urban center (1990 population around 52,000) that lies south of the densely populated Black Sea coastal plain. We learn from İsmail Hakkı Uzuncarşılı's work that at least until the 1930s, Kastamonu was also a relatively lively cultural and intellectual center.[2] The ports of İnebolu and Sinop on the Black Sea coast facilitated the development of moderately strong intellectual as well as economic ties with Istanbul. Furthermore, in recent years, the architectural characteristics of the town and its environs (especially Safranbolu) have, to a certain extent, stimulated a touristic and academic interest in Kastamonu.[3]

Nevertheless, it would still be difficult to argue that the average person in Turkey knows a great deal more about Kastamonu than Çankırı unless, of course, he or she happens to live there. This is sad, if not surprising, since the history of the region that contains Çankırı and Kastamonu is long and colorful. For example, we know that circa 6 BC ancient Çankırı, then known as Gangra, constituted the center of the Paphlagonian kingdom. The territories of Paphlagonia, which also included what is now Kastamonu, were later incorporated into the Roman province of Galatia.[4]

---

[1] İsmail Hakkı Uzunçarşılı, *Kastamonu Meşahiri* (Ankara: Kastamonu Eğitim Yüksekokulu Yayınları, 1990).

[2] Ibid.

[3] See Kenan Bilici, *Kastamonu'da Türk Devri Mimarisi ve Şehir Dokusunun Gelişimi (18. Yüzyıl Sonuna Kadar)*, Unpublished Ph.D. Dissertation, Ankara Üniversitesi, 1991; Kemal Kutgün Eyüpgiller, *Bir Kent Tarihi: Kastamonu* (Istanbul: Eren Yayınları, 1999).

[4] "Çankırı," *Yurt Ansiklopedisi*, vol. 3, pp. 1945–1948. Tayip Başer, *Dünkü ve Bugünkü Çankırı* (Ankara: İstiklal Matbaası, 1956), p. 7.

Mordtmann states that in antiquity Çankırı was a fortified place, occasionally used by the Byzantines as a place of exile.[5] The toponym of Kastamonu, however, remains obscure in its origins. Although it was situated on an important Roman route in north Anatolia and was regarded as an important city in Byzantine times, Colin Heywood insists that it was never mentioned in Roman or early Byzantine documents.[6] Later, during the seventh and eighth centuries, we find Çankırı and Kastamonu changing hands first between the Byzantines and the Persians, and then between the Byzantines and the Umayyads.[7] The region apparently remained under the domination of the Byzantine Empire between the late eighth and late eleventh centuries.[8]

Sources indicate that after the Byzantines were defeated near Malazgird (Manzikert) in 1071 by the Seljuks, the Danishmendids, a Turkic tribe moving in Anatolia during the eleventh century, began to spread over and control the northern half of Anatolia from Amasya to Kastamonu. According to Heywood, the Danishmendid forces captured Kastamonu around 1074.[9] Osman Turan and Mordtmann, however, contradict each other about exactly when this group took Çankırı. Whereas the latter states that they captured the region between 1075 and 1076, the former claims that a Danishmendid commander (Karatigin/Karatekin) conquered Çankırı sometime between 1082 and 1083.[10] Çankırı and Kastamonu were recaptured and briefly controlled by Byzantine forces between 1132 and 1134, and then again retaken by the Danishmendids. Subsequently, we find the region first in the hands of the Seljuks of Anatolia (after 1142) and then, during the thirteenth century, in the hands of another Turkish group, the Chandarlids.[11] It is not clear, however, when exactly the region was incorporated into the Ottoman Empire. The

---

[5] J.H. Mordtmann, "Çankırı," *Encyclopedia of Islam*, 2nd edition (from now on *EI*²), vol. 2, p. 13.

[6] Colin Heywood, "Kastamonu," *EI*², vol. 4, p. 737.

[7] Talat Mümtaz Yaman, *Kastamonu Tarihi I (XV inci Asrın Sonlarına Kadar)* (Kastamonu: Ahmed İhsan Matbaası Ltd., 1935), p. 44; Mordtmann, p. 13.

[8] Hacı Şeyhoğlu Ahmet Kemal, *Çankırı Tarihi* (Çankırı: Çankırı Vilayet Matbaası, 1930), passim; Başer, pp. 8–12; Yaman, pp. 43–44.

[9] Heywood, op. cit.

[10] Mordtmann, op. cit.; Osman Turan, *Selçuklular Zamanında Türkiye: Alp Arslan'dan Osman Gazi'ye (1071–1318)* (Istanbul: Turan Neşriyat Yurdu, 1971), p. 67 and passim.

[11] Mordtmann, op. cit.; "Çankırı," *Yurt Ansiklopedisi*, p. 1960; Yaşar Yücel, *XIII–XV. Yüzyıllar Kuzey-Batı Anadolu Tarihi; Çoban-Oğulları Çandar-Oğulları Beylikleri* (Ankara: Türk Tarih Kurumu, 1980), pp. 33–51.

sources indicate that the Ottomans initially began to control the region sometime between 1383 and 1398. The storm that Timur brought to Anatolia, however, is responsible for the reestablishment of Chandarlid control in the area for some time; then, Mehmed II reincorporated Çankırı into the Ottoman Empire in 1461 and Kastamonu in 1462 on his way to the conquest of Trabzon.[12]

In the fifteenth century, we find Çankırı and Kastamonu as two sub-provinces (*sancak*) in the province (*eyalet*) of Anatolia.[13] This situation continued until the nineteenth-century administrative reorganization of the Ottoman provincial structure. According to the court records, the sub-provinces of Çankırı and Kastamonu were assigned as *arpalıks*[14] in the seventeenth and early eighteenth centuries to members of the military with the ranks of *mirliva* and *mirmiran*. Although these individuals usually sent their agents (*mütesellim*: lieutenant governor) to administer and collect the revenues of the sub-province,[15] there is evidence that at least a number of them came to Çankırı and Kastamonu and personally administered the sub-provinces.[16]

The court records indicate a change in the status of the sub-province of Çankırı in 1730s. An order from Istanbul indicates that in 1731 Çankırı was assigned to Selim Paşa and, after him, to his son Seyyid Mehmed Gazi Beşe for their lifetimes (*ber vechi malikane*) in return for a fifteen-thousand *guruş* lump-sum and ten-thousand *guruş* yearly payments. Selim Paşa and his son were also required to attend military campaigns with their retinues.[17] We also have documentation

[12] Mordtmann, op. cit.; Heywood, op. cit.

[13] See Metin Kunt, *The Sultan's Servants; the Provincial Transformation of Ottoman Provincial Government, 1550–1650* (New York: Columbia University Press, 1983), chapter two for a brief description of the Ottoman provincial administration.

[14] Literally, "fodder money." Metin Kunt suggests that beginning from the early seventeenth century, *arpalıks* began to be assigned to the out-of-office governors-general (*beylerbeyis*) to keep them in funds while they waited for a province appointment befitting their rank; see Kunt, p. 87.

[15] Yaşar Yücel argues that these lieutenant governors were usually chosen from local families in the eighteenth century. According to my observations, however, they always came from outside the sub-province and were usually members of the governor's household. See Yaşar Yücel, "XVIII. Yüzyılda Mütesellimlik Müessesesi," *Ankara Üniversitesi Dil ve Tarih-Coğrafya Fakültesi Dergisi*, vol. XXVIII, nos. 3–4 (1970), pp. 369–85. Also see Musa Çadırcı, "II. Mahmut Döneminde Mütesellimlik Kurumu," *Ankara Üniversitesi Dil ve Tarih-Coğrafya Fakültesi Dergisi*, vol. XXVIII, nos. 3–4 (1970), pp. 287–96.

[16] See, for example, Çankırı Court Records (hereafter ÇCR), vol. 6, 23–?; ÇCR, vol. 6, 66–116 and ÇCR, vol. 9, 85–129.

[17] ÇCR, vol. 9, 62–88.

that from 1735 onwards, the revenues of Kastamonu began to be assigned as a lifetime tax farm (*malikane*) to persons of high military status.[18] Two or more individuals could claim the tax revenues of Kastamonu simultaneously; on such occasions, the revenues of Kastamonu were distributed among these people.[19]

Unfortunately we do not have many sources about the social, economic, and political history of Çankırı and Kastamonu after the Ottoman conquest.[20] The following discussion is based on scattered comments found in the studies of various scholars and my own observations from the archival materials.[21]

Primary and secondary sources indicate that Çankırı and Kastamonu were not centers of great importance from an economic perspective. It is possible that a sub-branch of the silk route between Bursa and Tabriz passed through Tosya and Çerkeş, two districts [*kaza*s] located in the sub-province of Çankırı, and contributed to the development of these urban centers in the fifteenth and sixteenth centuries.[22] We are aware of the existence of another, less important, route between Ankara and a Black Sea port, Sinop, which passed through the boundaries of the two sub-provinces and was used mainly for the shipment of agricultural products from these areas to Istanbul.[23] Suraiya Faroqhi mentions that Çankırı and Kastamonu were located on two alternative routes from Diyarbakır and Erzurum to Istanbul through which flocks of sheep were transported, although I do not have any evidence of this situation in the *sicil*s of the seventeenth and eighteenth centuries.[24]

---

18 Kastamonu Court Records (hereafter KCR), vol. 34, 99–122.

19 An imperial order (dated 1740) indicates that the tax revenues of Kastamonu were divided between vizier Yusuf Paşa and Elhac Mustafa Ağa who was a "gate-keeper of the Porte" (*Dergah-ı muʿalla kapucıbaşısı*); see KCR, vol. 38, 151–239.

20 Mordtmann claims that "during the subsequent peaceful period under Ottoman rule, Çankırı is very much in the background. Historians hardly mention it, though Evliya Çelebi and Katib Çelebi left descriptions of the town. The first mention by a European visitor dates from the years 1553–55, and is by Dernschwam . . . There is an eye-witness description by Ainsworth, almost 300 years later." Mordtmann, p. 13.

21 See Mustafa Akdağ, *Türk Halkının Dirlik ve Düzenlik Kavgası: Celali İsyanlari* (Ankara: Bilgi Yayınevi, 1975), for example, for the effects of Celali Rebellions on this region.

22 Halil İnalcık, "Bursa'nın XV. Asır Sanayi ve Ticaret Tarihine Dair Vesikalar," *Belleten*, XXIV/93 (1960), p. 51. It is probable that the Ottomans used this route in their military expeditions against Persia even after the decline of its economic importance in the seventeenth century.

23 "Çankırı," *Yurt Ansiklopedisi*, p. 1962.

24 Suraiya Faroqhi, *Towns and Townsmen of Ottoman Anatolia; Trade, Crafts and Food*

According to the secondary literature on the economic characteristics of the two sub-provinces, agricultural production seems to have been the most important kind of economic activity in the region. In addition to a significant amount of staple and fruit production, the court records indicate that there was a substantial amount of rice production around the river of Kızılırmak and in the district of Kargı (of Çankırı) during the early eighteenth century.[25] Faroqhi reports that hemp production was an important economic activity in the districts of Küre and Taşköprü in Kastamonu during and after the sixteenth century.[26] Also according to the fiscal documentation in the court records, animal husbandry constituted another major economic activity in both Çankırı and Kastamonu.[27]

In terms of manufacturing, Tosya, a district of Çankırı, was the most important center in the region. Faroqhi emphasizes in her work that cloth production from angora wool in Tosya rivaled that of Ankara in the sixteenth century.[28] However Tosya's trade suffered severely from the unrest and insecurity caused by the Celali rebellions by the end of the sixteenth and the early seventeenth centuries.[29] Nevertheless, according to the first thirteen court registers of Çankırı, textile production and related activities continued during the seventeenth and eighteenth centuries.[30] The court records also indicate the existence of tanning, sandal production, and candle making in Çankırı.[31]

In Kastamonu we are aware of the existence of rope making (especially in and around Küre and Taşköprü) as well as linen, silk, and woolen cloth production between the sixteenth and the eighteenth centuries.[32] Copperware production constituted an important trade in

Production in an Urban Setting, 1520–1650 (Cambridge, London, New York: Cambridge University Press, 1984), pp. 225–227.

[25] See, for example, ÇCR, vol. 6, 126–214, for a document regarding a tax-farm agreement of rice production in Çankırı.

[26] Faroqhi, *Towns and Townsmen*, p. 131. I have not encountered any evidence of hemp production in the Kastamonu court records of the late seventeenth and early eighteenth centuries.

[27] ÇCR, vol. 6, 140–234.

[28] Faroqhi, *Towns and Townsmen*, pp. 140–141.

[29] Ibid.

[30] Woolen thread production and weaving of woolen and cotton cloth were major economic activities in two districts of Çankırı, Kurşunlu and Karacaviran. See ÇCR, vol. 5, 35–75; ÇCR, vol. 6, 136–226; ÇCR, vol. 8, 38–71; ÇCR, vol. 11, 15–20.

[31] ÇCR, vol. 4, 7–30.

[32] Faroqhi, *Towns and Townsmen*, pp. 134–135.

the towns of Kastamonu and Küre.[33] One court record indicates the existence of wine and liquor (*rakı*) production in the late seventeenth century, presumably by and mostly for the Christian population of the sub-province.[34] Finally, as in Çankırı, there existed some dye-making, tanning, as well as candle and sandal making in Kastamonu.[35]

Copper mining has traditionally been a major economic activity in the sub-province of Kastamonu, and in particular in the district of Küre. In the sixteenth century most of the copper extracted in the area was either shipped from the port of İnebolu (in the sub-province of Kastamonu) to Istanbul, or was transported to the south towards Syria via the route of Amasya, Tokat, and Sivas.[36] Copper production generated a significant amount of labor movement within the region.[37] In Çankırı, on the other hand, there existed salt mines, which were regularly farmed by different contractors (*mültezim*s).[38]

Information regarding demographic characteristics of Çankırı and Kastamonu is even sketchier. We learn from a tax-related entry that the sub-province of Çankırı had seventeen districts in 1076/1665–66 (Bucura, Çankırı [district], Çerkeş, Karacahisar, Karacaviran, Kalecik, Kargı, Karıbazarı, Keskin, Koçhisar, Kurşunlu, Kurubazarı [sic], Milan, Şabanözü, Toht, Tosya, and Ünüz).[39] The tax registers in the court records specify the number of quarters in the district of Çankırı as seventeen, and this number does not change in the thirteen volumes studied in this book.[40] On the other hand, the number of villages that were located within the boundaries of the district of Çankırı changes over the course of time: Whereas a tax-related entry of 1064/1654 gives the number of Çankırı's villages as seventy-six,[41] an entry of 1106/1695 mentions seventy-four villages as being within the district of Çankırı,[42] and in an entry of 1144/1731 we find this number to be sixty-nine.[43]

---

[33] Ibid.
[34] KCR, vol. 1, 120.
[35] KCR, vol. 3, 28–62.
[36] Faroqhi, *Towns and Townsmen*, p. 175.
[37] Ibid., p. 177.
[38] See, for example, ÇCR, vol. 6, 141–239.
[39] ÇCR, vol. 2, 18–54.
[40] See, for example, ÇCR, vol. 4, 25–93.
[41] ÇCR, vol. 1, 8–13.
[42] ÇCR, vol. 4, 16–66.
[43] ÇCR, vol. 9, 19–22.

Another indicator of the demographic situation is the *ʿavarızhane* (*ʿavarız* household)[44] figures that are found in the court records. Although it is difficult to determine the actual population sizes of particular regions by using *ʿavarızhane* figures, they are the only indicators that can provide some clues about the demographic characteristics of the region. Table 2.1 presents the number of *ʿavarızhanes* for all seventeen districts of Çankırı, as reported in the court register of 1077/1667, and several calculations that I made in order to convert this information to real household and population figures.

Table 2.1: Population of the Sub-province of Çankırı in 1665

Districts	*ʿAvarız* households (1)	Real households (2)	Population lower (3)	Population upper (4)
Çankırı	*248.5*	*3,727.5*	*10,102*	*16,066*
Kalecik	141.75	2,126.25	5,762	9,164
Tosya	164	2,460	6,667	10,603
Kurşunlu	64.5	9,67.5	2,622	4,170
Çerkeş	105	1,575	4,268	6,788
Milan	53.25	798.75	2,165	3,443
Kargı	24.5	367.5	996	1,584
Karıbazarı	65.5	982.5	2,663	4,235
Koçhisar	40	600	1,626	2,586
Keskin	60	900	2,439	3,879
Şabanözü	35	525	1,423	2,263
Karacaviran	21.25	318.75	864	1,374
Toht	93	1,395	3,780	6,012
Bucura	36.5	547.5	1,484	2,360
Karacahisar	51.5	772.5	2,093	3,329
Ünüz	35	525	1,423	2,263
Kurubazarı	29	435	1,180	1,875
Total	1,268.25	19,023.75	51,554	81,992

Source: The information about the *ʿavarız* households presented in the first column is from ÇCR, vol. 2, 18–54.
Note: The second column is calculated by multiplying the *ʿavarız* households figures by fifteen. The third and the fourth columns demonstrate my calculations of the lower and upper limits for the population based on the information presented in the second column.[45] My assumption is that the actual populations of the districts remained between these lower and upper limits. For example: the actual population of Kalecik was not less than 5,762 and not more than 9,164 in 1665. These lower and upper boundaries are calculated by multiplying the "Real households" figures by 2.71 and 4.32 respectively. See footnote 45.

---

[44] *ʿAvarız* constituted, at least at the beginning, an irregular tax category that was collected for various purposes. It was used to support military campaigns, to maintain the post system, the imperial kitchens or the navy, to guard the mountain

We can infer from the second column that Çankırı, Tosya, Kalecik, and Çerkeş were the most populous centers of the sub-province in the late seventeenth century. In the third column, I multiply the number of *ʿavarız* households by fifteen, which is, of course, the largest possible number of real households that an *ʿavarız* household could contain. I have no real basis to make the assumption that each *ʿavarız* household in Çankırı contained fifteen real households since the sources provide no information about the actual proportion. The only reason I choose fifteen as the multiplier in converting *ʿavarız*

---

passes and to uphold bridges, roads, and waterworks. Beginning in the late sixteenth century, *ʿavarız* was regularized and began to be collected annually in cash. See Bruce McGowan, *Economic Life in Ottoman Europe; Taxation, Trade and the Struggle for Land, 1600–1800* (Cambridge: Cambridge University Press, 1981), pp. 105–114; Linda Darling, *Revenue-Raising and Legitimacy; Tax Collection and Finance Administration in the Ottoman Empire, 1560–1660* (Leiden: E.J. Brill, 1996), p. 87 and passim; Ömer Lütfi Barkan, "Avarız," *İslam Ansiklopedisi*, vol. 2, pp. 13–19. In the court records the amount of *ʿavarız* tax levied on a particular locality was determined according to the number of *ʿavarızhanes* (*ʿavarız* households) in that area. Although we know that each *ʿavarız* household consisted of a number of real households (*hanes*), the exact proportion between these units varied from one place to another. Barkan ascertains that each *ʿavarız* household could comprise three to as many as fifteen real households depending on their sizes and relative prosperity of the district; ibid. According to the secondary literature the proportion between *ʿavarız* household and real household did indeed vary among different places. For example, Özer Ergenç establishes in his work that each *ʿavarız* household comprised five real households in early seventeenth-century Ankara; see Özer Ergenç, *XVI. Yüzyılda Ankara ve Konya* (Ankara: Ankara Enstitüsü Vakfi, 1995), p. 54. Bruce McGowan calculated this ratio as 1 to 2.7 for Karaferye (located in present-day eastern Greece) of 1730s; see McGowan, p. 106. And finally, Süleyman Demirci has recently calculated that each *ʿavarız* household contained ten to twelve real households in Konya and fifteen real households in Kayseri during the mid-seventeenth century (personal communication).

[45] There are different approaches to convert real household figures to actual population figures. The most common way to make this conversion is to multiply the numbers of households in a particular location by five. This approach, however, has been criticized and alternative methods have been suggested by a number of scholars; see Bekir Kemal Ataman, "Ottoman Demographic History (14th–17th Centuries): Some Considerations," *Journal of the Economic and Social History of the Orient*, vol. 35 (1992), pp. 187–198 for an analysis of alternative approaches. Here, I will follow the methodology of Leila Erder and Suraiya Faroqhi. In their work these scholars calculate a number of demographic multipliers to produce a range of estimates indicating the general trends of demographic growth. According to Erder's models and calculations, these multipliers are confined to a range between 2.72 and 4.31, depending on the assumptions that we make regarding the characteristics of Ottoman households. According to these multipliers the population of Çankırı must have been between 114,000 and 168,000 in the late sixteenth century. See Leila Erder and Suraiya Faroqhi, "Population Rise and Fall in Anatolia, 1550–1620," *Middle Eastern Studies*, vol. 15 (1979), pp. 322–345.

household numbers to real household numbers is that among all other possibilities, it is this multiplier that produced the most conservative estimate of the demographic change in Çankırı between late sixteenth and late seventeenth centuries. Even with this large multiplier, the estimated size of the population for the late seventeenth century (3,800 real households for the district and 19,000 for the sub-province) barely reaches half of its size in the late sixteenth century.[46]

The record I used to prepare the table above is unique in the sense that there are no other entries in the first thirteen volumes of Çankırı that provide similar information about the districts of Çankırı. For this reason, it is impossible to observe the demographic fluctuations that these districts experienced after the 1660s. The rest of the *ʿavarız*-related entries in the Çankırı court records provide information about the number of *ʿavarızhanes* only within the district of Çankırı, in addition to the total numbers of *ʿavarızhanes* within the sub-province. The following table shows how these numbers changed over time.

Table 2.2: *ʿAvarız* households in Çankırı

	1654	1667	1695	1698	1710	1732	1737
District	248.5	248.5	201	193.5	190.5	187.25	187
Sub-province	1,268.25	1,258.25	1,100.5	1,092	1,006	928.5	926.5

If we assume that neither the proportion between the *ʿavarız* households and real households, nor the ratio of the tax-exempt groups to the tax-paying classes changed in Çankırı between 1654 and 1737, it follows that there occurred a substantial decline in the populations of the district as well as the sub-province of Çankırı (25 and 27 per cent respectively).

Kastamonu *sicils* do not offer the equivalent of the information presented in table 2.1. Nevertheless the following observations might provide some basis to understand the demographic situation in the region: The court records of the late seventeenth and the early eighteenth centuries report the number of districts within the sub-province

[46] What we know regarding the population size of Çankırı in the sixteenth century is based on information in the 1578 fiscal survey (*tapu-tahrir defteri*) of the sub-district. See my "Local Court, Community and Justice in the 17th- and 18th-Century Ottoman Empire," Unpublished Ph.D. Dissertation, Ohio State University (2001), chapter two.

as thirty-two, and this number remains constant in all the registers that I have studied.[47] Also, between 1684 and 1741 the number of quarters in the district of Kastamonu decreased from forty-five to forty-one and the number of villages increased from seventy-two to seventy-seven. These findings confirm the conclusions of Bilici and Eyüpgiller, who both argued that during the seventeenth and the early eighteenth centuries the town of Kastamonu remained, at best, stagnant in terms of urban development.[48]

Let us now look at the *ʿavarız* household figures:

Table 2.3: *ʿAvarız* households in Kastamonu

	1685	1692	1713	1735	1736	1738	1741
District	2,525	–	–	268	260	258.5	–
Sub-province	4,210	2,248	2,025	2,042	2,172	2,041	2,040

It is not easy to interpret the changes in the *ʿavarızhane* figures above, but it seems clear that they do not solely reflect demographic variations within the sub-province and the district. Indeed, it is probable that the sub-province of Kastamonu experienced an administrative and financial reorganization between 1684 and 1692.[49] Unfortunately the nature of this reorganization is not clear. It is possible that, for some reason or other, the proportion between the *ʿavarız* households and the real households had increased by the end of the seventeenth century. Or it might be the case that some of the *ʿavarız* households of Kastamonu were released from paying *ʿavarız* taxes during this period in return for the payment of specific levies or the performance of specific services in the region. Unfortunately, I cannot validate either of these hypotheses for the lack of sources. Furthermore, the exact numerical proportion between the *ʿavarız* houses and real households in Kastamonu during this period is unclear. If this pro-

[47] However, Bruce McGowan implies in his study that this number increased to thirty-four sometime between 1688 and 1698. My documents, however, do not indicate such an increase. See McGowan, p. 119.

[48] Bilici, pp. 272–277; Eyüpgiller, pp. 98–101.

[49] The figures Bruce McGowan provides in his book indicate a similar trend in the *ʿavarız* households of the sub-province of Kastamonu. He reports that the number of *ʿavarızhanes* in the sub-province was 4,562 in 1662, 4,559 in 1677, 4,211 in 1688, 2,159 in 1698, 2,024 in 1718, 2,036 in 1755, and 2,025 in 1786. See McGowan, p. 119.

portion is assumed to be 1 to 15, the population of the district would be about 4,000 and the sub-province about 30,000 to 33,000 real households at the turn of the century.[50] The figures presented in the above table also indicate that both the district and sub-province possibly lost some population between 1692 and 1742.

At this point it seems safe to assume that by the mid-eighteenth century, Kastamonu was a relatively larger urban and administrative center than Çankırı. The census conducted in 1831 also demonstrate this situation. According to this census, the district and the sub-province of Çankırı had about 24,000 and 37,000 "adult" inhabitants, respectively.[51] The district and the sub-province of Kastamonu, on the other hand, had populations of about 30,000 and 95,000 "adults" at the same date.[52]

Finally, I should emphasize the fact that the twenty-five volumes of court registers covered in this study are not extremely useful in reflecting the socioeconomic relations in Çankırı and Kastamonu and the structural evolution that the Ottoman provincial system was experiencing during this period. On the one hand, and in parallel with what has been stated in the literature regarding the process of decentralization and the emergence of local power-holders during the seventeenth and eighteenth centuries,[53] these sources confirm the existence of a group of notables (explicitly identified in the documents as *aʿyan*)

[50] Again, my choice of selecting fifteen as the appropriate multiplier is based on the observation that among all other possibilities, it is this figure that produces the most conservative estimate of the demographic change in Kastamonu between the late sixteenth and early eighteenth centuries: Even with this large multiplier, the populations of the district and the sub-province do not reach two-thirds of their sizes in 1580s. Our information of the demographic situation of Kastamonu in the sixteenth century is based on the information presented in three fiscal surveys of Kastamonu prepared in 1580s. See Ergene, "Local Court, Community, and Justice," chapter two, for a detailed discussion of these sources.

[51] "Çankırı," *Yurt Ansiklopedisi*, p. 1962. It is indicated in the yearbook of 1869 that the population of non-Muslims (mainly Christians) was about one-thousand; see Türkoğlu, p. 19.

[52] "Kastamonu," *Yurt Ansiklopedisi*, vols. 6–7, p. 4588. It is also indicated in this article that by 1870 the sub-province of Kastamonu had about 16,000 to 19,000 non-Muslim inhabitants (including the children) by the end of the nineteenth century; ibid.

[53] On *aʿyan* see Deena R. Sadat, "Urban Notables in the Ottoman Empire: The Ayan," Unpublished Ph.D. Dissertation, Rutgers University, 1969; idem, "Ayan and Ağa: The Transformation of the Bektashi Corps in the Eighteenth Century," *Muslim World*, vol. 63, no. 3 (1973); idem, "Rumeli Ayanları: The Eighteenth Century," *Journal of Modern History*, vol. 44, no. 3 (1972); and Yuzo Nagata, *Tarihte Ayanlar: Karaosmanoğulları Üzerine Bir İnceleme* (Ankara: Türk Tarih Kurumu Basımevi, 1997).

who were active in the legal, financial, and administrative affairs of the two locales. In addition to representing their communities in the court and supervising the distribution of tax levies to individual districts, quarters, and villages, the documents indicate that these notables commonly served as court witnesses.[54] On the other hand, what we may infer about the extent of their influence in provincial politics, the nature of relations they established with local administrators and the common people, and the sources of their wealth is rather impressionistic, given the limited information on the *aʿyan* in the court records.[55]

At a different level, the court records provide some indications of sociopolitical disorder. For example, these sources frequently report the actions of the bandits (*eşkiya*) and the troubles caused by independent mercenaries (*kapusız levendat*) and nomadic Turkoman and Kurdish groups in the countryside.[56] Although it is not clear whether the numbers and activities of these people were increasing during the period under study, it seems from the orders sent to Çankırı, Kastamonu, and other places that these people constituted a source of trouble for the central and provincial governments. These documents urged the provincial administrators to capture and punish the bandits and force the nomadic groups to settle in specific locations.[57]

It is obvious in such orders that the central government was concerned about the increasing numbers of migrants to Istanbul who were arriving from various locations in Anatolia and Rumelia. The reasons for this movement are unclear.[58] Yet it seems that these newcomers undermined the security of the capital and depleted its

---

[54] See, for example, KCR, vol. 39, 12–15; KCR, vol. 35, 123–139; KCR, vol. 35, 310–307; KCR, vol. 35, 303–298 and KCR, vol. 35, 310–308.

[55] The court records indicate that many of these people occupied various provincial posts (such as the trusteeship of local endowments, wardenship (*kethüdayerliği*) of the local janissary corps, tax farmers, stewardship of the provincial treasury, etc.) in addition to holding substantial amounts of land and property in the urban center and the countryside. See KCR, vol. 4, 21–61 and 96–80; KCR, vol. 5, 111–226; KCR, vol. 36, 212–102; KCR, vol. 37, 59–84 and 63–90; KCR, vol. 38, 35–41; KCR, vol. 39, 11–12, 150–361, 121–216, 73–124. Also, some of the local notables had retail stores in the bazaars and were involved in commercial activities. See KCR, vol. 39, 37–61.

[56] There are a great number of documents related to this issue in Çankırı and Kastamonu court records. See, for example, ÇCR, vol. 5, 53–108; ÇCR, vol. 11, 20–29 and 38–57; ÇCR, vol. 9, 12–17.

[57] Ibid.

[58] See ÇCR, vol. 9, 55–82 and 56–83.

resources. For these reasons, the central government urged local administrators to stop immigrants from entering the city and to send back those individuals heading towards Istanbul without any legitimate reason. Those who were permitted to go to the capital were supposed to carry letters of permission from their local *kadıs*.

The Courts of Çankiri and Kastamonu

The court records indicate that for most of the late seventeenth and the early eighteenth centuries, the *kadıs* of Çankırı and Kastamonu were appointed by direct sultanic warrants (*berats*) and usually came to these sub-provinces from outside. An entry in the court records of Çankırı (dated 1154/1741) indicates that the *kadı*ship of Çankırı was assigned to a Seniullah Efendi with the rank of *salise* (which came after the ranks of *Sitte-i Mısır, Musul*, and *saniye* among the *kadıs* of Anatolia)[59] and with the salary of three hundred *akçes* per day.[60] Unfortunately I have not found similar information in the court records of Kastamonu. Nor does Uzunçarşılı indicate the rank of the Kastamonu *kadı*ship in his work. Nevertheless, since it was not one of the major judgeships (*mevleviyets*) in Anatolia, it can be assumed that it was an ordinary district *kadı*ship (*kaza kadılığı*).[61] Their warrants indicate that the *kadıs* of Çankırı and Kastamonu were appointed to twelve- to sixteen-month terms in their districts.[62]

---

[59] İsmail Hakkı Uzunçarşılı, *Osmanlı Devleti'nin İlmiye Teşkilatı* (Ankara: Türk Tarih Kurumu Yayınları, 1965), p. 93.

[60] ÇCR, vol. 13, 13–32; also see ÇCR, vol. 11, 104–168. This information fits well with what Uzunçarşılı reports about the *kadı*ship of Çankırı. Accordingly, the *kadı*ship of Çankırı was considered in the eighteenth century as a *Devriye Mevleviyeti*, a fourth class following the *Haremeyn Mevleviyetleri* (the *kadı*ships of Mecca and Medina; these constituted the highest class after the *kadı*ship of Istanbul), the *Bilad-ı Hamse Mevleviyetleri* (the *kadı*ships of Edirne, Bursa, Damascus, Cairo, and Plovdiv) and the *Mahreç Mevleviyetleri* (the *kadı*ships of Jerusalem, Aleppo, Tırhala Yenişehri, Galata, Izmir, Salonika, Eyüb, Üsküdar, Sofia, Crete, and Trabzon). Uzunçarşılı argues that in addition to Çankırı, the *Devriye Mevleviyetleri* included the *kadı*ships of Maraş, Baghdad, Bosnia, Antep, Erzurum, Tripoli (of the East), Beirut, Adana, Van, Ruscuk (Ruse), and Sivas in the eighteenth century. See Uzunçarşılı, *İlmiye Teşkilatı*, pp. 99–103.

[61] Uzunçarşılı lists all the *mevleviyets* in his work, and the *kadı*ship of Kastamonu is not one of them. Ibid.

[62] Some *kadıs* in the sub-provinces of Kastamonu and Çankırı were dismissed before the end of their terms in response to complaints against them and their illegal actions. See ÇCR, vol. 4, 3–12 and 13–52; KCR, vol. 35, 78–130. On one

In theory, the *kadı* not only represented the highest judicial authority in a particular region, but also partook of the political prerogatives of protecting the subjects against the oppression of local military and administrative officials. According to Ronald Jennings, he had the ability to accomplish the latter task because, in addition to being the "sultan's legal instrument for achieving the rational implementation of Ottoman law (*şer*ʿ and *kanun*),"[63] the *kadı* was also a representative of a centuries-old Islamic moral-legal tradition and was a legitimate executor of the holy law, which, in theory, relieved him from the control of those who represented political authority:

> The office of *kadı* was an institution that antedated the Ottoman Empire and presumably would outlast it as it had endured after all earlier Islamic empires. The law was a Law that came from God and was in its essence not subject to the whims of mundane and transitory sultans. Every *kadı* had full authority, divine and imperial, to enforce the Law within his district.[64]

In the subsequent chapters we will have a chance to check the validity of Jennings' claim that the Ottoman *kadı* was in theory able to maintain his autonomy in his judicial operations. For now, however, it is necessary to call attention to the fact that by identifying sultanic authority and divine law as the only sources of judicial legitimacy, Jennings implicitly disregards the importance of communal dynamics in determining the limits of the *kadı*'s authority. In an administrative structure where collective responsibility and self-government were the main operative forces,[65] the relationships that the *kadı* fostered within the provincial society must have been critical for

---

occasion the term of a *kadı* was extended for six months because of his exemplary service in Çankırı; see ÇCR, vol. 3, 19–23.

[63] Jennings, "*Kadı*, Court, and Legal Procedure," pp. 137–142.

[64] Ibid., p. 142. İlber Ortaylı indicates the practical limits of this theoretical structure as follows: "Even though the theoretical system of the state structure proposes the independence and direct connection of the qadi to central authority, in a feudal society no efficient organization existed which could provide such a mechanism. The sociological and technological structure of the society was an obstacle for the realization of this mechanism; therefore the qadi was subjected to the pressures that came both from the local officials and nobility." See İlber Ortaylı, "Some Observations," p. 62; also idem, *Hukuk ve İdare Adamı Olarak Osmanlı Devletinde Kadı* (Ankara: Turhan Kitabevi, 1994).

[65] See Amnon Cohen, "Communal Legal Entities in a Muslim Setting, Theory and Practice: The Jewish Community in Sixteenth-Century Jerusalem," *Islamic Law and Society*, no. 1, vol. 3 (1996), pp. 75–87. Also see Deena R. Sadat, "Urban Notables in the Ottoman Empire"; idem, "Ayan and Ağa"; and idem, "Rumeli Ayanları."

his local influence. Indeed, abundant evidence indicates that the ability to establish strong ties with particular groups and agents was one of the essential conditions for a successful judicial and administrative career in the seventeenth and eighteenth centuries.[66] In this sense, the policy of rotating *kadı*s among different provincial posts may be seen as a sign of these peoples' tendency to become part of the social environment in which they operated, rather than a way to prevent such a situation as has been assumed in the secondary literature.[67] What is more, we have evidence that the system of rotation did not always function properly: For example, in 1694, the *kadı*ship of the district of Toht in Çankırı was assigned to a Musa Efendi, who had been residing in the same district for more than fifteen years at the time of his appointment.[68]

We also need to remember that the *kadı* operated within the institutional context of the Islamic court. He was surrounded by his assistants (*na'ib*s), scribes (*katib*s), witnesses (*şuhudülhal*), and other court officials, who were usually recruited from the local community and were very much involved in local affairs. It is more than probable that these people influenced the decisions of the *kadı* so that they conformed with local beliefs, customs, and interests. In this sense they probably preserved the communal memory, complemented the legal expertise of the judge, and ensured the power of community norms in the legal arena.

Unfortunately, and despite their importance in the processes of dispute resolution, we do not find much information about the court officers in the secondary literature. What is found in the court records

[66] Cevdet Adliye 2311 provides the account of the *kadı* of İnebahtı, Osman Efendi, who was taken out of the court in 1785 by "some inhabitants of the locality," put in a boat with the rest of his household and driven out of the district. There are many such accounts in the Prime Ministry Archive; see, for example, Cevdet Adliye (hereafter CA) 1601; CA 2670; CA 3318; CA 3319; and Cevdet Zabtiye (hereafter CZ) 1305.

[67] Halil İnalcık argues that: "[I]t was a kind of 'constitutional' precept in the Ottoman patrimonial system not to allow government agents to hold a provincial position for too long, lest he establish local connections and be integrated into the community. In fact, having a key position in a town, a cadi could gain a particularly strong position, and thus secure economic advantages. Some of the dismissed cadis, taking advantage of the special conditions which arose in the eighteenth century, actually settled in the towns, and they, or their offspring became local notables. Many of the *a'yan*s then, were former *kadı*s or *kadızade*s." See Halil İnalcık, "The Ruznamçe Registers of the *Kadı*asker of Rumeli as Preserved in the Istanbul Müftülük Archives," *Turcica*, vol. 20 (1988), p. 264.

[68] ÇCR, vol. 4, 13–52.

and other archival material draws only an incomplete picture of their activities. According to these sources, not only were the *na'ib*s and the *katib*s usually members of the local community,[69] but many of them were also able to retain their posts for long periods under successive *kadı*s. For example, we find İbrahim bin Mustafa serving as scribe of the court of Kastamonu for at least six years.[70] Nor was this situation limited to Çankırı and Kastamonu; we understand from a 1762 document that a man by the name of Fethullah Efendi served as a scribe of the court of Mahmud Paşa in Istanbul for at least 40 years![71] Other documents indicate that the posts of *niyabet* (assistantship) and *kitabet* (scribeship) could be transferred from father to son.[72]

The identities of the *na'ib*s in Çankırı are unclear in the court records. Two *na'ib*s in Kastamonu, however, are identified as religious scholars (singular, *müderris*)[73] living in the district, and one other was a very prominent and wealthy notable active in the public affairs of Kastamonu for a considerable period.[74] Unfortunately, I do not have more information about the identities of the scribes in the courts of Çankırı and Kastamonu. It is indicated in one entry that a scribe of the Kastamonu court, Mustafa Efendi, was also a *müderris*,[75] and it is clear that many of the court scribes in eighteenth-century Anatolia were among the local notables.[76] This finding suggests that during our period, *na'ib*s and *katib*s were usually recruited from people of similar social and economic backgrounds. Indeed, on one occasion a single individual held the posts of both *niyabet* and *kitabet* in a particular town, albeit at different times.[77]

---

[69] KCR, vol. 38, 18–12 and 192–292; CA 4439, 4495, 4832, and 6080. It should be emphasized that the recruitment of *na'ib*s among the members of the local community was legally prohibited; see CA 4439 and 4495.

[70] Compare KCR, vol. 34, 14–24, KCR, vol. 35, 46–64, and KCR, vol. 39, 57–94.

[71] CA 4629.

[72] CA 1164 and CA 4658.

[73] This is consistent with what Özer Ergenç has found in sixteenth-century Ankara. See Ergenç, p. 85.

[74] These *na'ib*s were *Müderris* İshakzade İshak Efendi, *Müderris* Abdullah Efendi, and Çetinzade Elhac Ahmed Efendi; see KCR, vol. 37, 9–1, KCR, vol. 38, 16–10 and 18–12. The wealth of Çetinzade Ahmed Efendi is apparent from the entry of an inheritance dispute he was involved in; see KCR, vol. 37, 24–25. Also KCR, vol. 37, 93–147 (dated 1740) identifies Çetinzade Ahmed as an *a'yan* of Kastamonu since 1715.

[75] KCR, vol. 39, 18–25.

[76] CA 1674 and CZ 4174.

[77] Cevdet Dahiliye (hereafter CD) 3607.

Uzunçarşılı argues that *niyabet* was being farmed out more and more frequently during the eighteenth century.[78] This also seems to be the situation in Kastamonu after its *kadı*ship was assigned as *arpalık* to Mehmed Esad Efendi, the *kazʿasker* of Anatolia and the *kadı* of the imperial army (*ordu-yu humayün kadısı*), in June 1739.[79] Before then, Kastamonu was directly administered by the *kadı*s, but since Mehmed Esad Efendi could not come to Kastamonu because of his more urgent responsibilities, he appointed *naʾib*s to attend to his legal and administrative responsibilities in Kastamonu. Until the time when the *kadı*ship of Kastamonu was released again from being an *arpalık* (March 1741), it changed hands between three *naʾib*s.[80]

The court records of Çankırı and Kastamonu indicate that the *naʾib*s and *katib*s had great responsibilities in administering justice. In addition to their usual functions in the courts of Çankırı and Kastamonu,[81] they also traveled to nearby districts and villages to hear and adjudicate disputes. Surprisingly, in many such situations the *katib*s were not accompanied by the *naʾib*s; they heard and resolved these disputes personally.[82] This situation indicates how influential these people could be for the administration of justice in their own communities. Their control over local litigations must have further

---

[78] İsmail Hakkı Uzunçarşılı, "Naip," *İslam Ansiklopedisi*, vol. 9, p. 50.

[79] KCR, vol. 38, 16–10. Mehmed Esad Efendi also held the *kadı*ships of the districts of Sapanca and Siroz as *arpalık*s.

[80] KCR, vol. 37, 9–1; KCR, vol. 38, 16–10 and 18–12; KCR, vol. 39, 3–1. Unfortunately it is not clear how much it cost to acquire the *niyabet* of Kastamonu. However, in 1765 the *naʾib* of İstanköy was paying 320 *guruş* per month for his post; see CA 272. In 1795 the *naʾib* of Göynük was prepared to pay 1,350 *guruş* for the *niyabet* of Sultanhisarı; see CA 5320.

[81] We know that *naʾib*s assisted the *kadı*s in various ways and *katib*s were responsible for keeping the court records. In addition, they may have also served other functions. For example, they may have functioned as intermediaries between the court and the community by bridging the conceptual gaps between these different worlds. See Susan Hirsch, *Pronouncing and Persevering: Gender and the Discourses of Disputing in an African Court* (Chicago: The University of Chicago Press, 1998), pp. 123–4; Barbara Yngvesson, "Legal Ideology and Community Justice in the Clerk's Office," *Legal Studies Forum*, vol. 9 (1985), pp. 71–89; idem, "Making Law at the Doorway: The Clerk, the Court and the Construction of Community in a New England Town," *Law and Society Review*, vol. 22 (1988), pp. 409–448.

[82] See, for example, KCR, vol. 34, 14–24; KCR, vol. 35, 46–64, 88–140, and 98–156; KCR, vol. 37, 11–3. It seems that in some places in eighteenth-century Anatolia the difference between a *kadı* and a scribe in terms of their knowledge of legal matters could be trivial. Indeed, an entry in the court records of Kastamonu indicates that a scribe in the court of Mahmud Paşa in Istanbul also held the *kadı*ship of the district of Larende in Konya during the 1740s; see KCR, vol. 38, 25–22.

increased when the *kadı*ships were assigned as *arpalık*s, as was the situation in Kastamonu between 1739 and 1741. During such periods local notables like Çetinzade Ahmed Efendi occupied the highest-ranking legal posts within their districts.

Other participants in the court processes included the "expert witnesses" (*şuhudülhal*), who constituted another interesting group of people for the concerns of this study. Mustafa Akdağ claims that this was an "advisory council" that tried to influence the opinions of the *kadı* in keeping with the values and traditions of the community. Accordingly, *kadı*s consulted with these "witnesses," especially regarding local customs and traditions about which they might know very little.[83] According to Farhat Ziadeh, members of the community became involved in legal disputes through this process of consultation and hence made their views known to the court about matters brought before it.[84] Witnesses had the authority to confirm the integrity and reliability of individuals who came to the court, and this constituted a significant source of power for the members of the *şuhud*, and a means for discrimination against "undesirable" elements within the community.[85]

As in the case of other court officials, we do not know much about these *şuhud* or about their actual involvement in legal matters in the Ottoman Empire. Hülya Canbakal's recent work on sixteenth-century Antep court records, however, provides some relevant information in this regard.[86] According to Canbakal, these witnesses were a small, closed, and well-off group who monopolized the legal proceedings and manipulated the court system in accordance with their own interests, rather than (or perhaps, in addition to) acting as the social conscience of the community. Interestingly this representation is not consistent with the findings and conclusions of other researchers. Ronald Jennings, for example, argues that in seventeenth-century Kayseri no one at the court was ever identified as being a member of the "class" of *şuhudülhal*; witnessing was open generally to all

---

[83] Mustafa Akdağ, *Türkiye'nin İktisadi ve İctimai Tarihi*, vol. 1 (Istanbul: Cem Yayınevi, 1974), p. 404.

[84] Farhat J. Ziadeh, "Integrity ('Adalah) in Classical Islamic Law," in Nicholas Heer ed., *Islamic Law and Jurisprudence* (Seattle: University of Washington Press, 1990), p. 78.

[85] Ibid., p. 91.

[86] Hülya Canbakal, "Legal Practice and Social Hierarchy: The Truth-Bearers of 'Ayntab," presentation given in the workshop *Law and Its Applications in the Ottoman Empire*, Harvard University, 17 April 1998.

Muslims.[87] Karen Barkey also claims that the witnesses cannot be considered a select group, "since some are men who just attend court daily, or are just drawn into a case for no reason other than their physical presence."[88]

I have observed that a well-defined group of people regularly attended the judicial and administrative proceedings as witnesses in the courts of both Çankırı and Kastamonu, although they do not seem to be the only ones to serve in that capacity.[89] According to the court records, many of these people were among the local notables, and many carried military and religious titles. Furthermore, it seems that there was a temporal continuity in their involvement with the court proceedings: Not only were people like Kıbrısizade Elhac Ahmed Efendi, Gubarizade Ahmed Ağa, Şeyhzade Mehmed Efendi, and Rıftarizade Hafiz Mustafa Efendi (incidentally, all members of the *a'yan*) active as witnesses in the court of Kastamonu between 1735 and 1743, but so were their fathers, uncles, and other male relatives in the 1690s. The existence of Kıbrısizades, Çetinzades, Rıftarizades, and Gubarizades is a constant in the entire collection of Kastamonu court records here studied.

It also seems that some expert witnesses appropriated certain official responsibilities. An entry in the court records of Çankırı indicates that it was a group of court attendees (including several prominent members of the *şuhud*) that determined the identities of the post-station keepers (*menzilci*) in the sub-province.[90] Also, several witnesses accompanied the *na'ib*s and *katib*s when they left Kastamonu to hear and adjudicate disputes.[91] It is even likely that these people were regularly compensated for their legal and administrative services at the court.[92]

---

[87] Jennings, "*Kadı*, Court, and Legal Procedure," pp. 145–46.

[88] Karen Barkey, "The Use of Court Records in the Construction of Village Networks: A Comparative Perspective," *International Journal of Comparative Sociology*, nos. 1–2, vol. 32 (1991), p. 209.

[89] I believe that when a dispute was brought to the court from a particular quarter or village, some inhabitants of these areas also came or were brought to the court as witnesses in occasional instances. Many of the people were identified as the elders or religious leaders (*imams*) of these localities.

[90] ÇCR, vol. 8, 29–53.

[91] See, for example, KCR, vol. 4, 4–9, and KCR, vol. 38, 59–84.

[92] A petition from the Prime Ministry Archive indicates the fact that witnesses of the court of the town of Akçahisar in Anatolia were receiving regular salaries during 1710; see CA 902.

At least some of these witnesses must have been experienced and knowledgeable in religious and legal matters. A fair number of religious scholars served as members, and the fact that one of them, Çetinzade Ahmed Efendi, later received the most prominent legal post in the district supports this assumption. Yet it is not clear how these people used their experience and knowledge in manipulating the court for themselves or on behalf of others. Indeed, the number of disputes that they personally got involved in is very small, and although there are a number of occasions on which they acted as legal agents on behalf of others[93] their influence on the court processes is invisible. Needless to say, however, their influence must have been felt intensely in the court.[94]

It is also possible to identify other attendants in the court of Kastamonu (with the titles of *çukadar*, *muhzır*, *mübaşir*, *müteferrika*, etc.). However, the nature of their functions and responsibilities is not clear. It is likely that these people constituted what Ronald Jennings called a "police" force that enforced the orders of the court or summoned people before it. Nevertheless it should be emphasized that there is almost no evidence of the nature of "police" activities in Çankırı and Kastamonu.[95]

Finally, although they were not among the court officials, local *müftis* (jurisconsults) in Çankırı and Kastamonu need to be men-

[93] Şeyhzade Mehmed Efendi seems to be the most popular of such agents. He acted as a legal agent in four different trials. Kıbrısizade Ahmed Efendi also acted as an agent in two cases. The court records of Çankırı and Kastamonu indicate that quite a number of litigants made use of legal agents. Nevertheless these agents were usually related to the litigants. See Ronald Jennings, "The Office of Vekil (Wakil) in 17th Century Ottoman Sharia Courts," *Studia Islamica*, vol. 42 (1975), pp. 147–169.

[94] Several indicators suggest the validity of this assertion. For example, according to an order relayed from the capital, a number of complaint letters were sent to the central government from Kastamonu about two individuals (Boyacıoğlu Mehmed and Kara Hüseyinoğlu Mustafa) who were among the select group of *şuhud* in Kastamonu. These individuals were accused of "associating" (*düşüb kalkub*) with the *kadı*s, *na'ib*s, *mütesellim*s (lieutenant governors), and other military-administrative officials in Kastamonu and spreading false allegations about innocent people; see KCR, vol. 4, 169–226 (the order is dated evasıt Zilhicce 1103/August or September 1692). Also, on many occasions the court proceedings in Kastamonu were conducted in the house of Gubarizade Ahmed Ağa, although it seems that he had nothing to do with the cases that were adjudicated during these proceedings. This situation is indeed indicative of the strong relationship that existed between the court and some members of the *şuhud*; see KCR, vol. 35, 150–236 and KCR, vol. 37, 35–41.

[95] See Ronald Jennings, "*Kadı*, Court, and Legal Procedure," pp. 148–157.

tioned since their legal opinions (*fetvas*) played a noteworthy role in the processes of dispute resolution. In theory, these jurisconsults, who were accessible to the population at large, provided short answers to legal questions brought to their attention. In this sense their functions involved stating the law as well as explaining and applying it in practical situations.[96] Although the opinions of the *müftis* were not legally binding in the court, the court records indicate that they were used with relative frequency by the litigants, and that they carried significant weight in the proceedings, winning legal cases for their bearers almost every time. Unfortunately, however, the court records resist disclosing more about the relationship that existed between the *müfti* and the court officials and about the ways in which the former became involved in the court processes formally or informally, other than by responding to legal questions. For this reason, much about the nature of the *müfti*'s legal presence and activities in the processes of dispute resolution constitutes a mystery.

[96] Uriel Heyd, "Some Aspects of the Ottoman Fetva," *Bulletin of the School of Oriental and African Studies*, vol. 32 (1969), pp. 53–54.

CHAPTER THREE

A COMPARATIVE ANALYSIS OF THE OPERATIONS OF ÇANKIRI AND KASTAMONU COURTS

There is a consensus in the existing literature on the duties of Islamic courts in the Ottoman Empire. It seems that every study of the Ottoman courts reiterates the same list of judicial and administrative responsibilities when describing the operations of the courts. There is nothing wrong with this, especially if the objective of the study is to provide a general understanding of court operations. Nevertheless, if we wish to attain a deeper insight of the role of the court in a provincial context, we need to be aware that this tendency eliminates as yet unrecognized distinctions in the function of different courts and, therefore, obscures the variations in their "characters."

In this chapter I aim to examine the nature of services that the courts of Çankırı and Kastamonu provided in their respective localities, and to check whether it is possible to distinguish between these courts in terms of their operations. There is, of course, no a priori reason to expect that the two courts played different roles in their own settings. However, as we shall see shortly, there exists a significant disparity between the *sicil*s of Çankırı and Kastamonu in terms of the proportions of different kinds of documents in these collections. Since specific kinds of documents correspond to specific court operations, this disparity indicates a variation in both the major functions of these courts and in how they were utilized by their clients.

The first section of the present chapter provides a detailed statistical analysis of the documentation found in the court records. This analysis will indicate that the administrative and notarial activities of the court of Çankırı overshadowed its judicial operations. In the second section, I will explore the social and political impact of these activities in some detail and assess the ways they might have affected how the courts were perceived by the local community.

Contents of the Court Records

The variety of documents that make up a "typical" *sicil* is considerable. This variation results from the multifunctional role of the Ottoman magistrate (*kadı*) who was, on the one hand, responsible for the administration of his district (*kaza*) and the execution of the state's orders, and was, on the other hand, obligated to solve local disputes and serve other necessary judicial functions.[1] In this sense, his court, *mahkeme*, represented a platform where autonomy from and dependence on the state coexisted: Sometimes the court acted as an autonomous body where the decisions of the "holy law," the court clients, or the community were determined and enforced quite independently from outside. At other times, the court had to convey the imperial will and execute decisions that were ordered by higher authorities.

This dual-faced character of the Ottoman court can be demonstrated through the kinds of documents found in the *sicil*s. In a typical volume of court records, we find documents composed in the local court by the *kadı*, by other court officials, and by the participating members of the community. These documents include summary accounts of the cases heard and adjudicated in the court, copies of contracts, records of inheritance, divorce cases, suretyship (*kefalet*), support after divorce (*nafaka*), and guardianship (*vesayet*), etc. In addition, the court records also contain documents that were not originally composed in the local *mahkeme* but were sent there for fiscal, military, and administrative purposes and recorded in the *sicil* mainly for notarial reasons. In general, these documents demonstrate the nature of interaction and the degree of dependency between the "center" and the "province" through the mediation of the local court.

[1] It is for this reason that scholars such as Gyula Kaldy-Nagy are hesitant to use the word "judge" when translating "*kadı*" into English: "The authority of the *kadı* covered such a large area of responsibility that the full meaning of the title cannot be accurately rendered by the word 'judge'." See Gyula Kaldy-Nagy, "Kadı," *EI*[2], vol. 4, p. 375. On the other hand İlber Ortaylı warns us that "the unity on the duties of the Qadi (in civil-penal cases, in administrative, municipal, and financial affairs) should not be taken as a distinctive characteristic of the Qadi of Middle Eastern countries. It should be born in mind that a similar situation existed in the European cities of the Middle Ages. Let it suffice to say that Burgermeister and the Lord Mayor of London also performed the above mentioned duties." See Ortaylı, "Some Observations," p. 57.

My research has shown that, although the types of documents in the registers of individual courts are similar, the statistical proportions between various kinds of documents can differ from court to court. I believe it is this difference in proportions that reveal some of the distinctions between the courts of Çankırı and Kastamonu. In tables 3.1 and 3.2 below, I compare locally composed records with those generated outside the sub-provinces. As obvious in these tables, the proportions of the types of records appearing in the Çankırı and Kastamonu registers vary dramatically. In each and every volume of the first thirteen volumes of Çankırı *sicil*s, the number of entries drafted outside the court of Çankırı is significantly higher than those that were composed there. In Kastamonu registers, however, the numbers of local documents are consistently and substantially higher than non-local ones: In nine of the twelve volumes of Kastamonu *sicil*s studied in this book, locally composed entries constitute the majority of the documents.

Table 3.1: Documents Sent by Higher Authorities versus Documents Composed in the Court of Çankırı

Volumes	Period	Documents Sent by Higher Authorities	Documents Composed in the Court
Volume 1	1063–65/1652–55	133 (77%)	39 (23%)
Volume 2	1069–77/1659–66	109 (81%)	25 (19%)
Volume 3	1091–92/1680–81	87 (70%)	38 (30%)
Volume 4	1105–06/1694–95	115 (53%)	102 (47%)
Volume 5	1109–10/1697–98	95 (58%)	70 (42%)
Volume 6	1120–27/1708–15	228 (55%)	155 (45%)
Volume 7	1141–42/1729–30	71 (63%)	41 (37%)
Volume 8	1141–43[a]/1729–31	188 (71%)	62 (29%)
Volume 9	1143–45/1731–32	105 (72%)	40 (28%)
Volume 10	1145–47/1732–34	82 (74%)	29 (26%)
Volume 11	1148–51[b]/1735–38	153 (78%)	44 (22%)
Volume 12	1153–54/1740–41	33 (75%)	11 (25%)
Volume 13	1154–57/1741–44	96 (65%)	53 (35%)

a – In the last twelve pages of this volume there are documents from 1151 and 1152.

b – There are documents from 1139, 1140, and 1143 in the last two pages of this volume.

Table 3.2: Documents Sent by Higher Authorities versus Documents Composed in the Court of Kastamonu

Volumes	Period	Documents Sent by Higher Authorities	Documents Composed in the Court
Volume 3	1095–97/1684–86	107 (43%)	144 (57%)
Volume 1	1099–02/1688–91	134 (57%)	101 (43%)
Volume 4	1102–03/1691–92	163 (72%)	62 (28%)
Volume 5	1103–05a/1692–94	108 (42%)	148 (58%)
Volume 12	1115/1703–04	34 (37%)	59 (63%)
Volume 19	1124–25/1712–13	49 (28%)	126 (72%)
Volume 34	1148/1735–36	29 (16%)	136 (84%)
Volume 35	1148–50/1736–38	141 (34%)	266 (66%)
Volume 36	1151–52b/1738–39	111 (61%)	72 (39%)
Volume 37	1153–54/1740–42	24 (20%)	98 (80%)
Volume 38	1153/1740–41	83 (28%)	209 (72%)
Volume 39	1154–55/1742–43	138 (38%)	226 (62%)

a – There are documents from 1158 and 1132 in the first forty-two pages of this register.
b – There are documents from 1213 between pages fifty-seven and sixty-seven.

What does this picture imply regarding the "characters" of individual courts? In order to answer this question, a more detailed numerical analysis of the court records is necessary.

Table 3.3: Documents Sent to the Court of Çankırı: Classification

Volumes	Orders			Warrants	Total entries
	Milt. Tax. Sec. (1)	*Zulm* (2)	Disputes (3)	(4)	(5)
Vol. 1	10 (6%)	1 (1%)	5 (3%)	110 (64%)	172
Vol. 2	24 (18%)	6 (4%)	5 (4%)	45 (34%)	134
Vol. 3	9 (7%)	3 (2%)	3 (2%)	44 (35%)	125
Vol. 4	52 (24%)	6 (3%)	9 (4%)	25 (12%)	217
Vol. 5	19 (12%)	6 (4%)	3 (2%)	53 (32%)	165
Vol. 6	65 (17%)	8 (2%)	13 (3%)	91 (24%)	385
Vol. 7	23 (21%)	4 (4%)	19 (17%)	22 (20%)	112
Vol. 8	56 (22%)	11 (4%)	9 (4%)	63 (25%)	250
Vol. 9	30 (21%)	4 (3%)	9 (6%)	39 (27%)	145
Vol. 10	37 (33%)	– (0%)	2 (2%)	20 (18%)	111
Vol. 11	88 (45%)	6 (3%)	4 (2%)	124 (63%)	197
Vol. 12	14 (32%)	3 (7%)	3 (7%)	8 (18%)	44
Vol. 13	58 (39%)	4 (3%)	1 (0%)	23 (15%)	149
Total	484 (22%)	62 (3%)	77 (4%)	667 (30%)	2206

Table 3.4: Documents Sent to the Court of Kastamonu: Classification

Volumes	Orders			Warrants	Total entries
	Milt. Tax. Sec. (1)	*Zulm* (2)	Disputes (3)	(4)	(5)
Vol. 3	36 (14%)	5 (2%)	1 (0%)	61 (24%)	251
Vol. 1	43 (18%)	10 (4%)	9 (4%)	47 (20%)	235
Vol. 4	63 (28%)	8 (4%)	8 (4%)	70 (31%)	225
Vol. 5	33 (13%)	2 (1%)	5 (2%)	53 (21%)	256
Vol. 12	4 (4%)	– (0%)	1 (1%)	27 (29%)	93
Vol. 19	21 (12%)	2 (1%)	4 (2%)	19 (11%)	175
Vol. 34	9 (5%)	1 (1%)	2 (1%)	10 (6%)	165
Vol. 35	72 (18%)	– (0%)	5 (1%)	52 (13%)	407
Vol. 36	60 (33%)	2 (1%)	4 (2%)	33 (18%)	183
Vol. 37	10 (8%)	– (0%)	2 (2%)	11 (9%)	122
Vol. 38	19 (7%)	1 (0%)	3 (1%)	45 (15%)	292
Vol. 39	84 (23%)	1 (0%)	7 (2%)	33 (9%)	364
Total	454 (16%)	32 (1%)	51 (2%)	461 (17%)	2768

Tables 3.3 and 3.4 provide a numerical distribution of the documents sent from the central government, the capital of the province of Anatolia (Kütahya), or from higher authorities elsewhere. These documents can be divided into two broad categories: orders (*fermans* and *buyuruldus*) and copies of warrants (*berats*) recorded in the court registers. The orders received by the courts of Çankırı and Kastamonu also constitute a variegated subset of documents. I have categorized these orders according to their contents to draw a picture of the functions of the *kadıs* in these courts.

In the tables above, the first columns list the numbers of orders sent to the provinces for military, fiscal, and security reasons. Those orders that were military in nature generally demanded the mobilization of troops from the provinces, the punishment of soldiers who failed to report to the imperial army, and the provision of necessary supplies and equipment during campaigns. Orders that were fiscal in nature, on the other hand, usually demanded the collection of various (regular and irregular) taxes and payments levied upon the inhabitants of Çankırı and Kastamonu. Finally, there are documents that relate to the security of Çankırı, Kastamonu, and neighboring areas. These orders are usually about preventing banditry, protecting travelers and merchants from attacks, and maintaining peace in the countryside as well as in the urban areas.

Zulm, which means "injustice" in modern and Ottoman Turkish, was used in Ottoman administrative terminology to describe illegitimate taxation and excessive violence committed by local military and administrative officials. There are numerous orders in the *sicil*s sent to prevent these kinds of actions. These orders were usually drafted in response to personal, written complaints of the taxpayers. The columns with the *zulm* sub-heading provide the numbers of such orders found in Çankırı and Kastamonu court records.

Under the sub-heading "Disputes" we find the numbers of orders about various kinds of contentions between different individuals or groups within Çankırı and Kastamonu that had initially been brought to the attention of the central government, governor-general of the province of Anatolia, or other legal or administrative authorities such as the *kazʿasker* of Anatolia.[2] These orders indicate that the contentions reported to non-local authorities were usually directed back to the local *mahkeme*s to be heard and resolved according to the law. Occasionally, and especially in the cases of endowment (*vakıf*) or tax allotment disputes, the center shared its own records and demanded that the local *kadı* resolve the issue according to this information as well as to the claims and evidence supplied by the litigants.

The fourth columns provide the second major category of documents that were not drafted in the courts. They give the numbers of warrants (*berat*s) in the *sicil*s for different religious, military, and administrative posts in the two sub-provinces. These posts include lieutenant governorships (*mütesellimlik*s), trusteeships (*mütevellilik*s) of different endowments, wardenships of Çankırı and Kastamonu fortresses (*dizdarlık*s), prayer leaderships (*imamet*s), etc. These warrants announced the value, the duration, and the salary of the office that was presented to the new appointee. As is obvious from the tables, these documents constitute a sizable portion of the records drafted outside

[2] Uriel Heyd describes the office and duties of *kazʿasker* as follows. "*(K)adi-ʿasker*, lit 'judge of the army'; from 1481 onwards two in number, 'of Rumeli [Rumelia]' (the senior) and 'of Anadolu [Anatolia]', both being permanent members of the Imperial Divan [Council]. Besides their duties on campaign, they appointed the cadis (up to a certain rank) in their respective provinces and had the oversight of various legal matters, civil and criminal, concerning all members of the *ʿaskeri* class." See Uriel Heyd, *Studies in Old Ottoman Criminal Law*, edited by V.L. Ménage (Oxford: Clarendon Press, 1973), p. 339. Brackets added.

the courts of Çankırı and Kastamonu. The last columns remind us of the totals of all the documents in each court register for the purpose of comparison.

Before we proceed to the interpretation of the above tables, I should give two warnings about my method of classification. First of all, the sub-categorizations used in the tables do not exhaust all the variations in the orders received by the courts in question. Although these sub-categories include the most common kinds of orders in the records, there also exist a few other types that do not belong to any of the categories presented in the table. For example, an order to build or turn a small mosque (*mescid*) into a Friday mosque and an imperial command to provide horses for messengers passing through are excluded from the above table. For this reason, the numbers of orders presented in the tables are less than the total numbers found in the *sicil*s.

Secondly, the boundaries between some of the sub-categories presented in the tables above are somewhat fluid. This is especially true for military and fiscal orders since a significant number of the orders received by the courts of Çankırı and Kastamonu had both military and fiscal purposes. It is difficult to decide, for example, whether an order to collect the levies of *imdad-ı seferiyye* or *sürsat akçesi* from the inhabitants of Çankırı and Kastamonu should be assigned to the sub-category of "military" or "taxation." Nevertheless such a decision is not really critical for my concerns here, since in the orders of both of these sub-categories, the duties and functions of the *kadı* were unambiguously similar in nature.

The numerical distribution presented in the tables above provides an understanding of the balance among the judicial, administrative, and notarial functions of the courts of Çankırı and Kastamonu. Such an understanding is possible because these documents relate to different functions and responsibilities of the provincial *kadı*s. The orders included in the combined set of "Military-Taxation-Security" point out the administrative responsibilities of the courts. Orders sent in relation to the local disputes and acts of "injustice," on the other hand, evoke the judicial duties of the courts since these documents urge the court officials to consider and resolve those cases brought to the attention of the central government and other higher authorities. Finally, warrants were brought to the court and recorded in the *sicil*s mainly for notarial and archival purposes, and, unlike orders, they did not necessitate the involvement of the *kadı* or other members of the court in any administrative or judicial process unless their arrival generated a conflict within the community. Occasionally, certain appointments were eagerly pursued by specific individuals and were subject to local contentions. When warrants were offered for these kinds of appointments, the *kadı*s were asked to check the validity of the claims and counter-claims reported to the center by different parties against rival individuals or groups.

What we find in the numerical distribution of these documents in both tables is an emphasis on the courts' administrative and notarial functions; those records that relate to the courts' judicial responsibilities make up less than ten percent of the total number of documents originally drafted outside the local courts. This observation is not surprising since the majority of records that illustrate the judicial responsibilities and functions of a provincial court were drafted in the *mahkeme*. Yet the similarities between tables 3.3 and 3.4 end at this point; from my point of view, a more critical observation is the proportional difference between the numbers of administrative and notarial documents that were sent from imperial and provincial headquarters to these two courts. In the case of Çankırı, these documents constitute more than half of all the entries found in the *sicil*s. In the court records of Kastamonu, on the other hand, they make up less than one third of all the documents.

The same system of categorization used in tables 3.3 and 3.4 can be applied to those documents that were locally composed. The following tables provide the numerical distribution of the three most common kinds of documents that were drafted in the courts of Çankırı and Kastamonu.

Among the three columns of the tables above, column three is the most removed from the judicial functions of the court. This column offers the total number of tax rosters in each *sicil* volume where we find the amounts of monetary and in-kind taxes levied upon the neighborhoods, villages, and districts of Çankırı and Kastamonu. Usually the tax allotments of these fiscal units were determined by the *kadı* and by the prominent members of the sub-province in a "town meeting" held in the court.

Column two provides the numbers of disputes brought to the court for legal resolution; the technical term for these documents is *iʿlam*, and they include records of both civil and criminal cases. Finally,

Table 3.5: Documents Drafted in the Court of Çankırı: Classification

Volumes	Contracts (1)	Disputes (2)	Tax Records (3)
Volume 1	21 (12%)	14 (8%)	– (0%)
Volume 2	14 (11%)	8 (5%)	6 (4%)
Volume 3	18 (14%)	18 (18%)	1 (1%)
Volume 4	25 (12%)	14 (6%)	55 (25%)
Volume 5	41 (25%)	11 (6%)	11 (6%)
Volume 6	84 (22%)	10 (3%)	36 (9%)
Volume 7	14 (13%)	1 (1%)	22 (20%)
Volume 8	20 (1%)	3 (0%)	31 (12%)
Volume 9	11 (8%)	2 (1%)	24 (17%)
Volume 10	6 (5%)	– (0%)	23 (21%)
Volume 11	15 (8%)	2 (1%)	25 (13%)
Volume 12	– (0%)	– (0%)	11 (25%)
Volume 13	21 (14)	– (0%)	22 (15%)
Total 2	90 (13%)	83 (4%)	267 (12%)

Note: Statistics in parentheses denote the percentage proportions of the preceding figures to the total number of entries in a particular register.

Table 3.6: Documents Drafted in the Court of Kastamonu: Classification

Volumes	Contracts (1)	Disputes (2)	Tax Records (3)
Volume 1	41 (18%)	53 (22%)	4 (2%)
Volume 4	28 (12%)	29 (13%)	1 (0%)
Volume 5	56 (21%)	77 (30%)	1 (0%)
Volume 12	27 (29%)	26 (28%)	– (0%)
Volume 19	86 (49%)	29 (16%)	1 (1%)
Volume 34	76 (47%)	37 (22%)	2 (1%)
Volume 35	134 (33%)	66 (16%)	30 (7%)
Volume 36	34 (19%)	20 (11%)	6 (3%)
Volume 37	65 (53%)	28 (23%)	1 (1%)
Volume 38	96 (33%)	82 (28%)	7 (2%)
Volume 39	127 (35%)	64 (17%)	16 (4%)
Total	834 (30%)	572 (21%)	72 (3%)

Note: Statistics in parentheses denote the percentage proportions of the preceding figures to the total number of entries in a particular register.

we find in column one the numbers of contracts—*hüccet*s—enacted in the *mahkeme* and recorded in the court records. These contracts were of various kinds, ranging from personal agreements (marriage, divorce), to commercial transactions, and even to agreements of compensation between legal heirs of a victim and his or her murderers (blood money, *döm-ü-diyet*).[3] Although the enactment of these contracts did not necessarily require judicial action by the *kadı*, their recognition was dependent on their agreement with the law. For this reason, we can assume that the legal guidance and supervision of the *kadı* guaranteed the validity of the contracts that we encounter in the court records. I contend that of those records composed in the court, only the *iʿlam*s and *hüccet*s demonstrate the judicial activities of the *kadı*.

Tables 3.5 and 3.6 demonstrate that the most notable difference between the *sicil*s of Çankırı and Kastamonu appears in the numbers of disputes brought to and contracts enacted in the two courts, although the total numbers of entries found in the records of these courts are comparable. This difference has important implications regarding the roles and functions of the *kadı*s of these courts. According to what we find in the *sicil*s of Çankırı and Kastamonu, the judicial functions of the *kadı* of Kastamonu were more pronounced than those of his counterpart in Çankırı. This point is substantiated by the following tables, which distinguish between those documents that reflect the administrative and notarial responsibilities of the two courts and those records that relate to their judicial functions.

The figures in the following tables are calculated by using the data presented in the previous tables (tables 3.3 to 3.6), and they aim to draw an *approximate* picture of the balance between different responsibilities of the court.[4]

---

[3] "Contracts" in tables 3.5 and 3.6 also include the records of estates divided by the court among the heirs of the deceased (*tereke*s).

[4] The emphasis in this sentence is on the word "approximate," as it can be very difficult to decide whether a document relates to the administrative or judicial responsibilities of the *kadı*.

Table 3.7: Division of Labor in the Court of Çankırı

Volumes	Administrative – Notarial (1)	Judicial (2)	Column 2 / Column 1 (3)
Volume 1	128	41	0.32
Volume 2	104	33	0.32
Volume 3	82	42	0.51
Volume 4	155	54	0.35
Volume 5	97	61	0.63
Volume 6	243	115	0.47
Volume 7	73	35	0.48
Volume 8	197	43	0.22
Volume 9	116	26	0.22
Volume 10	103	8	0.07
Volume 11	168	27	0.16
Volume 12	38	6	0.16
Volume 13	113	26	0.23
Total	1617	692	0.43

Table 3.8: Division of Labor in the Court of Kastamonu

Volumes	Administrative – Notarial (1)	Judicial (2)	Column 2 / Column 1 (3)
Volume 3	116	135	1.16
Volume 1	119	116	0.97
Volume 4	147	73	0.49
Volume 5	109	147	1.35
Volume 12	37	54	1.46
Volume 19	51	124	2.43
Volume 34	49	116	2.37
Volume 35	201	207	1.03
Volume 36	123	60	0.49
Volume 37	37	83	2.24
Volume 38	105	190	1.81
Volume 39	165	199	1.21
Total	1259	1501	1.19

Clearly, the Çankırı court's responsibilities and workload differed significantly from those of the Kastamonu court. Whereas judicial entries constitute a fraction of the number of administrative and notarial documents in the Çankırı *sicil*s, they are the majority in the *sicil*s of Kastamonu. This situation is especially noticeable in the last six volumes of Çankırı court records, which suggests that the administrative character of the court of Çankırı became more dominant over the course of time.

To state the obvious, the most important implication of these findings is that the "character" of different courts, even those located relatively close to each other, might vary considerably. Indeed, according to the court records, the court of Kastamonu was able to provide a forum for communal and individual decision-making as well as for dispute resolution. The court of Çankırı, however, acted more as a conveyor between the center and the local community and lacked, in relative terms, the capacity to act as a stage for judicial and civil autonomy.[5]

Why do we have relatively few documents that relate to the judicial activities in Çankırı? The difference in the populations of Çankırı and Kastamonu might have been a factor: As demonstrated in chapter two, the *kaza* of Kastamonu was larger and more crowded than the *kaza* of Çankırı. This means that the court of Çankırı must have had relatively few clients and disputes to deal with; this may be partly why the documentation sent from the imperial and provincial centers for mainly military and administrative purposes constitutes a high percentage of the Çankırı court records. Moreover, and as I will demonstrate in a subsequent chapter, the existence of alternative sites of dispute resolution must have also impinged on the popularity of the courts, at least to a certain extent.[6] At this point I am unable to offer more satisfactory explanations for the relative lack of judicial documents in the *sicil*s of Çankırı.

The *Kadi* as an Intermediary

Given what we have just discovered in the preceding tables, it is plausible that in Çankırı the administrative stature of the *kadı* over-

---

[5] It is possible that this situation was not peculiar to the *sicil*s of Çankırı. Indeed Virginia Aksan claims that the majority of the entries in the *sicil*s of eighteenth century Sofya were also sent from Istanbul or the army headquarters at the border, or were probate records of soldiers in the area (private communication). According to Beshara Doumani, the special condition of the Sofia *sicil*s could be a consequence of Sofia's critical location in a frontier region, which is obviously not applicable to Çankırı (personal communication).

[6] However, there is no reason to assume that such alternative sites did not exist in Kastamonu.

shadowed his image as a representative of the sharia: If the court of Çankırı was indeed relatively underutilized for judicial purposes, as I tend to assume, it would be reasonable to claim that the influence Çankırı *kadı* had over the local community was mainly based on his administrative functions and responsibilities.

How, then, did the Ottoman *kadı* affect his socio-political environment as an administrative agent of the state? And how did his administrative activities shape his image in the eyes of the local people? Unfortunately, not many historians have dealt with these questions, which may be due to a tendency among Ottomanists to regard the *kadı* as primarily a judicial functionary and to disregard his non-judicial operations. In places like Çankırı, where the non-judicial responsibilities of the court far exceeded its judicial functions, this tendency conceals the ways the *kadı* and other members of the court influenced the local society. In subsequent chapters, I shall examine in detail the judicial activities of the Ottoman *kadı*. For now, though, let us turn our attention to his administrative operations, which highlight his role as an intermediary between the local and the center.

Ronald Jennings is one of the few scholars who recognized the place of the Ottoman *kadı* in the bureaucratic structure of the provincial administration. He demonstrated in his work that among his other functions, the *kadı* was also a bureaucrat who represented the authority of the sultan and his government at the local level, not only by transmitting and executing the orders conveyed from the center, but also by maintaining peace and order in his locality, regulating the prices, and supervising the quality of the products sold and bought in the market, all in the name of the sultan.[7] My observations indicate that this assessment of the *kadı*'s administrative functions is only partially accurate because his representation of the center to the local community was not his only responsibility as an intermediary. In theory, he was also obligated to represent the local to the center in judicial and administrative matters, and it is this role of the *kadı* that I am going to examine in this section.

According to the court records of Çankırı and Kastamonu, a major function of the court in representing the local to the center was a

[7] Jennings, "*Kadı*, Court, and Legal Procedure," pp. 137–138. Here, I am not interested in providing a detailed discussion of these activities and their impact on the local society, which are well documented in the contributions of Jennings, Uriel Heyd, and others.

specific sort of guidance and intercession. Most of the orders and warrants that *sicil*s contain were sent in response to petitions that were frequently (but not always) drafted in the court. In this process of petitioning, the *kadı* and other court officials must have performed important services both to the petitioners and the government. Local people probably benefited from the scribal skills of the court personnel and their ability to draft formal petitions that conformed to pre-established bureaucratic and scribal conventions. Although we cannot be sure how seriously these conventions were observed, it is apparent from the material in the *sicil*s that the subjects attempted to make their petitions credible in the eyes of the central and provincial authorities by conforming to these conventions.

From the viewpoint of the central and provincial authorities, the involvement of the local *kadı* in these petitions probably guaranteed some degree of assurance regarding the accuracy of the allegations. Indeed, there exist orders from the government demanding that provincial authorities bar appellants who were trying to reach Istanbul from presenting their petitions, unless they prove that they had already obtained the "endorsement" (*ʿarz*) of their *kadı*s.[8] In this sense, provincial *kadı*s usually acted as official witnesses on whose testimony the government had an understandable tendency to depend. And for this particular reason the endorsement of a *kadı* became one of the most sought-after documents in the struggle between different parties in Çankırı and Kastamonu who were competing for provincial offices. Although the *kadı* was not officially expected to get involved in local appointments, he was usually an active participant in the hunt for office.

It is true that the endorsement of the *kadı* was not absolutely essential in this process: Numerous warrants were given out without such an endorsement and in response to direct petitions of those who were willing to acquire or re-acquire certain provincial posts.[9] Never-

[8] See, for example, ÇCR, vol. 7, 9–13 and ÇCR, vol. 12, 20–21.

[9] For example, in 1091/1680 the government ordered the *kadı* and the lieutenant governor of Çankırı to reappoint a certain Abdülmecid to the prayer leadership (*imamet*) of the mosque of Şeyh Osman. This order was sent in response to a petition that Abdülmecid had previously sent to the government to complain against certain unnamed individuals who had been able to seize the *imamet* from him illegitimately. See ÇCR, vol. 3, 8–10. In 1109/1697 the wardenship (*dizdarlık*) of the fortress of Çankırı was given to Elhac Mehmed Ali, who had personally gone to Istanbul to complain against the previous *dizdar* of the fortress, Mehmed bin Ömer, and to request appointment to the office. See ÇCR, vol. 5, 10–22.

theless, the fact that an endorsement of an individual by a particular *kadı* was frequently prompted by the endorsement of another *kadı* on behalf of another individual indicates that their support must have carried some significance. There are repeated examples of situations in which subsequent *kadı*s in a particular locality endorsed the applications of rival parties for a specific office. In fact, it seems that a new *kadı* could give a chance to those who were unable to gain the support of the previous *kadı*. For example, it is indicated in an order that was sent to Çankırı in 1142/1730—in response to a petition from certain unidentified inhabitants of the town—that one İsfendiyar was able to seize the much-sought-after trusteeship of the Sultan Süleyman Han endowment illegally. According to this petition (as reported in the order), İsfendiyar had obtained this post despite the disapproval of the inhabitants of Çankırı and the refusal of the previous *kadı* of the town to support his appointment. Yet after the dismissal of the previous *kadı*, İsfendiyar was able to influence the new *kadı* "because of the strength of his financial situation" and get a letter of endorsement from him before anybody knew about it.[10]

There are also many examples of situations where a man who could not get the endorsement of the *kadı* for a local office would obtain the support of a neighboring *kadı*. For example, in 1141/1729 Şeyh Mehmed Halife from Çankırı acquired the endorsement of the *na'ib* in Toht[11] when the *kadı* of Çankırı refused to support his appointment to the *imamet* of the Kayser Beğ mosque in Çankırı.[12] It is also pointed out in the same entry that when the *kadı* of Çankırı endorsed the appointment of one Seyyid Mehmed to the *imamet* of Mirahor mosque, "all the inhabitants of the neighborhood" asked the *kadı* of nearby Kurupazarı[13] district to report the corruption of Seyyid Mehmed and the *kadı* of Çankırı to the government and stop this appointment.[14]

[10] ÇCR, vol. 8, 27–51. Also see ÇCR vol. 1, 1–1, 3–5; vol. 8, 26–50; 43–80; 57–103 and 116–201; KCR, vol. 12, 25b–1, 36a–1, 36a–2.

[11] A *kaza* in the *sancak* of Çankırı that was located about 30 kilometers away from the Çankırı *kaza*.

[12] See ÇCR, vol. 8, 39–73.

[13] This too was a *kaza* in the *sancak* of Çankırı.

[14] See ÇCR, vol. 8, 116–201. For other examples see ÇCR, vol. 7, 29–41; ÇCR, vol. 8, 57–103; ÇCR, vol. 11, 102–163, 111–179, 113–181, 74–117. KCR, vol. 12, 31b–2.

In fact, this second example suggests that the endorsement of the *kadı* was not limited to those offices within the boundaries of his jurisdiction. And the lack of evidence that local contenders, rival *kadı*s, or the central government protested such interventions might indeed imply that the endorsement of a *kadı* was something different—perhaps less formal—from an official letter of support by a state functionary who was authorized to give such endorsements for offices located within his jurisdiction.[15] In other words, in the eyes of the government, the endorsement of a *kadı* might have meant nothing more than the support of a figure of some stature and prominence whose influence was not based on the office he occupied.

This, however, does not change the fact that the office of the local *kadı* was significantly politicized, and, consequently, his active involvement in the process of office hunting occasionally made him open to contempt. Accusations of bribery and corruption are frequent in the *sicil*s in relation to the roles the *kadı* played in assigning local offices; the central government repeatedly found it necessary to warn the *kadı*s, as well as the other provincial functionaries, against such illegal and illegitimate practices.[16]

Admittedly, it is difficult to claim that the government really cared about the identities of the appointees or whom the local *kadı*s endorsed for different provincial offices. Quite the contrary, the entries in the court records of Çankırı and Kastamonu give the impression that local offices changed hands frequently in response to petitions with contradictory claims. In many cases, contenders for local offices sent

---

[15] I have evidence that jurisdictional boundaries of local courts were protected vigorously in the cases of legal hearings and judicial decisions. For example the *kadı* of the island of Sisam (Samos, in the Aegean Sea) sent a letter to the center in 1118/1706 to request an imperial order compelling the inhabitants of Sisam not to take their legal disputes anywhere other than the court of Sisam; see CA 4851. Also see CA 2072 and 3152 for other examples.

[16] In an imperial rescript of justice dated 1141/1729, the most frequent complaints against the *kadı*s and their assistants (*na'ib*s) were listed as follows: ignorance on the part of the *na'ib*s and the *kadı*s of most basic legal rules and issues; their corruption and immorality; the tendency of the *kadı*s to farm their offices to their *na'ib*s in return for big sums of money; their tendency to benefit illegally from state revenues and to pocket those taxes that should be collected for the government; their neglect in the execution of the imperial orders; fabrication of false reports in relation to provincial issues. See ÇCR, vol. 7, 8–12. There are also many reports of individual cases of corruption. See, for example, KCR, vol. 1, 244; KCR, vol. 4, 162–231; KCR, vol. 38, 56, 111; KCR, vol. 39, 140–37, 136–377; ÇCR, vol. 8, 116–201; ÇCR, vol. 9, 2–1; ÇCR, vol. 11, 131–? etc.

petitions against their rivals and accused them of acquiring certain posts illegally and usually with the illicit help of certain *kadıs*. The central government rarely hesitated to grant the wishes of these petitioners and offer the posts in question to them. Yet, when the dismissed parties sent similar reports to the center, they, too, were granted their requests and were reappointed to the same offices following the dismissal of the previous holders.[17]

It is interesting that many members of the community did not hesitate to replace the intermediary functions of the *kadı* with his judicial authority. This is especially noticeable in the court records of Çankırı where it seems that the people preferred to employ their *kadıs* as official scribes and witnesses rather than adjudicators with the authority to solve judicial contentions immediately. Certain problems or disputes were initially taken to the court not to be legally resolved by the *kadı* but to be drafted and then petitioned to the imperial or provincial centers through his intermediacy. For example, we learn from an order sent to the lieutenant governor and the *kadı* of Çankırı in 1119/1707 that the inhabitants of the village of Kayı had previously come to the court of Çankırı and complained against certain individuals with military titles "who owned land and property" in their village. Reportedly, these individuals had been refusing to join in the collective tax burden of the village because they claimed to have tax exemptions. Through the intermediacy of the *kadı*, the villagers asked for an imperial order from the central government to pressure the accused parties to pay their tax shares. In the order sent in response to this petition, the government made it clear that "if these individuals did really own land and property in the aforementioned village, they should be compelled by the authorities to pay the required taxes."[18]

It is not clear why the villagers did not demand the resolution of the dispute in the local court. This was possible in legal terms, and there are examples of such resolutions in the court records of Çankırı and Kastamonu. For the reasons that will be discussed later, the military status of the parties against whom the villagers complained might have discouraged the villagers from seeking a resolution in the local court. It is likely that the disproportionate balance of power in

[17] See for example, ÇCR, vol. 3, 13–17, and 53–68; vol. 3, 22–30 and 65–86; ÇCR, vol. 7, 58–82 and 62–93; ÇCR, vol. 7, 44–63 and vol. 8, 34–64.

[18] ÇCR, vol. 6, 105–177.

the court frequently led weaker parties to request that their complaints be forwarded to the center instead of asking the *kadı* to act as an adjudicator.

Apparently, the subjects were well aware of their rights to appeal to the government and demand justice. Indeed, in the court records of Çankırı and Kastamonu, there exist quite a number of orders from the government and higher provincial authorities concerning the local disputes and acts of injustice brought to their attention, many of which could have been resolved at the local level. The following tables demonstrate that the inhabitants of Çankırı were especially willing to take their cases initially to the provincial or central authorities (with or without the intermediacy of the local *kadı*) rather than to the local court for resolution. Although the same cannot be claimed for the inhabitants of Kastamonu, the total number of relevant documents that we encounter in the *sicil*s of Kastamonu is not insignificant, either.

Table 3.9: Preference between Alternative Judicial and Administrative Offices in Dispute Resolution (Çankırı)

Volumes	Numbers of complaints directly brought to the local court	Numbers of orders issued in response to the complaints reported to higher authorities
Volume 1	14	6
Volume 2	8	11
Volume 3	18	6
Volume 4	14	15
Volume 5	11	9
Volume 6	10	21
Volume 7	1	23
Volume 8	3	20
Volume 9	2	13
Volume 10	–	2
Volume 11	1	10
Volume 12	–	6
Volume 13	–	5
Total	83	147

Table 3.10: Preference between Alternative Judicial and Administrative Offices in Dispute Resolution (Kastamonu)

Volumes	Numbers of complaints directly brought to the local court	Numbers of orders issued in response to the complaints reported to higher authorities
Volume 3	61	6
Volume 1	53	19
Volume 4	29	16
Volume 5	77	7
Volume 12	26	1
Volume 19	29	6
Volume 34	37	3
Volume 35	66	5
Volume 36	20	6
Volume 37	28	2
Volume 38	82	4
Volume 39	64	8
Total	572	83

We know that the local *kadı*s, whose primary responsibility was to hear and resolve legal and administrative contentions, were not supposed to intervene in local disputes or confrontations unless the litigants explicitly sought their assistance. When the litigants preferred to report their problems to Istanbul, Edirne, or Kütahya (the provincial center), the *kadı* did not have any authority to prevent them from doing so. Yet knowing that their petitions would probably be directed back to the local court for resolution, as was usually done by the central government, why did the inhabitants of Çankırı and Kastamonu choose to send so many appeals to the imperial center or the governor-general?[19]

It seems that a significant portion of the petitions and complaints sent to the imperial and provincial centers were about acts of injustice—illegal or excessive taxation by local officials and subsequent

[19] The central government played an important role in the resolution of disputes regarding the administrative and usufruct rights over the assets of charity endowments and the distribution of tax allotments among different individuals and local communities. Also initiated by the appeals of the populace of Çankırı and Kastamonu, the government involvement in these kinds of disputes seems to be less overtly political and controversial in its nature since it was primarily oriented towards guidance and clarification of the matters at the local level with reference to the records kept in the archives and records in the center.

violence and physical abuse—inflicted upon the inhabitants of these two sub-provinces.[20] This pattern might indicate an inclination among the provincial people to secure the support of higher authorities in their confrontations with local military administrators. In the *sicil*s, I found more than ninety orders that demand these complaints be carefully investigated and resolved. Furthermore, on many occasions the central government or the governor-general sent special inspectors (*müfettiş*) with their orders to supervise the legal processes.

By reporting their legal contentions to higher authorities, the petitioners attempted to guarantee the objectivity of the court processes: The orders that were received by the same court demanded in forceful language that if the allegations against the executive officials were proven to be accurate, the *kadı* was to force the guilty official to return what he had extracted illegally. The *kadı* was also urged to report the disobedience of this official to the central government or the headquarters of the province of Anatolia, if the latter chose to disregard this order.

It is not that the people of Çankırı and Kastamonu took no cases of illegal taxation or abuse by the provincial officials directly to the local *mahkeme* during this period of approximately one hundred years.[21] Nevertheless, only thirteen such cases are reported in the *sicil*s of Çankırı and Kastamonu, and most of them were initiated against minor provincial officials such as the members of the provincial cavalry units (*sipahi*s), local janissaries, or village constables (*karye zabiti*). These observations suggest that the subjects generally were not optimistic about the effectiveness of the legal process initiated against members of the higher echelons of the local military-administrative officials, especially if not conducted under the watchful eyes of the agents of the government.[22]

---

[20] This is implicit in the information presented in tables 3.3 and 3.4 above. Columns two and three in these tables provide the numbers of those orders that were sent from higher authorities in response to previous petitions and complaints filed by individual parties or small groups of people. According to the information provided in these columns, about 45 per cent of all those orders that were sent in response to local petitions and complaints are related to the acts of "injustice" in Çankırı. In Kastamonu this figure is about 39 per cent.

[21] For examples of such situations see ÇCR, vol. 2, 9–22; ÇCR, vol. 3, 32–45; ÇCR, vol. 4, 19–71; ÇCR, vol. 6, 45–72; KCR, vol. 3, 115–22; KCR, vol. 3, 117–27; KCR, vol. 3, 135, 74; KCR, vol. 1, 95; KCR, vol. 4, 128–274; KCR, vol. 35, 63–98; KCR, vol. 38, 85–134.

[22] See KCR, vol. 3, 115–22, 117–27 and 135–74 for examples of such trials.

It was not impossible for the inhabitants of Çankırı and Kastamonu to have their cases transferred to other and presumably more independent judicial platforms. And although this seems to have happened only rarely, some of the petitioners may have hoped to do so since it probably neutralized the disproportionate power balance in favor of influential opponents in the local court. There is evidence that this was a possible way to diminish the capacity of local power-holders to influence the legal processes: In 1715, for example, when the military commander (*serdar*) of Drama in Rumelia was ordered to go to the Rumelia court to face the accusations of the inhabitants of his locality, he refused to obey this order and demanded to be tried in Drama. In a second order the government asked the governor-general of Rumelia to summon the commander to his headquarters since "it was obvious that he will not be tried in his own locality."[23]

Other documents indicate that the local court may have lacked the ability to try certain individuals or, even if it could do so, enforce its decisions upon them. The case of Mustafa, a lieutenant governor of Çankırı, is an example of the first situation: According to an imperial order, Mustafa, who was accused of committing robbery, kidnapping, and assault could not be adjudicated in the court of Çankiri because of his "tyranny."[24] The following order sent to the lieutenant governor and the *kadı* of Kastamonu, on the other hand, demonstrates the other possibility:

> A retired *sipahi*, Elhac Ali, sent a petition to my felicitous threshold and reported that he had made a contract with the trustee of the endowment of İsmail Beğ in Kastamonu to rent the inn of the endowment (Kurşunlu Han) in return for the payment of one hundred *guruş* per day for a period of three years. After the enactment of the contract, Elhac Ali had also spent a substantial amount of money for necessary repairs and further constructions in the inn. Although there was no legal reason for anybody to interfere, the leader of the local janissaries (*Ocak Ağası*) Mehmed and another janissary, Kundakçıoğlu Hüseyin, occupied the inn, claiming that they had the right to do so. When Elhac Ali had taken the issue to the local court, the janissaries were ordered by the *kadı* to vacate the inn immediately. Nevertheless accord-

[23] CZ 1041.
[24] ÇCR, vol. 11, 37–55.

> ing to what Elhac Ali reported in his petition, the janissaries, being among the unjust people of their locality (*zalemeden olmalarıyla*), refused to obey the decision of the court, broke the lock [of the inn], and occupied it once again. In his petition, Elhac Ali stated that he had also acquired a legal opinion (*fetva*) and begged us to issue an order commanding the jannisaries to return the inn to him in accordance with the title-deed (*temessük*) and the *fetva* that he holds . . .[25]

In the rest of the document, the government orders the *mütesellim* and the *kadı* of Kastamonu to hear and adjudicate the case once again and return the inn to Elhac Mehmed if what he reported in his petition was accurate.

It is interesting that only a very small number (nine) of petitions were actually drafted in the courts of Çankırı and Kastmonu to report the incidents of "injustice," although petitions for other types of disputes were frequently drafted in the two courts. Furthermore, almost none of those few petitions were against the higher echelons of provincial officials, such as the governor or the lieutenant governor of the sub-province.[26] It seems that the *kadı*s of Çankırı and Kastamonu were willing to draft petitions against provincial officials only if the accused were among the lower-ranking members of the military and the administrative elite, or if, as was the case in one instance, the lieutenant governor against whom the petition was written had already been deposed.[27] This observation suggests that the courts of Çankırı and Kastamonu lacked not only the ability to disregard the disproportionate balance of power in the process of adjudication, but at least in some occasions, the capacity to link the local to the center, and to represent the former to the latter.

Did fear play a role in this situation? We cannot be sure about the answer. Nevertheless, there is some evidence that the highest military-administrative officials of the sub-province might have had

[25] KCR, vol. 4, 132–169, entry of CI 1102/February 1691.

[26] There are only two complaints against a governor or lieutenant governor drafted in the court. Both of them were drafted in the court of Kastamonu. See KCR, vol. 3, 57–125 and KCR, vol. 36, 191–126.

[27] ÇCR, vol. 8, 60–109. In a petition that was sent to Istanbul in December 1746, more than one hundred inhabitants of the *kaza* of Zagre reported that it was because of their *kadı*'s inability to "protect them" from the oppression of their subgovernor that they were forced to appeal to the central government. It seems that the *kadı* was not even involved in the drafting of this petition. See CA, 4111.

the ability to intimidate or to pressure members of the court. For example, according to a 1712 order, the governor of Kastamonu jailed the *kadı* and fined him when the *kadı* refused to withdraw his allegations against some of the governor's men in relation to a dispute regarding the blood money of the *kadı*'s son.[28] My findings in the Prime Ministry Archives of Turkey also indicate that before the nineteenth century, threats and acts of violence were not uncommon between the court officials (especially the *kadı*) and local military-administrative officials:[29] A notable example of such violence can be found in a letter of complaint sent to the capital in 1767 by the wife and two sons of Ahmed Efendi, the former *kadı* of Niğbolu. According to this letter, the lieutenant governor of Niğbolu had asked for Ahmed Efendi's support against the petitions of the local populace to Istanbul, reporting his acts of oppression. Ahmed Efendi, however, refused to write such a perjurious letter, and in response, the lieutenant governor, through bribery and his connections in Istanbul, had the *kadı* dismissed and forced him to leave Niğbolu. Furthermore, the lieutenant governor had the *kadı* and his household followed and attacked after their departure. The *kadı* and one of his sons were killed during this attack. The letter indicates that even after these incidents and repeated letters of complaint by the members of Ahmed Efendi's family, the lieutenant governor continued to hold his post in Niğbolu. The wife and sons of Ahmed Efendi begged for justice in their letter.[30]

The inhabitants of Çankırı and Kastamonu usually drafted petitions against high-ranking military-administrative officers themselves without any help from their *kadı*. More interestingly, perhaps, although the orders issued by the central government or the governor-general invariably dictated that disputes between the people and the provincial officers needed to be settled in the local court, only a small

[28] ÇCR, vol. 6, 116–192.

[29] See, for example, CA 1022, 2978, 4808, 5002, 5320, 5709, 6116 and CD 13019 and 16582.

[30] CA 4822. Other documents indicate that physical violence might not necessarily constitute the only type of threat against the *kadı*s and other members of the courts. For example, according to several orders sent to different provincial centers some "governors, lieutenant governors and other military authorities" were very much involved in the appointment and dismissal (literally: "appointing and dismissing") of the *kadı*s, their assistants and other court offlcials in their locality. See CA 1775, 4634 and 6116.

number (six) of such disputes was actually brought to and resolved in the court following the arrival of such orders. Does this mean that these orders were generally ineffective in solving disputes between the people of Çankırı and Kastamonu and their military-administrative officers by judicial means, and in preventing injustice? Again, we cannot be sure about the answer to this question, yet the information found in the *sicil*s is unsettling.

Those issues that were most commonly resolved in the local *mahkeme* without intervention by the central government or the governor-general involved disputes about inheritance, debt, property, and different sorts of assaults usually resulting in rape, injury, and less frequently, murder. This does not mean that the inhabitants of Çankırı and Kastamonu never attempted to report such problems to Istanbul or Kütahya. In fact, in cases involving robbery, the number of complaints brought to the court (five) is less than the number of complaints sent to the imperial center and the governor-general (seven). Nevertheless this finding seems to be an exception; such matters were usually handled locally.

Conclusion

This chapter has raised several points. First of all, the "characters" of individual courts, in terms of their major occupations and responsibilities, could be very different from one another. Such a difference is especially noteworthy between the courts of Çankırı and Kastamonu: Whereas notarial and administrative services occupied nearly all the time of the former, judicial services constituted the greater part of the latter's operations. I believe that this difference is important: Although the issue of how the local *kadı*s and courts were perceived by the community is something that we cannot be really sure about, it is probable that this perception had a great deal to do with the "character" of the court.

Secondly, I have argued that the intermediary position the courts occupied between the local and the center, and in particular, the responsibility of the court to convey local requests and complaints to the center, is a factor that needs to be taken into account in assessing the social and political influence of the courts in their localities. It must have been possible that even when they were unable to disregard the disproportionate balance of power in their platforms and objectively adjudicate the cases between the weak and the strong, the courts could still have helped weaker parties report their complaints to higher authorities. If and when the courts could not do so for any reason, they must have significantly lost their ability to influence the social and political settings in which they operated.

CHAPTER FOUR

LITIGANTS, LITIGATIONS, AND RESOLUTIONS: A STATISTICAL ANALYSIS

Chapter three has discussed in detail the administrative responsibilities of Ottoman courts. Chapter four will shift our focus on the courts' judicial operations with reference to the disputes found in the *sicils* of Çankırı and Kastamonu. In this context, I will first classify the *iʿlams* (summary accounts of the trials) according to their nature and contents, and then examine the frequency of their appearance in the *sicils*. Doing so will help identify which types of disputes were brought to the courts of Çankırı and Kastamonu most frequently and which were resolved elsewhere. It is probable that the court was better suited for the litigation of certain kinds of disputes than others.

I will also investigate in this chapter the socio-economic backgrounds and residential affiliations of the litigants and check whether there was any kind of correlation between the identities of litigants and the outcomes of litigations. This analysis should offer an understanding of the kind of justice administered in the courts of Çankırı and Kastamonu, and indicate to what extent that the court decisions reflected the socio-economic balance of power among different classes in their localities.

Classification of the Disputes in the Court Records

Tables 4.1 and 4.2 provide information about the frequency of various kinds of disputes that often appear in the court records of Çankırı and Kastamonu; they do not, however, exhaust all kinds of contentions appearing in the *sicils*. For example, whereas tax-related contentions are negligible in Çankırı documents, they constitute a sizable set in the records of Kastamonu, and this is why they are excluded from table 4.1 and included in table 4.2. Other kinds of contentions excluded from both tables because of their infrequency include disputes over the distribution of endowment (*vakıf*) revenues, cases of prostitution, and guild-related conflicts.

Table 4.1: Types of Disputes in the Court Records of Çankırı

	Inheritance (1)	Land (2)	Debt (3)	Property (4)	Theft-Usurpation (5)	Assault-Murder (4)	Rape (5)	*Zulm* (6)	Marital[1] (7)
Vol. 1	3	4	–	2	1	1	–	1	2
	20%	27%		13%	6%	6%		6%	13%
Vol. 2	2	–	1	–	1	1	1	1	–
	29%		14%		14%	14%	14%	14%	
Vol. 3	7	2	2	3	1	–	–	–	3
	39%	11%	11%	17%	6%				17%
Vol. 4	2	1	2	4	–	–	3	1	–
	15%	8%	15%	31%			23%	8%	
Vol. 5	–	–	1	4	2	2	1	1	–
			9%	36%	18%	18%	9%	9%	
Vol. 6	1	–	–	1	1	3	1	2	–
	10%			10%	10%	30%	10%	20%	
Vol. 7	–	–	–	–	–	–	–	–	–
Vol. 8	–	–	–	–	–	1	–	2	–
						33%		66%	
Vol. 9	–	–	–	–	1	–	1	–	–
					50%		50%		
Vol. 10	–	–	–	–	–	–	–	–	–
Vol. 11	–	–	1	–	–	1	–	–	–
			50%			50%			
Vol. 12	–	–	–	–	–	–	–	–	–
Vol. 13	–	–	–	–	–	–	–	–	–
Total	15	7	7	14	7	9	7	8	5
	18%	8%	8%	17%	8%	11%	8%	10%	6%

As is obvious in the tables, there are some remarkable differences between the records of Çankırı and Kastamonu. Perhaps the most noticeable is the total number of disputes brought to these courts for resolution: The total number of disputes heard and adjudicated by the court of Kastamonu in twelve volumes is about 6.5 times more than the total number of disputes reported in the first thirteen volumes of the Çankırı court records (see tables 3.5 and 3.6 in the previous chapter).

[1] The term "marital" might be deceptive. The cases under this category generally, if not always, reflect those disagreements that emerged before or in the process of the enactment of the marriage contract. A change of mind on the part of the bride or her family regarding the person whom she was supposed to marry usually constituted the reason for such contentions. Non-monetary disputes between already married couples were seldom brought to the court for resolution.

Table 4.2: Types of Disputes in the Court Records of Kastamonu

	Inheritance (1)	Land (2)	Debt (3)	Property (4)	Theft-Usurpation (5)	Assault-Murder (6)	Rape (7)	*Zulm* (9)	Marital (9)	Tax (10)
Vol. 3	12	–	20	9	1	4	–	1	2	2
	20%		33%	15%	2%	6%		2%	3%	3%
Vol. 1	6	6	12	7	2	6	–	3	3	8
	11%	11%	22%	13%	4%	11%		6%	6%	15%
Vol. 4	4	4	8	6	2	1	1	1	1	1
	14%	14%	27%	21%	7%	3%	3%	3%	3%	3%
Vol. 5	10	1	14	23	3	1	–	–	2	5
	13%	25%	18%	30%	4%	1%			3%	6%
Vol. 12	5	1	3	7	–	3	2	–	3	2
	19%	4%	12%	27%		12%	8%		12%	8%
Vol. 19	6	5	11	2	1	2	–	–	–	2
	21%	17%	38%	7%	3%	7%				7%
Vol. 34	14	4	10	2	4	2	–	–	1	–
	38%	11%	27%	5%	11%	5%			3%	
Vol. 35	14	4	8	11	5	5	1	1	5	2
	21%	6%	12%	17%	8%	8%	2%	2%	8%	3%
Vol. 36	2	1	6	2	2	1	–	–	1	–
	10%	5%	30%	10%	10%	5%			5%	
Vol. 37	6	4	7	5	1	2	–	–	3	–
	21%	14%	25%	18%	4%	7%			11%	
Vol. 38	20	5	21	17	3	7	–	2	5	2
	24%	6%	26%	21%	4%	9%		2%	6%	2%
Vol. 39	13	7	12	9	1	11	–	–	6	5
	20%	11%	19%	14%	2%	17%			9%	8%
Total	112	60	132	100	24	47	4	8	32	29
	20%	10%	23%	17%	4%	8%	1%	1%	6%	5%

Furthermore, although the number of civil cases is greater than the number of criminal disputes in the *sicil*s of both Çankırı and Kastamonu, the proportion of these documents varies considerably in each collection. For every entry of a criminal hearing, there are 1.7 entries of civil contention in Çankırı court records. In Kastamonu court records, on the other hand, the number of civil disputes brought to court for resolution is about 5.5 times greater than the number of recorded criminal hearings. There is no way to know which of these figures is closer to the general pattern (if there was one) in other places because no comparable information is provided in the literature on the Ottoman administration of justice. Nevertheless, proportional differences between civil and criminal registries serve as important numerical indicators of how particular communities used their courts.

The information provided in the tables indicates that the inhabitants of Çankırı and Kastamonu *generally* made use of the courts in resolving disagreements on the issues of inheritance, indebtedness, property ownership, and claims over land usage. Although this is an interesting piece of information, it needs to be interpreted carefully: The number of disputes in the court records probably does not reflect the actual number of such disputes occurring among members of the community, since we can assume that not all disputes were brought to the court for resolution.

There may be several reasons for the lack of documentation for a wider variety of disputes in the *sicil*s. On the one hand, we should expect that certain kinds of disputes arose less often than others, and that the documentation in the court records about them reflects their actual frequency of occurrence. I believe that disputes on the distribution of *vakıf* revenues and cases regarding prostitution- and guild-related conflicts are examples of these kinds of contentions. On the other hand, it seems that other kinds of disputes were deliberately kept out of the court. Sources of contention among members of the same family or relatives, with the exception of issues relating to money or property, were brought to the courts rarely.[2] Even in the money- and property-related disputes, there seems to be a tendency to keep contentions among kinsfolk out of the courtroom. Whereas 37 per cent of all money- and property-related contracts (180 of 481 *hüccet*s) seem to have been enacted among kin, only 17 per cent of all the money- and property-related conflicts (75 of 450 *iʿlam*s) involved relatives or members of the same family.

Under-representation is not limited to disputes between related parties. Indeed if we focus on the Çankırı court records for a moment, we notice this situation very clearly. As table 3.5 demonstrates, the first six volumes of the Çankırı court records contain more than 75 per cent of all disputes found in the thirteen Çankırı *sicil*s. In the next seven volumes, the number of disputes recorded in the court records is only eight, and seven of these cases are criminal in nature.

[2] These might include persistent discord among the spouses and acts of physical and sexual abuse among the relatives or members of the same family.

The reasons behind this tendency are not clear. It is arguable that the system of record keeping in the court of Çankırı went through some sort of transformation, and a division of labor had emerged in the registers after 1127/1715. The existence of specialized registers in some other provincial centers suggests the possibility of this situation in Çankırı too. According to Beshara Doumani, these specialized registers contain only documents about administrative and fiscal matters as well as orders from the government demanding the collection and delivery of tax revenues and wartime provisions.[3] If the last seven Çankırı volumes were indeed the products of such a transformation in record-keeping practices, this would explain why certain kinds of disputes were recorded in them and others were not. As indicated above, seven of the eight disputes found in these volumes were criminal in nature, and they concerned the security of the locality. From the viewpoint of the local administrators these cases had a certain administrative relevance.

Nevertheless, deeming volumes seven to thirteen as some sort of specialized registers generate a number of problems. First of all, had such a transformation really occurred in record keeping, there should be other collections of court records for the period between 1141/1729 and 1157/1744 that were specifically designated to contain "non-military/non-administrative" documents, including the accounts of judicial disputes. The archival catalogues and my research at the National Library in Ankara, however, indicate that no other registers exist for Çankırı for this period. It is possible that such registers existed at the time, but were lost before modern archivists and librarians catalogued them. The fact that the first six volumes of the Çankırı court records do not constitute an unbroken chronological series, as do the last seven volumes, or as do the court records of Kastamonu, indeed suggests the possibility that we are missing many volumes of Çankırı court records.

On the other hand, although volumes seven through thirteen do not contain many records of disputes, the presence of other kinds of judicial documentation in them weakens the likelihood that these volumes are specialized in the way suggested by Doumani. In

[3] Doumani claims the existence of such registers for Damascus, Aleppo, and Jerusalem from the early nineteenth century (personal communication).

addition to the accounts of eight trials mentioned above, there are also a number of contracts indicating that non-administrative matters and legal engagements between individual parties were not categorically excluded from these volumes. The presence of entries for amicable settlements (*sulh*) in these volumes strengthens this conclusion. Perhaps, then, what we encounter in these volumes suggests a transformation of the judicial practice, or of how the community made use of the courts, rather than—or in addition to—a possible change in the system of record keeping. Since it is unlikely that non-criminal disputes ceased to exist in Çankırı after 1141/1729, they were either not brought to the court at all, or, when they were brought to the attention of the *kadı*, they were not recorded in the court registers.

If this was the case, under-representation of specific kinds of disputes might not be limited to the last seven volumes of the Çankırı court records. Indeed, the ratio between civil and criminal cases in the first six Çankırı volumes is also significantly low (2.2 to 1) in comparison to what is observed in the Kastamonu court records. Assuming a) that the ratio between civil and criminal disagreements—brought to court or not—did not vary greatly from one location to another, and b) that criminal disagreements among the community were statistically better represented in the court records than civil disputes because of the more serious nature of these allegations, we can suppose that the number of civil cases is also under-represented in the first six volumes of Çankırı court records.

Courts, Clients, and "Justice"

In this section I will turn my attention to the outcomes of disputes brought to the courts of Çankırı and Kastamonu and try to discover patterns that not only demonstrate how these courts operated but also suggest how the inhabitants of these localities may have perceived the courts and their operations. This analysis should help us understand why people with different socioeconomic backgrounds tended to choose or avoid using local courts, if and when they did so.

In the thirteen volumes of Çankırı studied for this book, there exist 73 entries of adjudication and 10 entries of amicable settlement. The twelve Kastamonu registers contain 442 entries of adjudication and 130 entries of amicable settlement. The inhabitants of the towns of Çankırı and Kastamonu are better represented in these records than the people of neighboring villages. In 39 of the cases (52 per cent) recorded in the Çankırı records, plaintiffs were residents of the town. Villagers acted as plaintiffs in 34 cases (46 per cent). Similarly, defendants were the inhabitants of the town of Çankırı in 45 cases (62 per cent) and were from the villages in 28 cases (37 per cent). The situation is not very different for Kastamonu; townsmen and townswomen acted as plaintiffs in 312 cases (72 per cent) and residents of the surrounding villages acted as plaintiffs in 129 cases (27 per cent). Likewise, defendants were townspeople in 309 cases (71 per cent) and village residents in 131 cases (28 per cent).[4] This variation implies that the residents of the towns of Çankırı and Kastamonu were more inclined than the villagers to take their disputes to court in spite of the fact that the populations of the two districts constituted only a fraction of the populations of the subprovinces.[5]

Women did bring their disputes to the court but not as often as men did. In Çankırı, they acted as plaintiffs in 13 cases (18 per cent) and as defendants in 10 (14 per cent). The numerical representation of the women in the Kastamonu court records seems to be somewhat higher: In 118 cases (27 per cent) they acted as plaintiffs, and in 76 cases (17 per cent) they acted as defendants.[6] Again, a majority of the female litigants (13 of 23 litigants in Çankırı and 153 of 194 litigants in Kastamonu) were town residents.[7]

According to the *sicils*, both of the courts served the interests of the plaintiffs well. This is especially the case for Çankırı: About 55 per cent (46) of the disputes (litigations and amicable settlements)

[4] Amicable settlements are not added to these numbers since many of the preceding disputes were not initially brought to the court for resolution. In such settlements it is not clear who would have acted as the plaintiff or the defendant, had they been brought to the court for resolution.

[5] See chapter two for population numbers. See the appendix for the places from where the out-of-town plaintiffs came to the courts of Çankırı and Kastamonu.

[6] Resort to the court by the women of Çankırı and Kastamonu was not limited to dispute settlement processes. Indeed, they came to the court more frequently to register the economic transactions they were involved in. In 10 of the 48 records (20 per cent) of such transactions that we find in Çankırı, women constituted either one or both of the parties. In six of these agreements their proxies (*vekils*) represented them.

[7] Again, amicable settlements registers are not included in the figures presented in this paragraph.

reported in the Çankırı court records resulted in favor of plaintiffs. The disputes were resolved in favor of defendants in only 23 cases (28 per cent), and 10 cases (12 per cent) were settled amicably (verdicts are unclear in 4 litigations). In Kastamonu, the situation was more balanced, although not radically different: 244 of the 572 disputes (litigations and amicable settlements) recorded in the Kastamonu court records (43 per cent) were resolved in favor of plaintiffs. 198 cases (35 per cent) were resolved in favor of defendants, and 130 (21 per cent) disputes were settled amicably.

This finding suggests that individuals who were willing to take their disputes to the court usually made sure that they could substantiate their claims in front of the *kadı*. In Çankırı plaintiffs usually supported the validity of their claims by witness testimonies (29 cases, 69 per cent of the 42 cases that resulted in favor of the plaintiffs). In 9 cases (21 per cent), defendants acknowledged the validity of plaintiffs' claims, and in 5 cases (12 per cent) plaintiffs used documentary evidence such as copies of contracts and warrants in their possession. Only in 14 cases (19 per cent of the 73 cases reported in the court records) were plaintiffs unable to produce any evidence to support their claims. In these situations defendants managed to acquit themselves by taking oaths proclaiming their innocence. In 10 cases, defendants denied the claims of plaintiffs and made counter-accusations against them. By doing so, they implicitly accepted the burden of proof according to Islamic litigation procedures. In 8 of these cases defendants succeeded in finding witnesses to prove their counter-claims and win the case. They were unable to do so only in 2 cases; in these cases the courts ruled in favor of plaintiffs after making them take an oath in which they asserted the validity of their claims.

The court records of Kastamonu also confirm the importance of witnesses in the process of litigation. Plaintiffs used witness testimonies to document their claims in 146 of the 244 cases (60 per cent) that were concluded in their favor. And although this percentage is lower in cases that were resolved in favor of defendants (74 cases, 37 per cent of the 198 cases), witness testimonies still appear to have been more popular than other forms of evidence brought to court by the defendants. Oath taking seems to have been the second most popular form of judicial documentation used by defendants in those cases that ended in their favor (61 cases, 31 per cent). Plaintiffs, on the other hand, won their cases by oath taking in only 11 cases (5 per cent of the 244 cases).

Plaintiffs in Kastamonu benefited from the confessions (*itiraf*) or acknowledgements (*ikrar*) of defendants in 31 cases (13 per cent of 244 cases) and produced documentary evidence in 23 cases (10 per cent). In return, defendants used documentary evidence 27 times (14 per cent of 198 cases). In 14 cases (7 per cent) they were able to force plaintiffs to acknowledge the validity of their responses and counter-claims against the initial allegations in the court. Both plaintiffs and defendants lost 5 times in court because they refused to take oaths to document the claims that they had previously made in the court. Finally, in 9 cases that resulted in favor of plaintiffs and in 15 others that resulted in favor of defendants, no legal evidence was produced except for the *fetva*s (legal opinions of jurisconsults) submitted by the litigants to the court. This is unusual since, according to established legal procedures, *fetva*s are not considered legitimate forms of evidence.

Before proceeding, I would like to emphasize that my observations square with some critical remarks made by Western observers of the Ottoman administration of justice. Dominance of plaintiffs in the court and a high degree of reliance upon witness testimonies have been pointed out in these accounts as two characteristics of the Ottoman judicial process. Interestingly, one such account established a connection between these two observations: Sir James Porter claimed that plaintiffs had "almost a certain advantage" over the defendants in law courts because it was extremely easy for them to secure witnesses "who will swear anything for pay."[8] Porter describes this process as follows:

> There are different species of witnesses; some your neighbors and old acquaintances; others, casual; and lastly, those who make a professed trade of attending courts of judicature, and live by it. On informing them of the merits of the cause, they first declare that they appear in it merely because they see the hardship and injustice intended against you; that, as they know you to be an honest man, on whose veracity they can absolutely depend, they will therefore affirm as truth whatever you shall aver to them as such. . . .

[8] Sir James Porter, *Observations on Religion, Law, Government and Manners of the Turks*, 2nd edition (London: J. Nourse, 1771), pp. 135–137.

> Or should it not have that effect; if the witnesses insist on better information, they are concealed in a private room, where they can hear all that passes in an adjoining apartment. Into this apartment the party with whom you are at variance is decoyed, and there such concessions, by interrogatories, and other artful managements, are drawn from him as he may make against himself: these the evidences report on the trial, and declare they have heard. Often indeed, on this occasion, instead of the real party, a friend of your own, who personates him, is introduced into the apartment, where he makes what concessions you please in the hearing of the concealed witnesses, who can neither see nor be seen, and who do not chuse to detect the fraud, but report to the judge what they heard, as spoken by the real person. . . .
>
> The last sort are those who make a professed trade of it, and are always ready at any man's service for a dollar or two. By habit and long practice these need no casuistry, no salvo to their conscience, but swallow their oath, true or false, and will stand or fall by their evidence.[9]

Balance of Power in the Court

By paying close attention to the identities of the litigants, we can make some observations about which parties wielded more power in the courts of Çankırı and Kastamonu. The following tables present relevant information on the social, economic, and geographical characteristics of the court clients. The first two tables characterize the frequency of litigation among people who held military and religious titles and those who did not. In these tables, we also find information about individuals who preferred to file their complaints at the court or initiate a litigation process as a group (*en masse*). As we will see later on, this strategy worked well against defendants with high social and/or economic statuses. Tables 4.5 and 4.6, on the other hand, present the frequency of litigation among the townspeople and villagers. In all four of these tables, amicable settlements have been excluded.

[9] Ibid., pp. 137–139. D'Ohsson's account supports Porter's observations: "Car il est aisé de se procurer des témoins. On trouve dans chaque ville des homes qui n'ont d'autre profession que celle de déposer en justice pour un salarie;" see Mouradgea Ignatius D'Ohsson, *Tableau général de l'empire othoman, divisé en deux parties, dont l'une comprend la législation mahométane; l'autre, l'histoire de l'empire othoman*, 7 volumes (Paris: De l'imprimerie de monsieur [Firmin Didot], 1788), vol. 6, p. 222.

Table 4.3: Litigations in Çankırı According to the Social and Economic Statuses of the Litigants

Plaintiffs	Defendants		
	A1: Notables & Military – Religious title holders	A2: People without any titles – individually	A3: People *en masse*
A1: Notables & Military – Religious title holders	12	10	1
A2: People without any titles – individually	7	12	–
A3: People *en masse*	6	5	2

Table 4.4: Litigations in Kastamonu According to the Social and Economic Statuses of the Litigants

Plaintiffs	Defendants		
	A1: Notables & Military – Religious title holders	A2: People without any titles – individually	A3: People *en masse*
A1: Notables & Military – Religious title holders	111	65	1
A2: People without any titles – individually	76	125	1
A3: People *en masse*	10	8	1

Table 4.5: Litigations in Çankırı According to the Residential Affiliations of the Litigants

Plaintiffs	Defendants	
	B1: Townspeople	B2: Villagers
B1: Townspeople	30	5
B2: Villagers	10	18

Table 4.6: Litigations in Kastamonu According to the Residential Affiliations of the Litigants

Plaintiffs	Defendants	
	B1: Townspeople	B2: Villagers
B1: Townspeople	235	33
B2: Villagers	40	94

Before interpreting these figures, I should explain how they were prepared. As we know, the titles of the litigants in the court records are the main indicators of their social and economic statuses. For example, there can be no dispute that those litigants with the titles "beğ," "paşa," or "ağa" were members of the higher echelons of the military class. It is also easy to infer that those individuals who carried the titles "efendi," "hoca," or "şeyh" before or after their names, were either members of the *ʿilmiyye* or had some sort of religious reputation. Some titles, however, are more difficult to classify; for example, titles like "beşe," "çelebi," or "dede" do not disclose, as much as the other titles do, the class backgrounds or socioeconomic characteristics of those individuals who used them. In this study, I have classified holders of the title "beşe" as members of the military class and categorized holders of "çelebi" and "dede" as men of significant religious claims, although some evidence indicates that people with military background also used the latter two titles occasionally. Finally, in a small number of cases it was impossible to clearly identify the social backgrounds of the litigants or to interpret their titles; these litigations are excluded from tables 4.3 and 4.4.

To identify the notables (*aʿyan*) of Çankırı and Kastamonu, it was necessary to investigate the continuities in the consecutive volumes of the *sicils*. The names of certain individuals appear frequently and consistently in the entries that are related to administrative and public matters. As representatives of local communities, these individuals played a role in the partition of tax liabilities to individual neighborhoods and villages; witnessed the arrival, recording, and enforcement of imperial orders from the central and provincial governments; and occasionally voiced the demands of the local people in the court. Luckily, I did not always have to rely upon my instincts to decide whether a particular individual was in fact a notable. Some entries explicitly identify certain individuals as being among the *aʿyan*, and these documents have been very helpful to me in recognizing the local prominence of specific individuals. Almost all of these individuals also carried military and religious titles.

At this point, one common drawback of tables 4.3 and 4.4 should be mentioned. The main objective of these tables is to provide a comparison of what we know about the legal processes that the elite (A1) and the non-elite (A2 and A3) were involved in. For this reason, by distinguishing between the local elite and the rest of the local community, these tables overlook the economic and social differences *within* (not among) the individual groups of people who constituted A1, A2, and A3. Anecdotal evidence indicates that such differences among different notables and titleholders could be significant. Still, according to what is observed in the court records, the socioeconomic differences among the elite were not as marked as those distinctions that existed between them and the common people. Since I am more interested in drawing a general picture of the balance of power in the court than in elaborating the differences within individual groups, I will limit my analysis to the distinctions between the local "elite" and the "ordinary" people.

Tables 4.5 and 4.6 offer information about resort to the court by the residents of the towns and villages—as well as it could be determined. To a certain degree, these tables also demonstrate the differences in court usage among people from different social and economic statuses. Once again, the division between townspeople and villagers embodies certain significant shortcomings. First of all it masks the internal socioeconomic differences among the members of each group. Secondly, according to the court records, many inhabitants of Çankırı and Kastamonu owned land both in the town and in the villages and therefore spent considerable time in both locations. Nevertheless, the ways in which the residential affiliations of these individuals were identified in the court records obscure this situation.

More important, perhaps, is the fact that the differences in how townspeople and villagers used the courts may not always represent the distinctions between rich and poor or between influential and weak. Physical proximity to the court, for example, must have been a significant factor in the frequency of resorting to the court among residents of the towns and the villages.[10] In this sense, tables 4.5 and 4.6 provide only an approximation of a phenomenon that we cannot directly discern from the court records. Unfortunately the court records do not generally supply information about litigants' social and economic situations and, therefore, there is no direct way to distinguish them from each other and observe their performances individually.

Tables 4.3 to 4.6 consistently demonstrate that the litigants in a particular dispute usually shared the same economic and social characteristics. In 60 per cent of the cases from the court records of Çankırı and Kastamonu, either both litigants held military or religious titles, or neither of them did. Again, in about 80 per cent of the cases, the plaintiffs and the defendants were either both townsmen or both villagers. We can conclude from these findings that legal interaction between the members of different status and residential groups was relatively infrequent.

I believe that several factors might have played a role in this situation. For one thing, it is possible that what is observed in the tables is a consequence of the economic and social isolation of different groups in Çankırı and Kastamonu. There is some evidence for the validity of this assumption in the court records: In 39 of the 47 (83 per cent) of the contracts found in the court records of Çankırı, the contracting parties were either both from A1 or both from A2. In only 8 contracts (17 per cent) do we observe an economic or financial transaction between members of A1 and A2. If we try to classify these transactions according to residences of the parties, the result is similar: In 38 of the 47 contracts (81 per cent) the contracting parties were either both residents of Çankırı (B1) or both villagers (B2).

[10] See the appendix.

The situation in Kastamonu, although more balanced, is not much different. In about 61 per cent of the commercial and financial contracts in the Kastamonu records, the contracting parties were either both individuals from A1 or both from A2. Again, if we categorize these contracts according to the residences of the parties, we would observe that in about 60 per cent of the cases the parties were either both residents of the town (B1) or both villagers (B2). These results suggest that individuals from a particular socioeconomic group interacted primarily with someone of similar status rather than with people from other groups. And if this observation accurately represents the nature of prevalent social and economic interactions in Çankırı and Kastamonu, it also explains the reasons behind what we encounter in the tables above. It is highly probable that the residents of Çankırı and Kastamonu clashed with their own kind in the court more frequently because they interacted with them more regularly.

Nevertheless, I believe that there may be other explanations of the patterns observed in tables 4.3 to 4.6. According to what we learn from other sources, the relative lack of legal contentions among individuals from different socioeconomic groups may indicate cultural and institutional barriers to the functioning of formal adjudication processes.[11] Accordingly, in Çankırı and Kastamonu the influence of notables and holders of military and religious titles on the court may have discouraged "ordinary" people from filing grievances against them with the *kadı*. On the other hand, prominent individuals may have avoided resolving their disputes with "ordinary" people in the public arena of the court for various reasons. Indeed, there is evidence that when they were forced to participate in the litigation process by less-than-prominent opponents, the members of the higher-ranking military class almost always used legal proxies to represent their interests.

Convincing evidence for the influence of the notables, titleholders, and the townspeople over the court can be found in the outcomes of their legal contentions with opponents from lower social and economic strata. According to our observations, individuals from A1 sued people from A2 10 times in Çankırı, and in 9 of these cases

[11] John Rothenberger, "The Social Dynamics of Dispute Settlement," in Laura Nader and Harry Todd (eds.), *The Disputing Process: Law in Ten Societies* (New York: Columbia University Press), p. 164; Harry F. Todd, "Status Disputing in a Bavarian Village," *Ethnologia Europaea*, no. 1, vol. 10 (1977/78), p. 62.

the court decided in favor of the plaintiffs (see table 4.7). On the other hand, individuals from A2 sued people from A1 7 times in Çankırı, and 4 of these litigations were decided in favor of the defendants. These statistics become more impressive if we remember that in Çankırı the number of cases decided in favor of the plaintiffs was twice the number of those decided in favor of the defendants.

Table 4.7: Resolutions in Çankırı: Classification According to the Social and Economic Statutes of the Litigants

Plaintiffs	Defendants		
	A1	A2	A3
A1	–	9–1	1–0
A2	3–4	–	0–0
A3	6–0	3–2	–

Note: The "scores" in the cells above denote the number of cases resolved in favor of the plaintiffs and the litigants. For example, the cell with the score "9–1" indicates that 9 of 10 cases, where A1 acted as plaintiffs and A2 as defendants were resolved in favor of the plaintiffs.

It is interesting that the legal domination of A1 was threatened only when people with no military or religious titles acted together and challenged their opponents as a group. Such contentions most frequently emerged in the realms of taxation and oppression (*zulm*) where the interests of the villagers could not be separated from each other and thus were represented collectively. In such situations, some of the most distinguished members of a village (or villages, if the matter at hand also concerned the inhabitants of other villages) or a neighborhood came to the court *en masse*, representing and, usually, accompanied by other inhabitants of the village. Their cases frequently involved complaints against a member of the military class, who was usually accused of extracting revenues illegitimately, abusing people physically or, more commonly, both.

What is most noteworthy is that the community (*ahali*) was able to win these cases every time thanks to their collective effort in the court. In technical terms, the courts did not recognize the inhabitants of the village or the neighborhood collectively as litigants in such cases. They accepted the testimonies of a few members of the village or the neighborhood as witnesses while remaining representatives of the community acted as plaintiffs. For this reason collective representation in the court was the surest way to win a case against an individual regardless of his or her social and economic conditions.[12]

The situation in Kastamonu is not much different (see table 4.8). People from A1 sued individuals from A2 65 times, and 41 of these legal contentions were decided in favor of the plaintiffs. Conversely, people from A2 sued the members of A1 in 76 cases, and 41 of these contentions were decided in favor of the defendants.[13] Again, as in Çankırı, an effective way to resist the legal domination of A1 was to act as a group in legal contentions. As is indicated in the table below, people with no military or religious titles in Kastamonu were able to defeat their opponents from higher status and economic groups in 8 of 10 cases when they acted as a group.

The pattern of resolutions of contentions between townspeople and villagers also indicate an imbalance of power among these parties in the court. In Kastamonu, townspeople won 22 of 33 cases (67 per cent) that they brought to court against villagers. Villagers, however, lost 24 of 40 litigations (60 per cent) that they initiated against townspeople. In Çankırı, the numbers are more confusing: As in Kastamonu, townspeople dominated the cases they initiated against villagers (3–2), but they also lost all of the contentions initiated by villagers against them (6–0).[14] This last finding, however, does not disprove

---

[12] Consider the following example. In CI 1076/November 1665 the inhabitants of the villages of Kavra and Hoca Hasan came to the court together (*cem'ihim*) and complained against the lieutenant governor of Çankırı, Mustafa Ağa, in his presence. They claimed that the tax revenues of their villages belonged to the Şeyh Cemal endowment in Çankırı, which was responsible for maintaining a religious school (*medrese*) that had been built by Şeyh Cemal himself. Nevertheless, although they had been paying their dues and taxes to the professors (*müderrisler*) of this *medrese* regularly and, therefore, they were supposed to be exempt from all kinds of irregular taxes, the aforementioned lieutenant governor had been forcing them to make payments for *resm-i yaylak, resm-i odun, resm-i otluk* (levies of pasturage, wood, and straw), etc. They requested that the court question the lieutenant governor and prevent him from making such demands. After the lieutenant governor denied these accusations, Şeyh Ahmed bin Elhac Musa, Abdülkadir Efendi bin Mehmed Efendi, and eighteen other individuals from these villages testified that the lieutenant governor had indeed been forcing the inhabitants of Kavra and Hoca Hasan to pay irregular taxes. The court ordered the lieutenant governor to stop asking for money from the villagers. See ÇCR, vol. 2, 9–22.

[13] Again, we need to remember the fact that in Kastamonu 244 (43 per cent) of all the disputes were decided in favor of the plaintiffs and 198 (35 per cent) of them were decided in favor of the defendants.

[14] Table 4.5 indicates the existence of 10 such contentions. 6 of these contentions

Table 4.8: Resolutions in Kastamonu: Classification According to the Social and Economic Statutes of the Litigants

Plaintiffs	Defendants		
	A1	A2	A3
A1	–	41–24	1–0
A2	35–41	–	0–1
A3	8–2	7–1	–

Note: The "scores" in the cells above denote the number of cases resolved in favor of the plaintiffs and the litigants. For example, the cell with the score "41–24" indicates that 41 of the 65 cases, where A1 acted as plaintiffs and A2 as defendants, were resolved in favor of the plaintiffs.

my suspicions regarding the nature of the power balance in the court in favor of the townspeople. After all, when Çankırı villagers brought complaints to court against townspeople (most of whom were notables and titleholders in these cases), they usually came as a group; in fact, in 6 of 10 instances where villagers acted as plaintiffs and townspeople acted as defendants, the villagers were litigating *en masse* against townsmen, who also had military or religious titles. And since people with no titles had a greater chance of winning their cases against notables and titleholders when they acted as a group, it is no surprise that we find such a win-loss ratio among villagers and townspeople in Çankırı.

Conclusion

In this chapter I have attempted to portray the power balance between different groups of people in the courts of Çankırı and Kastamonu. All of my calculations and observations have pointed to the legal domination of the local "elite" against the "common" clients of the courts. At this point, there is no way to know whether this situation was a reason for or result of the fact that a group of individuals who constituted only about 10 per cent of the local popu-

were resolved on behalf of the villagers. The decisions in other 4 cases, however, are not clearly stated.

lation supplied 43 per cent of the plaintiffs.[15] Nevertheless, there should be a direct relationship between the disproportionate balance of power in the court and the frequent court use among local power-holders.

Do the findings of this chapter offer any explanation for the differences between the court records of Çankırı and Kastamonu? Earlier, we have seen that in the court of Çankırı the number of cases won by plaintiffs was twice the number of cases won by defendants. Moreover local notables and holders of military and religious titles won all but 4 of the 17 legal contentions that they had with "ordinary" people as defendants or plaintiffs. These percentages are more even in Kastamonu: As indicated earlier, the number of cases won by plaintiffs and defendants is relatively close to each other (244–198). Also, trials won by common people (as plaintiffs or defendants) against local elite constituted a significantly greater percentage than what we observe in the court of Çankırı (59 cases, 42 per cent of 141 contentions between A1 and A2).

According to these statistics, the results of the litigation processes were significantly more predictable in Çankırı and were more consistently against the interests of the poor and the weak. One wonders whether it is possible that, because of the obvious partiality of its decisions, the court of Çankırı lost its appeal to many of its clients. If the registries found in the *sicils* of Çankırı accurately reflect the "bias" of the court, it is understandable why people who lacked the economic and social prominence of their opponents would be hesitant to use the court as a platform for dispute resolution. And when their opponents threatened to sue them, they probably were eager to resolve the dispute outside of the court through less formal mechanisms.

---

[15] It is impossible to estimate the populations of the military and religious title-holders in Çankırı and Kastamonu during this period. Many scholars, on the other hand, surmise that their populations varied between 5 per cent and 15 per cent in different locations before the nineteenth century. See Ömer Lütfi Barkan, "Essai sur les données statistiques des registres de recensement dans l'Empire ottoman aux XVe et XVIe siècles," *Journal of the Economic and Social History of the Orient*, vol. 1 (1958), p. 22; Rıfat Özdemir, *XIX. Yüzyılın İlk Yarısında Ankara (Fiziki, Demografik, İdari ve Sosyo-Ekonomik Yapısı), 1785–1846* (Ankara: Kültür Bakanlığı Yayınları, 1998), p. 87; Ergenç, pp. 57 and 60; Suraiya Faroqhi, "Ankara Çevresindeki Arazi Mülkiyetinin ya da İnsan-Toprak İlişkilerinin Değişimi," in Erdal Yavuz and Ümit Nevzat Uğurel (eds.) *Tarih İçinde Ankara: Eylül 1981 Seminer Bildirileri* (Ankara: ODTÜ Mimarlık Fakültesi Basım İşliği, 1984), pp. 75–77 and 79–80.

CHAPTER FIVE

COSTS OF COURT USAGE

One of the least-studied aspects of the Ottoman legal system is the cost of court use. Other than citing the compilations of court fees determined by the state, the secondary literature provides no information on this issue. And although these compilations represent official guidelines for the prices of different court services, we do not find a satisfactory discussion of the extent to which these guidelines were honored in real life.

The cost of court usage, on the other hand, is too important to ignore. We may safely assume that the appeal of the courts, especially to individuals from the lower segments of society, was inversely related to the legal and illegal fees charged in the court. In other words, to understand the degree of popularity of the courts among a significant portion of the provincial population, we need to ascertain the actual costs of different court services. This task, however, is easier said than done; the fact that the court records do not mention the fees charged for most services makes it difficult to develop an understanding of the actual costs of court usage. For example, we do not know how costly it was to get married or divorced in the court. Nor do we know about the amounts paid by the litigants to take their cases to the court and have them adjudicated there.

Although we cannot answer these questions, Çankırı and Kastamonu *sicil*s do enlighten us on certain relevant issues. These volumes provide information about how much the court charged for dividing the estate of a deceased person among his or her heirs. There is also information on the entitlements of the *kadı* and other court officials for supervising the distribution of tax assessments to individual districts, villages and neighborhoods, and for recording the tax allotments of these localities in the *sicil*s. Admittedly, information from inheritance and tax distribution records cannot provide a comprehensive understanding of the costs of a variety of legal, notarial, and administrative services provided in the court. Yet it is possible to compare this information with data from various law books (pl. *kanunnameler*) and conclude whether the official guidelines were honored in the courts or not. Moreover, we may also expect the time-trends in these records to reflect the time-trends in the costs of other court services that we do not know anything about. This chapter will explore both of these lines of argument.

Before we examine the data from inheritance and tax distribution records, I should summarize what I found about court fees in various sources. I was able to locate six different compilations of court fees for the period between the sixteenth and the eighteenth centuries.

Table 5.1: Court Fees According to Official Compilations

Services	Late 16th century (1)	Late 16th–early 17th century (2)	1644–5 (3)	1676–77 (4)	Early 18th century (5)	Dec. 1780 (6)
Manumission of slaves (*i'tak*)	–	62	66	–	62	–
Registration of marriage (*nikah*)	–	25 for virgins 15 for previously married	25	25 for virgins	25 for virgins 15 for previously married	–
Inheritance (*miras*)	25	15 for every 1000 *akçe*s of estate's value	15 for every 1000 *akçe*s of estate's value	15 for every 1000 *akçe*s of estate's value	15 for every 1000 *akçe*s of estate's value	–
Notary service (*hüccet*)	26	25	25	25	25	25
Signature (*imza*)	–	12	12	12	12	12
Regisration fee (*sicil-i kayd*)	–	8	12	8	8	8
Letters to authorities (*mürasele*)	7	6	8	6	6	6

Sources: 1st, 2nd, and 5th columns, İsmail Hakkı Uzunçarşılı, *Osmanlı Devleti'nin İlmiye Teşkilatı*, p. 85. 3rd column, Halil İnalcık, "Mahkama," *EI*[2]. 4th column, "Tevki'i Abdurrahman Paşa Kanunnamesi," *Milli Tetebbular Mecmuası*, no. 3 (1331/1913), pp. 541–542. 6th column, Cevdet Adliye, 3715.

Note: All the values are in *akçe*. The fees presented in the above table include the shares of *kadı*s and other members of the court such as *na'ib*s (assistants) and *katib*s (scribes).

If we assume that the figures in this table reflect the actual fees charged in the court, we should conclude that the costs of court usage did not change over a period of about two-hundred years. Nevertheless, there are reasons not to make such an assumption. According to the latest calculations, Ottoman prices in general increased about four-hundred per cent during this period.[1] It is more than probable that the court officials did their best to keep up with this trend. Indeed, archival sources indicate that high court fees and illegal revenue extraction constitute major sources of complaint against the courts during the eighteenth century.[2]

Tax Records

Before presenting the amounts charged by the courts of Çankırı and Kastamonu for the supervision of the tax assessments, several observations should be made about the tax documents in the court records. First of all, not all of the tax documents in the Çankırı *sicil*s were actually drafted in the court of Çankırı. When, for example, a specific levy was ordered to be collected for the governor-general of Anatolia province, tax shares of individual districts within the sub-province of Çankırı were occasionally determined in the court of Kütahya—the administrative center of the province. And since the court of Kütahya charged consistently more for the supervision of tax assessments than the court of Çankırı, the data that originate from these two courts should be distinguished. The information provided in the next table is constructed from those documents that were drafted in the court of Çankırı.[3]

Secondly, the tax assessments in the courts of Çankırı and Kastamonu can also be divided into two categories: Assessments made for the *sub-provinces* of Çankırı and Kastamonu that outline the tax shares of different districts within these sub-provinces, and assessments made for the *districts* of Çankırı and Kastamonu that denote the tax shares of neighborhoods and villages within these districts. Since the court

[1] Şevket Pamuk, "The Price Revolution in the Ottoman Empire Reconsidered," *International Journal of Middle East Studies*, no. 1, vol. 33 (February 2001), pp. 75–79.

[2] See, for example, CA, 349; CA, 533; CA, 1130; CA, 1781 and CA 3715.

[3] There seems to be no such problem with the tax records that we find in the *sicil*s of Kastamonu.

Table 5.2: Court Fees for the Supervision and Recording of Tax Assessments in Çankırı (in *guruş* [= 110–120 *akçes*])

Volumes/Dates	İmdad-ı Seferiye	İmdad-ı Seferiye (subprovince)	ʿAvarız ve Bedel-i Nüzül	Menzil İmdadiyesi	Yaylakiye
5/1109–1110	40		50		38
1697–1698					
6/1120–1127	39	70	60		
1708–1715			68		
8/1141–1143					
1729–1731	50	100			40
	100				
		150			
		100			
		77			
9/1143–1145	67	140	83	60	80
1731–1732	60	120	84		70
	65	120			
10/1145–1147	41		84	45	70
1732–1734	47				
	47				
	50				
11/1148–1151	43	55	84		70
1735–1738	37	70	60		55
	38	55	60		55
	32				
12/1153–1154			74		
1740–1741					
13/1154–1157	36	60	74	30	55
1741–1743					55

Note: *İmdad-ı seferiye* was assessed to finance the military expenses during campaigns; *menzil imdadiyesi* was assessed to provide funds for local post-stations. For *ʿavarız* and *bedel-i nüzül*, see chapter two, footnote 44. The figures include all the fees and levies that were collected by the members of the court (including *harc-ı defter, katibiye, kaydiye* [different kinds of scribal fees], *hüddamiye* [custodial fees], etc). The tax categories presented in the above table (unless mentioned otherwise) denote the assessments made for the district of Çankırı.

fees seem to be consistently higher for the sub-provincial assessments, we should classify them separate from district-based assessments.

Finally, and although this cannot be decisively proven by the available data, it seems plausible that court fees varied according to the types of taxes levied. To take this kind of variation into account, I have organized the data according to different tax categories. In the following tables, I provide information about the court fees for those kinds of tax records that are observed most frequently in the *sicils* of Çankırı and Kastamonu. Unfortunately, the kinds of taxes represented in these two tables are not identical because certain types of tax records appear with varying frequency in the Çankırı and Kastamonu court records. For example, whereas the records of *resm-i yaylakiye* (levy of pasturage) constitute one of the most frequent kinds of tax records in Çankırı records, there are none in the *sicils* of Kastamonu.

Table 5.3: Court Fees for the Supervision and Recording of Tax Assessments in Kastamonu (in *guruş*)

Volumes/Dates	İmdad-ı Seferiye (subprovince)	ʿAvarız ve Bedel-i Nüzül	Menzil İmdadiyesi
34/1148		101	89
1735–1736		97	
35/1148–1150	391		95
1736–38	390		114
			114
36/1151–1152	390	101	105
1738–1739			105
38/1153		101	114
740–1741			115
39/1154–55	390	101	77
1742–1743	285		116
	175		116

Note: The tax categories presented in the above table (unless mentioned otherwise) denote the assessments made for the district of Kastamonu.

Unfortunately, there exist no records of fees charged by the Kastamonu court prior to 1735. For this reason table 5.3 does not help explain how court fees changed between the late seventeenth and early eighteenth centuries. Hence, my discussion of this issue will be based on the interpretation of table 5.2. Before doing that, however, I need to emphasize the differences between the amounts charged by the courts of Çankırı and Kastamonu for supervising and recording the assessments of similar kinds of taxes. According to the tables above, the court of Kastamonu charged substantially higher fees to assess *imdad-ı seferiye* (for the sub-provinces), *menzil imdadiyesi*, and *ʿavarız ve bedel-i nüzül* than did the court of Çankırı. These differences might indicate distinctions between the two courts in the judicial and administrative hierarchy since they do not correlate with the amounts of taxes apportioned in Çankırı and Kastamonu.[4]

In the absence of other kinds of data, the information extracted from the Çankırı tax records supplies some useful clues for understanding changes in the costs of conducting court business. The following table provides the averages of the observations presented in table 5.2 for each volume in order to make the time-trend more recognizable.

Table 5.4: Court Fees for the Supervision and Recording of Tax Assessments in Çankırı (averages)

Volumes/Dates	İmdad-ı Seferiye	İmdad-ı Seferiye (subprovince)	ʿAvarız ve Bedel-i Nüzül	Menzil İmdadiyesi	Yaylakiye
5/ 1109–1110 1697–1698	40	–	50	–	38
6/ 1120–1127 1708–1715	39	70	64	–	–
8/ 1141–1143 1729–1731	50	105.5	–	–	40
9/ 1143–1145 1731–1732	64	127	83.5	60	75
10/ 1145–1147 1732–1734	46	–	84	45	70
11/ 1148–1151 1735–1738	37.5	62.5	67	–	60
12/ 1153–1154 1740–1741	–	–	74	–	–
13/ 1154–1157 1741–1743	36	60	74	30	55

Note: The tax categories presented in the above table (unless mentioned otherwise) denote the assessments made for the district of Çankırı.

[4] There might be some correlation between court fees and the amounts of assessments for particular taxes in specific volumes. For example, in the tenth volume of the Çankırı court records four different registries of the *imdad-ı seferiye* assessments are found for the district of Çankırı. According to these registries, the amounts of *imdad-ı seferiye* that were to be collected on each occasion were 2191, 2480, 2638, and 2620 *guruş*, and the amounts charged for court services for these assessments were 41, 47, 47, and 50 *guruş* respectively. On the other hand, I cannot explain all the variations in fees for *imdad-ı seferiye* or other taxes solely with reference to the differences in the amounts of tax levies. For example, according to the eleventh volume of the Çankırı court records, the court charged 43, 38, and 32 *guruş* for supervising and registering the divisions of 2395, 2600, and 2360 *guruş* of *imdad-ı*

Although it is difficult to make a clear evaluation, we can identify a tendency for the court fees to increase between 1697 and 1732. In the period between 1732 and 1743, on the other hand, fees were declining. I should point out that this trend was probably specific to the court of Çankırı since, according to table 5.3, the fees charged in Kastamonu were stable during this period.

Table 5.4 indicates that tax assessment fees *generally* increased between 1697 and 1743. In two of the three tax categories for which there is more complete information for this period (*yaylakiye* and *ʿavarız ve bedeli-i nüzül*), an increase of over 25 per cent is observed in the court fees. The decline in the fees for *imdad-ı seferiye*, on the other hand, is relatively insignificant (about 10 per cent).

The fluctuation in fees for all kinds of tax assessments is also a matter of interest. According to my findings, these fluctuations were steep (40 to 100 per cent increases followed by up to 50 per cent drops) and concurrent for all tax categories. This observation suggests that court fees for all tax assessments were subject to the influence of some common external variables, which I have no means of identifying at this point.

Yet it is probable that the fees charged for supervising and recording tax assessments was somewhat dependent on the ability of the *kadı* and other court members to negotiate and extract revenues for their services. Although there is no direct evidence for the validity of this hypothesis, it seems that different *kadı*s charged different fees for the apportionment of similar kinds and amounts of taxes. For example, six of the eight *imdad-ı seferiye* and *yaylakiye* assessments in the eleventh volume were made under the supervision of three different *kadı*s. Similarly, the assessments of the two *ʿavarız ve bedel-i nüzül* taxes appearing in the sixth volume were supervised by two different *kadı*s. Therefore, the relative influence of these *kadı*s on the community may explain the fact that the one who was able to charge a greater amount (68 *guruş* vs. 60 *guruş*) supervised the apportionment of the lesser amount of tax (2,390 *guruş* vs. 2,899 *guruş*).

---

seferiye respectively. Similarly, for dividing 1570 and 1555 *guruş* of *resm-i yaylakiye*, the court charged 70 and 55 *guruş* respectively.

There is also no correlation between the court fees for *ʿavarız* and *bedel-i nüzül* and the number of households that these two taxes were levied upon. Documents that relate to other tax categories do not indicate the number of households in the localities for which the assessments were made.

What is more obvious in the tables above is the immense difference between the actual fees charged for tax assessments and the rates listed in contemporary law books and other official documents for such services. According to the official price compilations, the courts were permitted to charge only a fraction of one *guruş* for supervising and recording the tax assessments in their localities (see table 5.1). The category of "signature," or *imza* in Turkish, denotes those fees that were supposed to be charged by the court for the supervision of the tax assessments. As can be seen in table 5.1, sources from different periods consistently give this amount as 12 *akçe*s. Charges for scribal and notarial services were not supposed to cost more than 40 or 50 *akçe*s according to the official price compilations, so according to the official guidelines, the fees for tax assessment and division could not possibly exceed 70 or 80 *akçe*s. Therefore what was actually charged in the court of Çankırı was about 40 to 126 times what was prescribed in official compilations. The discrepancy between the actual rates and prescribed fees seems to be even larger in the Kastamonu records.

Admittedly, this large difference might not necessarily apply to other fee categories, and there is very little information by which to judge how representative these fees are. Nevertheless the extremely limited examples that I have of other fee categories allow the possibility that the courts charged substantially more for their services than the official fees. For example, according to one inheritance registry from the Çankırı court records, the court charged one heir 120 *akçe*s for a notarial receipt of guardianship (*hüccet-i vesayet*). In the very next inheritance record another *hüccet-i vesayet* is registered for 240 *akçe*s—about ten times what was dictated in the law books of this period. Two other inheritance registries indicate that the cost of ordinary notarial receipts (*harc-ı hüccet*) varied between 120 *akçe*s and 180 *akçe*s.

The costs of such services were even higher in the court of Kastamonu. Indeed, between 1735 and 1743 the amounts charged by the court of Kastamonu for a *hüccet-i vesayet* varied between 3.5 *guruş* (= 420 akçes) and 10 *guruş* (= 1,200 akçes)![5] The difference between these values and the official fees are comparable to the

[5] A *guruş* was equal to 120 *akçe*s during this period.

differences between the actual amounts charged by the court for tax assessments and the amounts determined in the official compilations for such services.

Inheritance Registries

Tax records are not the only documents offering evidence about the costs of court use; there also are significant amounts of information in estate inventories (*terekes*). These records contain the rates of "ordinary tax" (*resm-i ʿadi*) charged by the court for dividing the estate of the deceased among his or her heirs. Also, we frequently encounter in these registries the records of those fees charged by members of the court for their scribal, notarial, and custodial services.

As with other types of services, the court records of Kastamonu and Çankırı are not equally helpful in providing information about the court fees for handling inheritances. Curiously, among the thirteen volumes of the Çankırı court records studied here, only the sixth volume contains a relatively substantial number of estate inventories; twenty-two of all the twenty-five Çankırı inventories in our possession are from this particular volume. For this reason the Çankırı inventories will provide information only for the brief period between 1708 and 1715. The court records of Kastamonu, on the other hand, contain a considerable number of estate inventories (125 overall) and consequently my discussion of the temporal fluctuations in the court fees as observed in the inheritance records will be based on the Kastamonu court records.

According to the official guidelines (see table 5.1) the courts were to charge only 1.5 per cent of the value of the estate that they were asked to divide among heirs. We cannot be absolutely sure whether this amount was supposed to include the fees for scribal (*kalemiye, katibiye*), notarial (*resm-i hüccet*), or custodial (*hüddamiye*) services in addition to the "ordinary tax" (*resm-i ʿadi*) charged by the court for dividing the estate.

The following table compares the values of the estates divided by the court of Çankırı with the fees charged. The category "cost of court use" (column 2) includes payments for "ordinary tax" in addition to scribal, notarial, and custodial fees. While it was not always possible to differentiate these fees in estate inventories, the amounts charged for scribal, notarial, and custodial services never constituted more than a fraction of the amounts charged for "ordinary tax" (usually between one fourth and one fifth of it). Payments to the court for notarized guardianship (*hüccet-i vesayet*), on the other hand, are not included in the calculation.

Table 5.5: Court Fees in the Estate Inventories of Çankırı

Volume/Period	Gross value of the estate before debt payments and division among inheritors (1)	Tax + scribal, notarial, and custodial fees (2)	Relative cost of court usage: (2/1) × 1000 (3)
6/1120–27	90,780	1,980	21.81
1708–15	90,667	2,217	24.45
	89,370	2,216	24.80
	72,240	1,440	19.93
	63,750	1,320	20.71
	46,800	1,440	30.77
	24,330	300	12.33
	21,840	720	32.97
	18,720	600	32.05
	18,500	500	27.03
	16,990	500	29.43
	14,290	360	25.19
	11,110	300	27.00
	10,291	620	60.25
	7,940	200	25.19
	7,925	360	45.43
	6,990	180	25.75
	6,800	520	76.47
	5,877	250	42.54
	5,520	380	68.84
	4,221	120	28.43
	3,847	162	42.11

Note: The values in the first two columns are in *akçes*. The values of the estates are arranged in descending order from higher to lower values.

Table 5.6: Court Fees in the Estate Inventories of Kastamonu

Volume/Period	Gross value of the estate before debt payments and division among inheritors (1)	Tax + scribal, notarial, and custodial fees (2)	Relative cost of court usage: (2/1) × 1000 (3)
3/1684–86	1,043	50	47.93
	950	39	41.05
	904	22	24.33
	621	20	32.21
1/1688–91	2,428.5	80	32.94
4/1691–92	1,412.5	30	21.24
5/1692–94	1,074.5	25	23.27
	882	25	28.34
12/1703–04	1,119	32	28.57
	878.5	35	39.84
19/1712–13	7,338	170	23.17
	2,616.5	36.5	13.95
	1700	43	25.29
	1130	23	20.35
	1000	30	30.00
	768	19	24.74
	680	21	30.88
	472	15	31.78
	416.5	5	12.00
	286	7	24.48
	236	6	25.42
	219.5	8	36.45
	193	7	36.27
	155	4	25.81
34/1735–36	10,219	230	22.51
	5,900	135	22.88
	2,719	80	29.42
	1,392	30	21.55
	1,373	33.5	24.40
	905	27	29.83
	848	22.5	26.53
	747	26	34.81
	605	17	28.10
	476	13	27.31
	454.5	19	41.80
	438.5	12	27.37
	426	17	39.91
	401.5	15	37.36
	317	19	59.94
	126	6	47.62
	123	6.5	52.85

Table 5.6 *(cont.)*

Volume/Period	Gross value of the estate before debt payments and division among inheritors (1)	Tax + scribal, notarial, and custodial fees (2)	Relative cost of court usage: (2/1) × 1000 (3)
34/1735–36	110	6	54.55
(cont.)	108.5	3	27.65
	106.5	5	46.95
	54	2.5	46.30
	33.5	2	59.70
35/1736–38	42,031	1,250	29.74
	6,279	163.5	26.04
	4,822	112	23.23
	4,605	116.5	25.30
	2,901	92.5	31.89
	2,852	75	26.30
	2,684	72.5	27.01
	1,774	73	41.15
	1,613.5	43	26.65
	1,473	40	27.16
	1,181	38	32.18
	1,148	37	32.23
	1,000	29	29.00
	769.5	25	32.49
	729	20	27.43
	599	17.5	29.22
	494	16	32.39
	464	22.5	48.49
	382	13.5	35.34
	351	10	28.49
	343	9	26.24
	255	8	31.37
	250.5	8	31.94
	227	7	30.84
	114	8	70.18
	97.5	4	41.03
	72.5	2	27.59
	38	2.5	65.79
36/1738–39	4,528	144	31.80
	687.5	15.5	22.55
	660	23	34.85
	378	11.5	30.43
	318	14.5	45.60
	146	6.5	44.52
	91	5.5	60.44
	75	4.5	60.00
37/1740–42	1,620	50	30.86
	1,530	45.5	29.74

Table 5.6 *(cont.)*

Volume/Period	Gross value of the estate before debt payments and division among inheritors (1)	Tax + scribal, notarial, and custodial fees (2)	Relative cost of court usage: (2/1) × 1000 (3)
37/1740–42	979.5	29	29.61
(cont.)	522	15	28.74
	454	10	22.03
	376	13	34.57
	275	10	36.36
	233	8	34.33
	128	6	46.88
38/1740–41	6,542	185.5	28.36
	2,384	60	25.17
	2,216	70	31.59
	2,033	95	46.73
	2,000	60	30.00
	1,027	36	35.05
	972	36	37.04
	701	22	31.38
	564	17.5	31.03
	503	23	45.73
	486	17	34.98
	419	14	33.41
	335	10	29.85
	107	4	37.38
	82	3	36.59
	76	4	52.63
	74.5	2	26.85
39/1742–43	1,912	37	19.35
	1,769	65	36.74
	1,000	31	31.00
	927	24.5	26.43
	552.5	19	34.39
	425	14	32.94
	402	14	34.83
	353	11.5	32.56
	342	13	38.01
	336.5	11.5	34.18
	333.5	9.5	28.49
	211.5	8	37.83
	178.5	6	33.61
	111	3.5	31.53
	88	3.5	39.77
	75	3	40.00
	68	3	44.12

Note: The values in columns 1 and 2 are in *guruş*. The values of the estates for each volume are arranged in descending order from higher to lower values.

On the average, the relative cost of court use seems to be similar in the Çankırı and Kastamonu inventories: In both places the courts charged for their services about 3.4 per cent of the gross value of the divided estates. This value is substantially higher than what was dictated in official prescriptions. Furthermore, this rate seems to have varied substantially within individual inventories and reached up to 7 per cent in Kastamonu court records and 7.5 per cent in Çankırı records. Based on these observations it seems clear that the official guidelines were not observed in the courts of Çankırı and Kastamonu during the late seventeenth and early eighteenth centuries.

The information found in the estate inventories of Kastamonu provides an opportunity to examine whether or not the amounts charged by the courts for their services increased over time. Recall that the court records of Kastamonu studied here span three different time periods. The first four volumes cover the period between 1684 and 1694. The next two volumes, on the other hand, cover periods from 1703 to 1704 and from 1713 to 1714 respectively. For the purposes of generalization, I will combine the information from these two volumes and assume that this combination represents the amounts charged as court fees in the first decade of the eighteenth century. Finally, the last six volumes span the period between 1735 and 1743.

Table 5.7: Relative Court Fees in Kastamonu Estate Inventories for Different Time Periods

Period	Relative costs of court usage: Court fees/ Gross values of the estates (times 1000)
1684–94	31.4
1703–13	28.2
1735–43	35.4

The value calculated for the years between 1703 and 1713 may not be representative because the volumes available for this period are not comprehensive. Yet, according to other figures presented in the table above, we may safely state that the court fees for dividing the estates increased about 12 per cent during a period of sixty years. This is a significant increase, especially since the Ottoman prices in general remained relatively stable between 1680s and 1740s.[6]

[6] See Şevket Pamuk, *A Monetary History of the Ottoman Empire* (Cambridge: Cambridge University Press, 2000), p. 236.

Rich and Poor in the Courts of Çankırı and Kastamonu

It seems that the fees found in the estate inventories were estimated according to the gross values of the divided estates.[7] Yet a comparison of the net values of the estates (= gross value of the estate minus all the debts of the deceased, burial expenses, and legal fees) and the amounts charged by the courts provide clues as to why the poorer inhabitants of Çankırı and Kastamonu preferred to avoid the court. In the next two tables I provide such a comparison. Note that since the main objective of these tables is to offer a comparison between the amounts charged by the courts for the division of richer and poorer estates in particular volumes of the court records, only those volumes with relatively high numbers of inventories are included in the tables.

Table 5.8: Court Fees in the Estate Inventories of Çankırı (Based on Net Values of the Estates)

Volume/Period	Gross value of the estate after debt payments other expenses (1)	Tax + scribal, notarial, and custodial fees (2)	Relative cost of court usage: (2/1) × 1000 (3)
6/1120–27	71,831	2,217	30.86
1708–15	71,434	2,216	31.02
	63,480	1,440	22.68
	62,280	1,320	21.19
	53,740	1,980	36.84
	29,640	1,440	48.58
	20,200	720	35.64
	23,258	306	13.16
	16,380	500	30.53
	15,720	600	38.17
	12,960	360	27.78
	10,150	300	29.56
	8,980	500	55.68
	6,160	520	84.42
	5,526	620	112.20
	4,200	360	85.71

[7] This is apparent in the ways that the estate inventories were recorded in the *sicils*. Net values of the estates were calculated by subtracting the debts of the deceased, expenses for his/her burial *and* the fees of the court. Also, according to my observations, court fees constitute a disproportionately high percentage of the net values of some estates. In one particular situation the court fees were even higher than the net value of the estate that was divided by the court.

Table 5.8 *(cont.)*

Volume/Period	Gross value of the estate after debt payments other expenses (1)	Tax + scribal, notarial, and custodial fees (2)	Relative cost of court usage: (2/1) × 1000 (3)
	4,010	200	49.88
	3,840	380	98.99
	3,820	252	65.97
	3,381	120	35.49
	2,887	172	59.58
	2,440	180	73.78

Note: The values in the first two columns are in *akçes*. The net values of the estates are arranged in descending order from higher to lower values.

Table 5.9: Court Fees in the Estate Inventories of Kastamonu (Based on Net Values of the Estates)

Volume/Period	Gross value of the estate after debt payments other expenses (1)	Tax + scribal, notarial, and custodial fees (2)	Relative cost of court usage: (2/1) × 1000 (3)
3/1684–86	933	50	53.59
	822	22	26.76
	758	39	51.45
	592.5	20	33.76
19/1712–13	5,308	170	32.03
	2,544	36.5	14.35
	1,400	43	30.71
	919	23	25.03
	655	21	32.06
	545	30	55.05
	470	19	40.43
	379	15.5	40.90
	340	13.5	39.71
	229	7	30.57
	209	6	28.71
	200	8	40.00
	184	7	38.04
	128	4	31.25
34/1735–36	5,651	135	23.89
	2,627	80	30.45
	1,207	30	24.86
	707	26	36.78
	572	17	29.72

Table 5.9 *(cont.)*

Volume/Period	Gross value of the estate after debt payments other expenses (1)	Tax + scribal, notarial, and custodial fees (2)	Relative cost of court usage: (2/1) × 1000 (3)
	511	33.5	65.56
	420	12	28.57
	370	27	72.97
	364.5	15	41.15
	353	19	53.82
	343	13	37.90
	305	17	55.74
	107	6	56.07
	101	5	49.50
	97	3	30.93
	96	6.5	67.71
	29	2	68.97
35/1736–38	37,081	1,250	33.71
	6,114	163.5	26.74
	4,375	116.5	26.63
	3,547.5	112	31.57
	2,788.5	92.5	33.17
	2,609	75	28.75
	2,510	72.5	28.89
	1,694	73	43.09
	1,268	43	33.91
	1,046	40	38.24
	995	38	38.19
	937	37	39.49
	839.5	29	34.54
	689	20	29.03
	625	25	40.00
	550	17.5	31.82
	371.5	16	43.07
	346.5	22.5	64.94
	345	13.5	39.13
	339	10	29.50
	319	9	28.21
	246	8	32.52
	226	8	35.40
	219	7	31.96
	86.5	8	92.49
	81.5	4	49.08
	45	2	44.44
	4	2.5	625.00
36/1738–39	4,138	144	34.80
	521.5	15.5	29.72

Table 5.9 *(cont.)*

Volume/Period	Gross value of the estate after debt payments other expenses (1)	Tax + scribal, notarial, and custodial fees (2)	Relative cost of court usage: (2/1) × 1000 (3)
	289	14.5	50.17
	46	11.5	250.00
	46	4.5	97.83
	23.5	6.5	276.60
	16	5.5	343.75
37/1740–42	1,473	50	33.94
	1,349	45.5	33.73
	912	29	31.80
	402	15	37.31
	351	13	37.04
	242	10	41.32
	209	8	38.28
	107	6	56.07
	37	10	270.27
38/1740–41	6,144	185.5	30.19
	2,160	60	27.78
	1,854.5	70	37.75
	1,292	60	46.44
	1,123	95	84.59
	990	36	36.36
	872	36	41.28
	530.5	17.5	32.99
	504	22	43.65
	445	23	51.69
	379	17	44.86
	370	14	37.84
	215	10	46.51
	92	4	43.48
	69	3	43.48
	60	2	33.33
	44	4	90.91
39/1742–43	1,778.5	37	20.80
	902	31	34.37
	861	24.5	28.46
	441.5	19	43.04
	337	14	41.54
	323	9.5	29.41
	280	11.5	41.07
	279.5	14	50.09
	276	11.5	41.67
	247	13	52.63
	179.5	9	50.14

Table 5.9 *(cont.)*

Volume/Period	Gross value of the estate after debt payments other expenses (1)	Tax + scribal, notarial, and custodial fees (2)	Relative cost of court usage: (2/1) × 1000 (3)
	162	6	37.04
	82.5	3.5	42.42
	74.5	3.5	46.98
	55	3	54.55
	50.5	3	59.41
	2	65	32,500.00 (sic)

Note: The values in columns 1 and 2 are in *guruş*. The net values of the estates for each volume are arranged in descending order from higher to lower values.

In the table above, the negative correlation between the first and the third columns is noteworthy because it implies that the courts in Çankırı and Kastamonu kept relatively greater portions of the poorer estates as fees and other kinds of legal payments.[8] This was of course contrary to the spirit of the official guidelines, which state that a set percentage is to be charged for all estates divided by the courts. By ignoring this rule the courts of Çankırı and Kastamonu must have alienated the poorer inhabitants of their localities, at least to a certain degree.

The following figures illustrate this point perhaps better than the above tables. The first two figures juxtapose net estate values and relative court fees derived from the sixth volume of the Çankırı and the nineteenth volume of the Kastamonu *sicil*s, and they do not contribute anything new to tables 5.8 and 5.9 other than converting them to percentage terms to compare their variations at the same scale. The third figure (figure 5.3) is less straightforward since it combines information found in six volumes of the Kastamonu court records (volumes 34, 35, 36, 37, 38, and 39, which cover the period from 1735 to 1743). Each value represented in this figure is an average of six actual observations from the court records. These averages are calculated after a total of ninety-five observations from six

[8] The correlation coefficients between the values in these columns are −0.6 and −0.33 respectively, and both of these coefficients are statistically significant.

Kastamonu volumes were arranged according to the net values of the estates, from highest to lowest, and the five most extreme ones at the upper and lower ends were eliminated. Accordingly, the first estate value in the figure is the average of the six highest estate values in our set of ninety observations, and the first relative court fee is the average of those relative court fees charged by the court for dividing and inventorying these six estates. This calculation reduces the number of observations represented in the figure and makes the figure comparable to the previous two. It also eliminates extreme fluctuations in the series and, therefore, helps to produce a better representation of the main trends in the two series. Like the previous ones, figure 5.3 presents the net estate values and relative court fees in percentage terms.

Figure 5.1: Net Value of Decedents' Estates and Relative Value of Court Fees for Inventorying and Dividing Them (Çankırı, volume 6, 1708–1715)

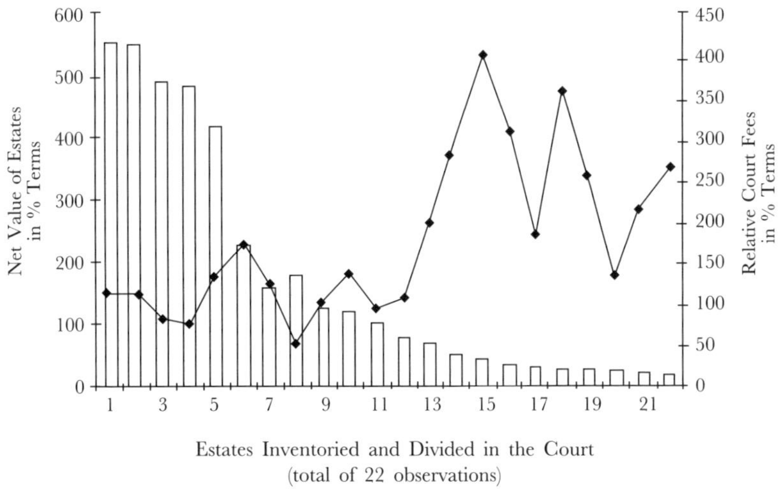

Note: Columns denote the net values of inherited estates in percentage terms (12,960 *guruş* = 100) and are plotted on the primary y-axis. Diamonds denote relative court fees (= actual fees/net estate values) in percentage terms (0.023 = 100) charged for the corresponding estate and are plotted on the secondary y-axis. Values greater that 1,000 per cent are omitted.

Figure 5.2: Net Value of Decedents' Estates and Relative Value of Court Fees for Inventorying and Dividing Them (Kastamonu, volume 19, 1712–1713)

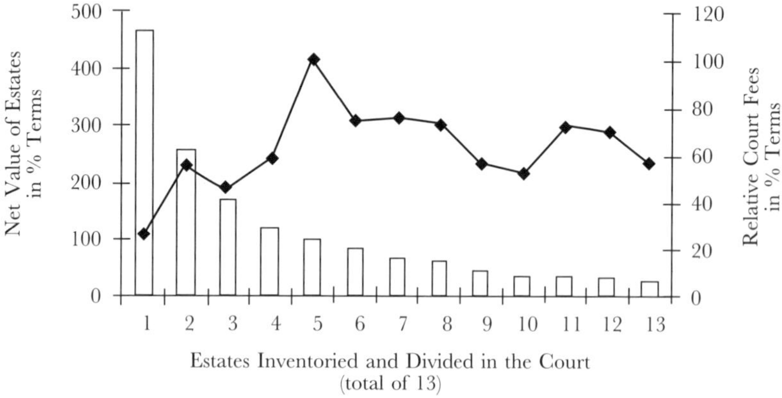

Note: Columns denote net values of the inherited estates in percentage terms (545 *guruş* = 100) and are plotted on the primary y-axis. Diamonds denote relative court fees (= actual fees/net estate values) in percentage terms (0.055 = 100) and are plotted on the secondary y-axis.

Figure 5.3: Net Value of Decedents' Estates and Relative Value of Court Fees for Inventorying and Dividing Them (Kastamonu, volumes 34–39, 1735–1743)

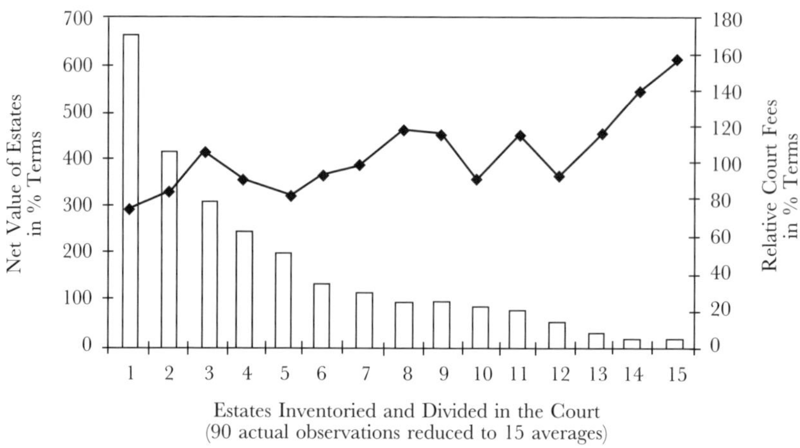

Note: Columns denote net values of the inherited estates in percentage terms (364.5 *guruş* = 100) and are plotted on the primary y-axis. Diamonds denote relative court fees (= actual fees/net estate values) in percentage terms (0.041152 = 100) and are plotted on the secondary y-axis.

Finally, I should also note that in Kastamonu court costs relative to net estate values increased over time more substantially than the court costs relative to gross estate values. Compare the following table with table 5.7.

Table 5.10: Court Fees in Kastamonu Estate Inventories for Different Time Periods (Based on the Net Values of the Estates)

Period	Relative costs of court usage: Court fees/ Gross values of the estates (times 1000)
1684–94	39.3
1703–13	41.5
1735–43	77.9

We know that the heirs of a deceased person were not required to use the courts for the division of the estates that they inherited; they were legally entitled to divide the inherited wealth and property themselves, independent from the courts. Usually, courts were invited to perform this service when it was difficult to estimate the overall value of the estate or when there were disagreements among the heirs about how to divide the estates fairly. The findings of table 5.10, on the other hand, suggest that not only the poor but also the relatively well-off must have developed greater reservations during our period about employing the courts to help them divide their estates. For this reason, it is possible that the heirs became increasingly more inclined to resolve their disagreements in a private manner by employing other non-official mechanisms of dispute settlement or intermediaries among the members of the community.

Conclusion

This chapter has demonstrated not only that the courts of Çankırı and Kastamonu charged substantially more for specific services than what was dictated in official price manuals, but also that the amounts that they charged for these services increased significantly over a period of sixty years. If this tendency was also valid for other services of the court, its use must have become more and more expensive for the inhabitants of Çankırı and Kastamonu during this period.

What could be the reason for the high court fees? As mentioned before, they may be related to the inflationary price movements in the provinces.[9] At the same time, intensifying competition for limited numbers of religious, academic, and judicial posts during the seventeenth and eighteenth centuries, as well as shorter tenures, must have also forced court officials to demand increasingly higher fees from their clients.[10]

I have also observed in this chapter that the division of estates by the court was more costly for the poorer parties than for richer ones. Again, if this kind of discrimination is generalizable to other court services, it would be naïve on our part to expect that the poorer segments of the community utilized the courts regularly or as frequently as richer parties did. This situation probably constitutes the greatest barrier to using the court records to write the history of the peasants and the urban poor in the Ottoman Empire "from below."

[9] Şevket Pamuk demonstrates in his work that prices in Istanbul remained relatively stable between 1650 and 1750. See Pamuk, *A Monetary History*, p. 236.

[10] Madeline Zilfi, *The Politics of Piety: The Ottoman Ulema in the Post Classical Age (1600–1800)* (Minneapolis: Bibliotheca Islamica, 1988).

CHAPTER SIX

THE COURT PROCESS I: ALTERNATIVE APPROACHES TO *KADI*SHIP, COURT, AND LEGAL "CORRUPTION"

This chapter constitutes an initial attempt to examine how law was practiced and how disputes were settled in Ottoman courts during the seventeenth and eighteenth centuries. It will seek this objective by replacing the macro-analytical framework developed in the last three chapters with a micro-analytical one, which will shift our focus from general trends and movements as observed in the court records to the details of individual cases.

The discussion begins with a general evaluation and critique of the secondary literature on the place and the functions of the courts in the Ottoman social and administrative structure. As already argued, not many students of the Ottoman courts have paid adequate attention to the relationship between the court and the community and to the ways in which the members of the community made use of the courts' services. Instead, Ottomanists have limited their analyses exploring the courts' functions in maintaining and reproducing the legitimacy of the regime. According to these scholars, the Ottoman regime was able to preserve its political legitimacy partly because of the courts' ability to administer justice in a relatively impartial manner.

Despite this positive image of the Ottoman courts in the secondary literature, archival and other contemporary sources indicate that court officials were generally considered to be "corrupt."[1] At the same time, this chapter will argue that legal corruption in the Ottoman Empire did not necessarily undermine the legitimacy of the state, nor did it render the employment of the courts useless or undesirable. I will demonstrate in the following pages how clients of the Ottoman courts found ways to handle corruption, and even benefit from it.

[1] The value-laden character of the word "corrupt" constitutes an issue that should be addressed here. As it should become clear in the following pages, the choice of this word to define certain aspects of Ottoman judicial processes does not entail a value judgment on my part. It is clear in our sources that the Ottomans themselves considered bribery, favoritism, evidence tempering, etc. as morally and legally unacceptable acts.

Some of the claims of this chapter are not based on and cannot be verified by the court records. Because of their formulaic makeup and condensed style, these documents themselves occasionally constitute an obstacle to fully understand Ottoman legal practices (more about this in chapter seven). Luckily, we find in Western accounts of Ottoman justice relatively complete and detailed descriptions of the Ottoman court processes. This chapter will draw heavily from these accounts.

The Ottoman *Kadı* and Court in the Secondary Literature

Many of those scholars who sought to define the place and the functions of the Ottoman *kadı* in the provincial administration seem to share a similar understanding of his importance for the stability of provincial society and for the legitimacy of the state. Amy Singer and Huri İslamoğlu-İnan, for example, characterize the *kadı* as an "arbiter between the peasants and the *sipahi*s [provincial cavalry]"[2] who "oversaw the activities of the *sipahi*s and made sure that the latter did not step beyond their rights in their interaction with the peasants and performed their administrative duties in accordance with the precepts of [the] state['s] legal codes."[3] As representatives of the "justice of the sultan," they were "clearly a separate arm of officialdom from the military-administrative officials,"[4] and therefore independently supervised the activities of the provincial military-administrative officials.

Indeed, parallel to the military-administrative chain of command, there existed in the Ottoman bureaucratic structure a separate judicial-administrative chain that ended in the provincial towns with the *kadı*. İslamoğlu-İnan argues that the separation of the judicial and administrative functions was one institutional characteristic of the Ottoman Empire, which made recourse to the ruler's justice possible for the subjects.[5] In this sense, the "*kadı*s represented the closest

---

[2] Amy Singer, *Palestinian Peasants and Ottoman Officials: Rural Administration around Sixteenth-Century Jerusalem* (Cambridge, New York: Cambridge University Press, 1994), p. 127.

[3] İslamoğlu-İnan, p. 7. Also see Barkey, *Bandits and Bureaucrats*, p. 103.

[4] Singer, p. 123.

[5] İslamoğlu-İnan, pp. 6–7.

and most reliable recourse for the peasant, short of going to the Porte and asking the imperial council for an audience. Courts were the main rural mechanisms for redressing wrongs."[6]

This role of the *kadı* was thought to be critical for the stability and legitimacy of the system, as it supported and contributed to the "patrimonial idiom" of the Ottoman socio-political structure.[7] İslamoğlu-İnan claims that the main objective of the Ottoman regime was to ensure the prosperity of all social groups while meeting the state's own financial needs. This goal involved the protection of rural cultivators and urban craft producers from fiscal and physical abuse by local officials. Accordingly, *kadı*s were responsible for mediating the relationship between the state officials and the tax-paying subjects (*re'aya*). They were expected to protect the fiscal basis of the empire, on the one hand, and the legitimacy of the system on the other. As long as the subjects expressed their grievances in terms of the patrimonial idiom of the system (which, she claims, was almost always the case before the nineteenth century), the courts served them as sites where they could take their complaints and seek justice in good faith.[8]

According to Karen Barkey, the provincial court was one of the main obstacles for the peasants in forming alliances with other rural groups (including other peasants and landholders) and, consequently, in generating rebellions in the countryside:

> The court system established throughout the Ottoman lands was the main alternative for direct contact with the state, and complaint to the state, about local conditions. Ottoman peasants made frequent use of the courts, which functioned to deflect anger from local tax-collecting patrons and acted as a safety valve for the Ottoman state. Peasants as well as nomads in rural society used local courts as recourse against those who abused their livelihood and privileges. Especially for the peasant, the court was the main foundation of mediation between himself and the timar-holder. It also weakened the tie between landholder and peasant, hampering their potential efforts at alliances.[9]

Barkey believes that the court, as a semi-independent institution outside the provincial administrative-military organization, lowered the chance and frequency of collective militancy while encouraging indi-

[6] Barkey, *Bandits and Bureaucrats*, p. 104.
[7] İslamoğlu-İnan, pp. 8–9.
[8] Ibid., p. 8.
[9] Barkey, *Bandits and Bureaucrats*, p. 103.

vidual action. She interprets the high number of court cases in the seventeenth-century Manisa *sicils* as evidence of peasant reliance on the court against incidents of oppression and the vagaries of the land tenure system.[10] Singer agrees with this conclusion, citing the social deference among the people of Palestine towards local *kadıs*. She claims that since they kept the state officials in line, *kadıs* won the respect of the Palestinian peasants in the sixteenth century.[11]

Be that as it may, neither Barkey nor Singer seems to be fully satisfied with the conclusions regarding the reverence shown to the *kadıs*. Barkey remarks at one point that "whereas court records demonstrate the peasantry's high reliance on the court, other records, especially rescripts issued by the sultans, paint an abusive image of the judge. The small-town judge in these rescripts is depicted as a rapacious, detestable man who abuses his tax-collection duties and makes alliances with unsavory mercenaries and bandits."[12] Singer, on the other hand, observes that the court records do not reflect the true feelings of the peasants towards the *kadı*, since they were recorded in his presence: "Naturally, peasants seeking assistance would be reticent to express unfavorable feelings toward the *kadı* in the same breath as their request. And any peasant outburst might not be considered germane to the recorded protocol of the case being judged."[13]

It is only Haim Gerber who appears fully confident about the great degree of respect shown to the *kadı* by the community. Based on his research in the court records of seventeenth-century Bursa, eighteenth-century Istanbul, and a seventeenth-century complaint register, he concludes that the *kadı* was highly revered by members of the community. Gerber states that he found very few records in his sources documenting examples of corruption.[14]

We have ample documentation of corrupt practices by the *kadıs* during the seventeenth and eighteenth centuries, and these documents are not limited to the imperial rescripts that Barkey mentions in her study. The accounts of Western observers of Ottoman legal practices unanimously represent the provincial courts as corrupt insti-

---

[10] Ibid., pp. 104–105.

[11] Singer, p. 122.

[12] Barkey, *Bandits and Bureaucrats*, p. 105.

[13] Singer, p. 122.

[14] Haim Gerber, *Economy and Society in an Ottoman City: Bursa, 1600–1700* (Jerusalem: The Hebrew University of Jerusalem, 1988), p. 205; idem, *State, Society and Law in Islam*, p. 66.

tutions that usually made decisions that benefited richer parties who could afford to bribe the *kadı* and other court officials. We also come across a number of documents on this matter in archival sources, including the court records. These documents consist of complaint letters and reports sent from different parts of the empire reporting the corruption of the *kadı*s. The court records also contain orders drafted in the capital in response to prior correspondences with the provinces. Although this documentation does not constitute the basis for a statistical analysis, it does draw an impressionistic picture of the time's judicial practices.

Admittedly, İslamoğlu-İnan acknowledges that her representation of the Ottoman legal and socio-political order portrays an "ideal image" that "the political authority had of itself and of the society over which it ruled."[15] Hence, she concedes that this view "parts company at many points with reality even in the sixteenth century when the state authority was at its zenith."[16] In other words, she never explicitly claims, as Gerber does, that the Ottoman courts were impartial and independent legal institutions that could and did diligently correct the injustices committed against the weak in everyday life. In this sense she is even more cautious than Barkey, who eventually chooses to ignore the implications of the rescripts that she herself mentions in her book, claiming that "we need to differentiate between the regularity and stability of the institution of the court and the instability and whims of its individual members."[17]

Despite her astuteness in differentiating between the reality and its idealized representations, however, there is no place for "legitimacy crises" in İslamoğlu-İnan's work, which should have emerged, according to her own analysis, when local courts failed to protect the rights of the tax-paying subjects. In fact, İslamoğlu-İnan implies that until the nineteenth century the paternalist model of the Ottoman state not only "provided the idiom of domination and a vocabulary for the political expression of different groups within the society," but also "provided the idiom of contestation of state power."[18] In other words, the hegemony of the paternalistic discourse of the Ottoman State was not questioned even when the state was challenged.

15 İslamoğlu-İnan, p. 9.
16 Ibid.
17 Barkey, *Bandits and Bureaucrats*, p. 105.
18 İslamoğlu-İnan, p. 9.

A Critique

When İslamoğlu-İnan, Barkey, Singer, and others emphasize the critical importance of the local court for the legitimacy and the stability of the system, they in fact repeat what was officially stated in the imperial rescripts of justice (*ʿadaletnameler*). Indeed, according to these rescripts, local *kadı*s were primarily responsible for enforcing the "justice of the sultan," which was generally understood as the protection of the safety and well-being of the subjects.[19] Nonetheless, according to the court records, the tendency to use local courts against the oppression of local authorities was not a universal phenomenon in the Ottoman Empire. In Çankırı and Kastamonu, for example, not many complaints against the military-administrative officials were initially brought to the court. As has been demonstrated in a previous section, subjects preferred to appeal to the central government or the governor-general of the province of Anatolia directly in both places if and when they had problems with local military-administrative officials.[20]

Contrary to what Barkey argues in her book, it is probable that local courts did not (or could not) always provide an alternative to appealing to Istanbul or the provincial capital, Kütahya.[21] On the

---

[19] See ÇCR, vol. 7, 8–12, 9–13 and vol. 12, 17–20, 20–21 for examples of these rescripts in the *sicil*s. Also see Boğaç Ergene, "On Ottoman Justice: Interpretations in Conflict (1600–1800)," *Islamic Law and Society*, no. 1, vol. 8 (Winter 2001), pp. 52–87 for a detailed discussion of the representation of imperial justice in these rescripts.

[20] There is evidence that this pattern was not limited to Çankırı and Kastamonu, and it might indeed be a manifestation of distrust towards local courts on the part of the community. For example, Heneage Finch, the British ambassador in Istanbul between 1660 and 1668, indicates in his correspondence that when the British consul and merchants in Aleppo could not get any help from the local *kadı* to prevent abuses by the governor, they, as well as the ambassador himself, used to appeal to the Grand Vizier for his intervention. The consul claimed in his letters to the ambassador that the governor controlled the *kadı*, and for this reason he could not protect them against the governor's oppression. See *Report on the Manuscripts of Allan George Finch, Esq., Burley-on-the-Hill, Rutland.* Vol. 1 Historical Manuscripts Commission (London: His Majesty's Stationery Office, 1913), pp. 214, 223, 224.

[21] The reasons for not taking complaints against local officials to the provincial courts were seldom made explicit in the petitions written to the capital or the governor-general in Kütahya, especially when these complaints involved specific accusations against local *kadı*s. The most we get in terms of an explanation is a brief remark indicating that it was impossible to resolve the problem within the locality according to law ("*mahallinde şerʿle halli mümkün olmadığından*"). See, for example, ÇCR, vol. 11, 37–55.

contrary, the inhabitants of Çankırı and Kastamonu sought secure channels to convey their complaints and demands to the government instead of letting the local court handle their grievances. Ironically, the court itself provided a means for this particular purpose: The court records indicate that many people brought complaints to the court not to obtain a fast legal resolution, but to have those complaints transcribed and sent to Istanbul or Kütahya. On other occasions, appellants used influential and powerful individuals at the capital to bring their complaints to the attention of the government. For example, the inhabitants of the villages of Ömer Şeyh and Kibir in the sub-province of Kastamonu benefited from the intermediacy and support of Darüssaʿade Ağası Yusuf[22] in 1096/1685 to obtain an imperial order against exactions of local military administrators.[23]

It would also be wrong to link the frequent use of the courts with judicial independence or legitimacy of the legal system. The basis of this connection lies in the assumption that cases brought to the court were resolved once and for all. It is assumed in the literature on the Ottoman judicial system that the litigants respected and obeyed the decisions of the courts regardless of the nature of these decisions. In fact, there is evidence that the very same disputes were taken over and over again to different courts for resolution. For example, in 1104/1693 Osman Beğ from Kastamonu agreed to settle a dispute

[22] Darüssaʿade Ağası (or Kızlar Ağası) is the official title of the chief black eunuch of the imperial palace. According to Jane Hathaway, Yusuf Ağa was one of the most politically active chief black eunuchs in the provinces. See Jane Hathaway, "The role of the Kızlar Ağası in 17th–18th Century Ottoman Egypt," *Studia Islamica*, vol. 75 (1992), pp. 141–158; and idem, *The Politics of Households in Ottoman Egypt: The Rise of the Qazdaglis* (Cambridge, New York: Cambridge University Press, 1997), *passim*.

[23] The revenues of these two villages belonged to the endowment (*vakıf*) of Sultan Bayezıt in Amasya, and Yusuf Ağa was the overseer (*nazır*) of the endowment at that time. See KCR, vol. 3, 27–60 and 28–61. There are many similar documents in the Çankırı and Kastamonu court records. If and when an act of injustice was actually heard and corrected in the court—which seems to have happened rarely according to the court records—this was not always a result of the administrative or legal authority of the court over military executives in the locality. For example, in 1099/1688, the sub-governor of Kastamonu agreed in court to return money he had forcibly extracted from the inhabitants of his district in return for the promise that they would not take their complaints to the government. In this particular example, as in many others, the court operated as a setting wherein different parties negotiated their differences and resolved their disputes. The supposed authority of the court over the provincial military administrators seems to have played no role in this process. See, KCR, vol. 1, 95.

with Mehmed Beşe amicably and pay sixteen and a half *guruş* to the latter, who had accused him of forcibly entering his house five years before the date of the document and stealing his money and property. According to what we learn from the same document, Mehmed Beşe had sued Osman Beğ immediately after the incident, but he could not document his claims in the court. Nevertheless, again according to the document, this outcome had not stopped him from taking the case to the court repetitively, presumably after the appointment of new *kadıs*. Finally, third parties convinced the two men to settle the dispute amicably.[24]

In another interesting example from the same volume, we find the wife and two daughters of the late Himmet bin Sefer suing Hüseyin Çelebi bin Elhac Ali, who had purchased a house from the deceased Himmet six years before the date of the document. The women claimed that the price that Hüseyin Çelebi had paid for the house was less than the actual value of the property, and they demanded that the defendant pay the difference to them. In response, Hüseyin Çelebi stated that Himmet had made the same claim himself before he died, but after an inspection of the property by the court officials and "learned" members of the community, the court had found his claim to be erroneous. Hüseyin Çelebi also claimed that Himmet had confessed to him after the trial that he had not actually wanted to sue him but had been forced to do by his wife and daughters. Indeed, Hüseyin Çelebi claimed that the women had sued him multiple times after the death of Himmet. Two witnesses confirmed the accuracy of Hüseyin Çelebi's statements in the court, and the court decided in his favor.[25]

What could be the objective of repeatedly bringing the same cases to the court? Presumably, it was hoped that the decision of the new

[24] KCR, vol. 5, 110–225.

[25] KCR, vol. 5, 126–270. There are numerous examples of similar situations in the sicils of Kastamonu. See, for example. KCR, vol. 4, 100–99; KCR, vol. 5, 106–209, 115–241, 117–245, 117–247; KCR, vol. 34, 48–81, 101–1; KCR, vol. 35, 31–38, 116–181, 251–380; KCR, vol. 36, 38–63, 43–75; KCR, vol. 37, 53–71; KCR, vol. 39, 39–64, 72–121. In the court records of Çankırı, on the other hand, there are numerous examples of those situations where subsequent *kadıs* endorsed different and rival parties for a particular office. In fact, it seems that the arrival of a new *kadı* gave a chance to those parties who were unable to gain the support of the previous *kadı*. See, for example, ÇCR, vol. 1, 1–1, 3–5; vol. 8, 26–1, 27–2; 43–80; 57–103 and 116–201.

kadı towards the case and the litigants would be different from those of the previous one. This situation is well documented in the account of Hans Ulrich Krafft, who remained incarcerated in Tripoli (in northern Lebanon) for three years because of complex financial disputes between his company and local merchants. In fact he was released only after the arrival of a new *kadı* who was sympathetic enough towards the German merchant to accept bribes from him.[26]

There is evidence that many cases were taken to neighboring courts after the initial trial for re-adjudication. For example, a petition sent to Istanbul from Aleppo in 1182/1768 demonstrates that after a dispute of unidentified nature had been taken to and decided by the court of Aleppo, the displeased party took the case to the court of Alexandria and was able to obtain a decision that was more favorable for him.[27] Although this type of action was clearly illegal, documents in the Prime Ministry Archive indicate that it happened frequently.[28] Indeed, an example from the Kastamonu *sicil*s proves that the ability to choose the court where the dispute was heard was critical in determining the outcome. An order from Istanbul (dated 1149/1736) indicates that a shop-owner from Kastamonu had sent a petition begging the government to order that a financial dispute involving his son and a group of nomads (*Türkmenler*) be heard and resolved nowhere else but in the court of Kastamonu. According to what he reported in his petition, the nomads had attempted to take his son to the court of Kütahya[29] for adjudication, "and to do injustice to my son; [in the court of Kütahya] some of [these nomads] will act as plaintiffs and the rest as witnesses."[30]

In short, the court was perhaps not a site of ultimate and unobjectionable justice and was not always considered to be so by its

[26] Hans Ulrich Krafft, *Türklerin Elinde Bir Alman Tacir*, translated by Turgut Akpınar (Istanbul: İletisim, 1997), pp. 67–131. See below for a more detailed discussion of Krafft's account.

[27] See CA 2072. Also see CA 1052 for a *kadı* petition which complains about this tendency among the "contemporary" (*zamane*) litigants (dated 5 CII 1137 / 24 October 1724).

[28] See CA 4025 and 4851 for two such incidents. D'Ohsson agrees with this observation in his account: "La loi n'admet point d'appel; cependant un plaideur qui a perdu sa cause, trouve souvent le moyen de la reproduire devant un autre tribunal, sous une forme différente," see D'Ohsson, vol. 6, p. 209.

[29] Kütahya was the administrative center of the province of Anatolia.

[30] KCR, vol. 35, 251–380.

clients. Indeed it seems that the administration of justice by a particular court was sometimes unfinished, temporary, and subject to challenge in other arenas. Hence, employing the local court did not necessarily imply an acknowledgement of its fairness. Rather, litigants sometimes shopped for alternate sites where their claims could find sympathetic ears. If this did not happen in a particular court, there were always other courts in which one could try his or her luck, especially if this person had some material means to pursue his or her interests insistently. In other words, we cannot be sure how well the legal component of İslamoğlu-İnan's patrimonial model functioned in the seventeenth and eighteenth centuries. Reversibility of justice gave a flexible character to Ottoman judicial system. It is probable that at least some court clients regarded the pursuit of justice as a creative process of legal and political contestation, rather than a quest for blind, impartial, and therefore, irreproachable justice. For this reason, frequent use of Ottoman courts does not necessarily imply an acknowledgement of the system's legitimacy. In many occasions, litigants approached provincial courts not because they constituted ultimate sites of justice, but because they privileged, if temporarily, certain claims over others in legal terms.

"Corruption" and Its Uses

In contrast to what has been generally stated in the secondary literature regarding the fairness of the Ottoman courts, we have significant archival evidence suggesting the corruption and the illegal practices of the *kadı*s in Anatolia and Rumelia during the seventeenth and eighteenth centuries.[31] This evidence includes reports, petitions, and orders regarding the practices of specific individuals as well as rescripts describing the general patterns of fraud among the

[31] There is documentation for such allegations both from the court records of Çankırı and Kastamonu and from elsewhere. See for example ÇCR, vol. 8, 26–52; 27–52; 39–73; 43–80; 112–193; 116–201; ÇCR, vol. 9, 2–1; ÇCR, vol. 10, 13–17; 75–125; KCR, vol. 3, 85; 244; KCR, vol. 1, 120–36; 130–60; KCR, vol. 34, 49–84; KCR, vol. 4, 4–9; 133–172; 162–231; KCR, vol. 5, 95–176; 116–244; 120–256; 141–303; KCR, vol. 35, 76–126; 251–380; KCR, vol. 37, 24–25; 53–73; KCR, vol. 38, 65–96; 77–122; 89–140; 152–241; 192–293; KCR, vol. 39, 136–377; 140–37; 177–335, 206–297; 252–232; CA 192, 196, 1014, 1038, 1305, 1601, 2311, 2620, 2759, 2968, 3318, 3319, 3797, 4082, 4564, 5312.

court officials. And although we cannot directly observe corrupt practices in court records, we have to keep in mind that these documents must have been designed to conceal such activities rather than to reveal them.

On the other hand, the objective of a fresh approach to Ottoman legal history should not be to prove that Ottoman justice was actually corrupt in its daily practices. There are two reasons for this assertion. First, there is nothing new in the argument that Ottoman justice was corrupt: As will be indicated shortly, many contemporary observers of Ottoman justice (western or non-western) complained about the problems and the corruption in the system. In fact, this assertion is perhaps older than the claim that the Ottoman courts functioned in a relatively uncorrupt manner.

Second, and more important, by changing the answer to the question of whether Ottoman justice was corrupt or not, we cannot step outside the paradigm that has occupied a central place in Ottoman historiography thus far. In other words, we need to rethink the questions we ask when trying to understand the functions and operations of local courts. For example, we need to explore the ways members of the community perceived and utilized the legal system, given its problems and perhaps even its corruption. Focusing on the relationship between the court and the community is one way to distance ourselves from the state-centered emphasis in the secondary literature.

The fact that justice could be purchased was probably advantageous for the rich rather than the poor. Indeed, the findings of chapter four demonstrate that wealthy and socially prominent parties in Çankırı and Kastamonu dominated the trials. On the other hand, there are some reasons weaker parties might not have been completely alienated from the provincial courts. For those who could afford the (legitimate and illegitimate) costs of adjudication, the "purchasability" of justice also implied relative autonomy from the prevalent patterns of social, cultural, and religious domination, and this might be why those individuals who were not among the local elite might have been willing to employ the local courts as much as they did. This point needs some clarification.

Melissa Macauley's inspiring work on litigation masters in late imperial China demonstrates that tendencies of "professionalization" in a legal structure could indeed be useful for the weak against the powerful—women against men, younger relatives against older ones, tenants against landlords, etc.[32] According to Macauley, professional litigation masters in China assisted the socially disadvantaged in lodging false accusations and unwarranted appeals in attacks on their opponents. They helped their clients of insignificant local stature engage in legal abuse as a form of defense strategy as well as a form of social attack. They wrote provocative letters of complaint to galvanize into action the courts that were, otherwise, unwilling to interfere with "petty" civil disputes on a local level. By doing that, these "inciters" drew the state into informal jurisdictions that were usually monopolized by prominent men, village headmen, and legal clerks, who would otherwise neutralize the grievances of the dominated.[33] In this sense the activities of litigation masters allowed the weak to break free of local systems of power and negotiation. Psycho-socially, they provided a formidable means of legal and social empowerment.[34]

Macauley mentions the existence of two rhetorical traditions regarding the activities of litigation masters. On the one hand, official sources and state authorities despised litigation masters because they helped to transform the courts into extended arenas of local contestation. According to Macauley, the local elite resented the fact that these men helped to draw the state into dispute resolution that the former group expected to dominate.[35] The alternative tradition of the politically alienated literati, on the other hand, tended to favorably portray litigation masters as artful, though morally flawed, champions to whom people threatened by the law or by evil officials and gentry could turn in desperation.[36] Their ability to strategize, cheat, and escape danger—which Macauley calls "cunning intelligence"—helped the weaker parties resist domination by their more powerful adversaries.[37]

We are not aware of such litigation masters in the courts of the Ottoman Empire although, of course, different members of the court or individuals who were knowledgeable in legal matters probably helped certain members of the community to exploit the loopholes

---

[32] Melissa Macauley, *Social Power and Legal Culture; Litigation Masters in Late Imperial China* (Stanford: Stanford University Press, 1998).
[33] Ibid., pp. 1–18 and pp. 325–330.
[34] Ibid., p. 329.
[35] Ibid., p. 330.
[36] Ibid.
[37] Ibid., pp. 330–331.

of the system.[38] The materials we find in our sources demonstrate that the assistants of the *kadıs*, scribes, translators, and other officials of the provincial courts were frequently reported to the central government for their illicit or unwarranted legal activities on behalf of certain individuals, including the weak as well as the powerful. Nevertheless, the documentation in the court records and in other archival sources is inadequate to prove the existence of a "cunning intelligence" in the Ottoman legal system that was for sale and that could, in theory, be employed even by the marginalized. This kind of information necessitates a different kind of documentation.

In this sense, Western observers' accounts of the Ottoman legal system are important, as they provide portrayals of Ottoman judicial practice based on their authors' personal observations or what they had heard from other people. These accounts relate how the legal system functioned, how the litigants were treated in the courts, how the disputes were resolved, and what the members of the community thought about the judicial officials. Hence, we find in them a cultural, political, and ethnographic substance missing from the court records and other archival documents. For this reason, the *kadı* and the operations of the court seem radically different in these accounts from the way they appear in court documents.

I believe that the portrayals of the *kadı* and the representations of his actions in these accounts are comparable to Macauley's description of Chinese litigation masters.[39] Like the first rhetorical tradition Macauley mentions, none of these Western accounts presents the Ottoman courts in a very positive light. The *kadıs* are generally characterized as dishonest and corrupt magistrates who were "well

---

[38] Among our sources it is only D'Ohsson who alludes to Ottoman "avocats." According to D'Ohsson, these individuals were as insidious as their Chinese counterparts: "On doit éviter le ministère des avocats, surtout de ceux qui sont pétris de ruses, d'artifices et de sophismes (*moufti-y-madjinn*); les hommes de cette espèce dovient même être bannis de toute société, aussi bien que les empiriques ignorants (*tabib djeahhil*), et les maquignons obérés (*mekiari-y-mufliss*). Le bien de l'humanité l'exige, pour garantir les peuples de l'art insidieux des uns, des funestes effets de l'ignorance des seconds, et du trafic vil et frauduleux des derniers." See D'Ohsson, vol. 6, p. 193.

[39] Again, it should be emphasized that my objective in this section is not to identify the Ottoman equivalent of the Chinese litigation master. Rather, I am interested in the consequences of the litigants' ability to employ those individuals (most notably the *kadı*, but also other court officers) who were knowledgeable about law and experienced in court processes.

acquainted with the means of promoting their private interests."[40] At the same time, however, they are also described as being "ingenious" in their ability to find legal loopholes to promote the interests of those who bribe them.[41] In fact, we are given very interesting accounts demonstrating this ingenuity. In his memoirs, Baron de Tott reports the following story:

> A Turk, in haste to inherit, had murdered his Father, and was condemned on the strongest Proofs to lose his Head. One of his Friends, the Companion of his Debaucheries, hastens to the Judge, with a large Sum of Money; where he learned that the Sentence had been already pronounced. Not discouraged by that, he continued to press the Cadi, whom the sight of such a Treasure had already persuaded. I cannot, said he to his Client, acquit your Friend without a Proof of his Innocence, stronger than the Evidence on which he has been convicted. Be bold enough to declare yourself the Murderer of his Father, procure two Witnesses, and I will condemn you to undergo the Punishment to which he has been sentenced; he will be immediately reinstated in all his Rights, and have the Power of granting you a Pardon. The Undertaking was certainly hazardous; no great Confidence could be reposed in a Parricide. Yet the convicted Criminal pardoned the pretended Murderer, and this Villainy, conducted in due Form of Law, was completely successful.[42]

If there is any truth in it, we witness in this account the "cunning intelligence" that Macauley talks about for Chinese litigation masters. Moreover, the fact that this "intelligence" was for sale made it a possible weapon for weaker parties who could afford it. The Western accounts provide many reports and stories that support this hypothesis. For example, William Eton narrates the following story:

> A Christian, subject to the Turks, was carried before a judge at Aleppo, accused by a Sherif of having one evening in the bazaar, or market place, knocked off his green turban, a crime punishable with death—the judge himself a Sherif—(this race have, in most places, the privi-

[40] A.L. Castellan, *Turkey, Being a Description of the Manners, Customs, Dresses, and Other Peculiarities Characteristic of the Inhabitants of the Turkish Empire*, trans. Fr. Shoberl (Philadelphia: H. Cowperthwait, 1829) vol. 3, p. 11. Also see W. Eton, *A Survey of the Turkish Empire . . .*, 3rd edition (London: T. Cadell & W. Daves, 1801), p. 31; Baron François de Tott, *Memoirs of Baron de Tott; Containing the State of the Turkish Empire and the Crimea During the Late War with Russia . . .* (London: G.G.J. and J. Robinson, 1785) vol. 1, pp. 199–201; and D'Ohsson, pp. 189–190.

[41] Eton, p. 31; Castellan, vol. 3, p. 12.

[42] Baron de Tott, vol. 1, pp. 199–200.

> lege of a judge of their own.) The Christian sent secretly, bribed him, and informed him of the truth, which was, that the Sherif's turban was of so dark a green that he took it for a dark blue, a colour which a Christian friend of his wore, and for whom he had taken him in the dark of the evening, and knocked off his turban in a joke: The accused was brought before the judge, and the plaintiff came into the judge's hall with a great number of other Sherifs. The judge addressed them; "*Do you come here in such numbers to ask justice, or to take it yourselves; go out all but those who are witnesses; and you Christian*," said he, addressing himself to the accuser (who had been privately pointed out to him) "*go you out, I suppose you are a witness for the accused; you shall be called when you are wanted*." The man exclaimed, that he was not only Mahomedan, but a Sherif, and the accuser himself. "*What*," says the judge, "*you a Sherif, and wear a turban of a colour that I myself in the day-time took for that of an infidel; how could the poor infidel in the dark distinguish it? You ought to wear the holy grass green of the prophet, and not be ashamed of it*." He acquitted the Christian, and ordered the plaintiff to be bastinadoed for not wearing a proper green turban.[43]

These accounts and several others not mentioned here portray the *kadı*s as dispensing justice and establishing relationships with litigants very differently from what court records suggest: The *kadı*s appear to take sides with specific parties, manipulate court proceedings, and determine their outcomes in ways that are not apparent in the *sicil*s. And if we assume that the court records reflect certain standards about how disputes were supposed to be heard and resolved in Ottoman courts (as will be argued in subsequent chapters), the discrepancies between the Western accounts of Ottoman justice and the court records could be indicative of the differences between judicial ideals and practices.

Admittedly, there are some points in the stories transmitted by the Western observers that could lead the reader to doubt the authenticity of these narratives and question their sources. For example, the act of sentencing a "Sherif" to bastinado for a crime that he did not intentionally commit does sound unrealistic, although, from a strictly legalistic point of view, this was not entirely impossible. Admittedly, many of these stories seem to have been borrowed by later authors from the accounts of the earlier ones and retold time and again to suggest that they personally witnessed the incidents recounted in the stories. What's more, there is the problem of language; even

[43] Eton, pp. 33–34.

if some Western observers had a chance to observe the court proceedings, a significant number of them lacked the language skills to comprehend the judicial processes.

Nevertheless, we should be careful about dismissing these accounts altogether. We know for fact that at least a number of them are based on first-hand observations of their authors, many of whom lived in the Ottoman Empire for considerable periods of time and were familiar with local languages.[44] Furthermore, even those stories whose sources are unclear can be considered as literary, if not historical, manifestations of the how courts operated in Ottoman society, with the potential of enlightening us about what was then "common-knowledge" about judicial processes. In this context, it is particularly noteworthy that how these stories depict the Ottoman administration of justice is generally consistent, despite the differences among these accounts in terms of their sources, and the variations among their authors' exposure to and attitudes towards Ottoman culture and society.[45]

The accounts of Western observers of the Ottoman judicial system do not necessarily indicate that the corruption of the judicial system was consistently beneficial for the weak or the innocent. Nevertheless, these accounts do demonstrate that the system was not so unpredictable, the rules of the game were actually not so difficult to master, and those who could understand these rules and "afford" the judicial process could actually succeed in spite of their lack of social status and/or power. Sir James Porter gives perhaps the clearest description of this situation:

> In general, let the cause be right or wrong, Christians or Jews have no chance against Turks but by dint of money; happy, if that can save

[44] One such example is Hans Ulrich Krafft's account, which will be discussed later in detail. Baron de Tott spent an extended period of time in the Ottoman Empire and spoke Turkish well; see Ezel Kural Shaw and Colin J. Heywood, *English Continental Views of the Ottoman Empire 1500–1800* (Los Angeles: University of California Press, 1972). Also see British Ambassador Finch's detailed and informed description of the activities of the local *kadı* in Aleppo in *Report on . . . Finch*, pp. 373–374.

[45] For the variations among Western attitudes towards Ottoman culture and society see Aslı Çırakman, "From Tyranny to Despotism: The Enlightenment's Unenlightened Image of the Turks," *International Journal of Middle East Studies*, no. 1, vol. 33 (February 2001), pp. 49–68; Brandon Beck, *From the Rising of the Sun: English Images of the Ottoman Empire to 1715* (New York: Peter Lang, 1987); Clarence Dana Rouillard, *The Turk in French History, Thought and Literature (1520–1660)* (Paris: Bouvin, 1938).

> them . . . They have no subpoenas; the law does not permit a summons, or oblige any person to give in their evidence; they must do it uncompelled. Turks, unless your dependants, will not appear in favor of a Christian or a Jew: the mere force of money must bring them in court. If they really know the justice of the cause, and had seen the fact, they generally expect the higher bribe; and that in proportion as they think their evidence material.[46]

In this context it should be emphasized that although most Western accounts of Ottoman legal practice mention the corruption of the system, in none of them do we find an image of the *kadı* "sitting under a tree dispensing justice according to considerations of individual expediency."[47] Instead we can identify a legal system with relatively concrete boundaries, pre-established procedures of litigation, and well-known evidentiary standards. It is for this reason that the legal knowledge or skill to manipulate the system or to prevent others from doing so was one of the prerequisites for obtaining a successful outcome in the courts. After all, in the account of Baron de Tott it was the *kadı*'s judicial expertise that enabled him to find a legal (although illegitimate) solution to the dilemma of the son who had killed his own father. In other words, "cunning intelligence" was required not only to take advantage of the loopholes of the system but also to remain within the limits of it and, therefore, to acknowledge the legitimacy of the judicial process.

A Case Study: Hans Ulrich Krafft's Memoirs

As informative as the Western accounts are in demonstrating aspects of the Ottoman administration of justice that were only alluded to in archival sources, they do not usually describe the *processes* of litigation and adjudication in a very detailed manner. And although these accounts provide an image of the power struggle in the court in ways that court records do not, they also fail to shed light on the

[46] Porter, pp. 140–141.

[47] A quote from Justice Frankfurter in Terminiello vs. Chicago (United States Supreme Court, 1949), p. 11; quoted in Rosen, *The Justice of Islam; Comparative Perspectives on Islamic Law and Society* (Oxford, New York: Oxford University Press, 2000), p. 3.

complete arsenal of litigation strategies as well as the operations of the *kadı* in his court. Hans Ulrich Krafft's memoir is an exception to this rule, and for this reason I would like to focus on this account in the rest of this chapter.

Summary of the Events

Hans Ulrich Krafft was a German merchant in the Middle East, and he wrote this account after his return to his country in 1577. He was jailed in Tripoli (in northern Lebanon) for three years because of his company's debts to local Jewish merchants.[48] Krafft gives a detailed description of these three years in his account, and although his experiences are extremely interesting, it is not necessary at this point to delve into the issue of how he survived in prison.[49] More critical for this study is his experience with the judicial establishment and the rules that he had to master in order to play the legal game successfully.

In short, his ability to establish connections with people who could make appeals on his behalf and instruct him on judicial processes was what made Krafft's release possible after three years in prison. The French consul in Tripoli and certain Venetian merchants were friendly and helpful towards Krafft during his imprisonment. Yet, perhaps the single most important connection he had was that with the commander of a fortress (*dizdar*) in which he was detained. He was able to attain this friendship by repairing a valuable clock for the commander and by demonstrating his knowledge of astronomy. The commander's support proved to be critical later on, since it was he who made an initial appeal to the *kadı* of Tripoli regarding the situation of the German merchant. Subsequently, and as a result of the suggestion of the commander, Krafft also had an opportunity to repair a golden watch of the *kadı* and gain his gratitude.

Krafft's account is useful for demonstrating how litigants struggled to gain the favor of the *kadı* in the litigation process. Indeed, Krafft indicates in his account that when his opponents, the Jewish creditors, heard about his services to the *kadı*, they felt obligated to send gifts to the *kadı*. Nevertheless, with the intensified lobbying efforts of

[48] Krafft, op. cit.

[49] Two of his friends, with whom he had been jailed, died during this period.

the commander on behalf of Krafft, the *kadı* took a step to help the German and suggested a legal way to make his release possible. The *kadı* told the commander that if Krafft could get loans from the European merchants in the region to pay at least a portion of his company's debt, he might force the Jewish creditors to negotiate an amicable settlement (*sulh*) with Krafft.

Although Krafft was initially encouraged by these comments, he was warned by the French consul not to trust the *kadı*, who, the consul claimed, could easily be bought by Krafft's opponents. Krafft then decided to make an appeal to the favorite wife of the *kadı* in hopes that she would influence her husband in his favor. Again, it was the commander who helped Krafft send two silk dresses to the *kadı*'s wife by a female servant. According to what this servant later reported, the wife accepted the presents and promised to make an appeal to the *kadı* on behalf of the German. She also promised to return the dresses if the *kadı* decided to take sides with Krafft's opponents.

Krafft reports that, according to what he later heard from the same servant, the wife had indeed made an appeal to her husband and asked the *kadı* to be lenient towards the German. Reportedly, the *kadı* had become visibly distressed upon this request and told his wife that the amount of debt attributed to Krafft was too large to make his release possible. In response, his wife suggested that he threaten to send the creditors and the German merchant to Istanbul to resolve their problems in the Imperial Council (*Divan-ı Hümayun*). She claimed that the creditors would be unwilling to take this chance, since the German merchant could easily secure the support of the German and French ambassadors in Istanbul.

Then the *kadı* asked his wife how he would benefit from the release of the German. His wife showed him the dresses that Krafft had sent and assured him that the German would be willing to reward him generously if he decided to support the German against his creditors. Consequently, the *kadı* promised his wife that he would summon the merchant and hear his side of the story.

When he learned about these developments, Krafft began to inquire about the amount that he should pay the *kadı*, should he agree to release him. The French consul told him that anything less than 100 gold pieces would be inadequate. The consul also advised him to pretend to be extremely poor and in need of the help of other Christians in Tripoli to pay even this "modest" amount. In reality,

Krafft had received a considerable amount of money from Europe immediately after his imprisonment. Yet, because he feared that the creditors would try to seize this amount, he left it in the safekeeping of the French consul and tried to live an impoverished life in prison.

Subsequently he was summoned to the court, where the *kadı* asked him about the amount that he could find to cover his debts. Krafft, hiding the fact that he had his own money in the custody of the French consul, told the *kadı* that he could borrow 1,000 gold pieces from the benevolent Christians in Tripoli. According to what Krafft reports in his account, the *kadı* was disappointed. He asked the German how he could expect to be saved from a debt of twenty-four thousand gold pieces with this small amount of money. Krafft responded by stating that this entire amount was not his responsibility; it was his two friends who had borrowed the greatest part of this sum from the creditors on behalf of the company.

Then the *kadı* asked Krafft, explicitly, how much he was willing to pay for his services. Krafft told him that he was hoping to be able to pay him as much as 100 gold pieces, which the *kadı* accepted. According to what was reported to Krafft by his friends later on, the *kadı* had made inquiries immediately after their conversation to learn whether Krafft would be able to pay the amount of money that he had promised him. When they were approached by the *kadı*, Krafft's friends guaranteed that he would be able to make the payment.

Later on, the *kadı* summoned the Jewish creditors to the court to meet with them privately. On their way to the court they were seen carrying silk dresses, presumably to counter the gifts sent by Krafft to the wife of the *kadı*. This news irritated Krafft and his supporters. Nevertheless, according to what was told to Krafft by a friend of the commander who had witnessed the interaction between the *kadı* and the creditors, the latter found an angry person in the court when they arrived. Reportedly, the *kadı* was upset because the creditors were late in arriving to the court. He reprimanded them severely for this and then began to force them to settle the case amicably.

He did this first by claiming to have discovered that the amount that Krafft owed them was significantly less than they had claimed, since a large portion of the debt owed to the company was actually the liability of the two other merchants, who had previously died in prison. Moreover, the *kadı* claimed, they had continued to charge interest during the period in which Krafft and his friends were in prison, and this was illegal. Thirdly, he emphasized the fact that two of the imprisoned merchants had already died, and he did not want the third one to die in prison as well. He also argued that the creditors would not benefit from the imprisonment of Krafft since, apparently, there was no one in Europe who was willing to pay his debts and save him from prison. Finally, he suggested that Krafft did not want to hurt them, nor did he personally benefit from the money borrowed by his company. It was the owners of the company who were responsible for the creditors' losses and the German should not be punished for their crimes. Then the *kadı* reportedly told the creditors that if they refused to accept 1,000 gold pieces and agree to reach an amicable settlement with Krafft, he would transfer the case to the Imperial Council in Istanbul and send a letter to the Grand Vizier reporting the unwillingness of the creditors to cooperate.

After the Jewish creditors were "persuaded" to accept the amicable settlement (*sulh*) offered by Krafft, the *kadı* summoned Krafft, the French consul, and two translators to the court. The *kadı* first asked the consul whether the Christians of Tripoli were willing to pay 1,000 gold pieces to save the German merchant. The consul replied that they were, and he was personally willing to guarantee this payment to the creditors. He also made it clear that this amount would be paid to the creditors only after Krafft's departure from Tripoli. Then the *kadı* turned to the creditors and asked them whether they were willing to accept 1,000 gold pieces from Krafft and absolve him of all accusations. They said "yes" three times in Turkish and Arabic. Then the *kadı* ordered a scribe to transcribe the settlement and record the names of the four creditors, the German merchant, and the French consul. At that point, seven "trustworthy inhabitants of Tripoli" appeared and declared that they would like to be witnesses to this settlement. After the scribe recorded their names on the document, the *kadı* asked the people in his presence whether they were satisfied or not. When they all confirmed that they were, he raised his hand and said, "set him free," in a clear and loud voice.

Discussion

Although Krafft's account predates the Çankırı and Kastamonu court records, it is an invaluable description of dispute resolution in an Ottoman court that is far more detailed than any archival source now known. We indeed learn a lot from this account about the objectives and strategies of the litigants as well as the process of adjudication itself. It is unfortunate that we do not have more sources like this one.

Krafft's memoirs represent the process of litigation as a course of protracted negotiation between the litigants as well as between them and the *kadı*. This process could (and, in Krafft's case, did) take considerable time, during which the litigants and the *kadı* found the opportunity to strategize and re-strategize in response to the operations of the other participants in the court process. It took even more time for Krafft to construct the much-needed social networks and personal connections to influence the *kadı* and obtain a favorable outcome in the court: He had to spend three years in prison before he became a friend of the commander and benefited from his support.

The influence of the *kadı*'s wife on her husband and her role in the legal process is particularly noteworthy. Indeed, her role in this case not only demonstrates that the personal relationships of the *kadı* could be critical for a particular outcome but also proves that the "cunning intelligence" needed in this kind of situation did not have to belong to the *kadı*: An intimate knowledge of law and legal practice could be possessed by anybody who had spent enough time observing or even hearing about the legal processes in the court.[50] If this was true for the wife of the *kadı*, it must also have been true for all the functionaries of the court.

It is arguable that the importance of the intermediaries was an exception in this situation since Krafft was a stranger who was alien to the language as well as the social protocols of interaction. Indeed, we saw that the Jewish creditors were able to interact with the *kadı* directly and without any help of third parties. Nevertheless the fact that they felt obligated to send gifts to the *kadı*'s wife, as Krafft had done, indicates their awareness of the importance of lobbying and social networks in the court. On the other hand, the leverage his personal connections provided for Krafft was definitely more critical than what they meant for the Jewish merchants. Before he had established his friendships with the commander and the consul and had gained the favor of the kadı's wife, Krafft was the disadvantaged party.

[50] It is unlikely that the *kadı*'s wife had any chance to observe the court proceedings. For this reason the basis of her legal experience must have been her conversations with her husband or other individuals who had the opportunity to participate in the court proceedings.

In fact, Krafft mentions at one point that immediately after the arrival in Tripoli of the same *kadı* who later released Krafft from prison, Krafft and the rest of the prisoners in the fortress had been taken to the court, and allegations against them had been reviewed in accordance with the usual judicial procedures. At that point Krafft had no connection with the commander, and the support of the consul proved to be useless; after hearing the accusations against the German merchant, the *kadı* sent him back to prison. It was only after gaining the support of the commander and, consequently, the wife of the *kadı*, that Krafft was able to neutralize the power differential in the court. And although the court records are generally silent about the importance of networking in the processes of dispute resolution, Krafft's account demonstrates how crucial they could be for a successful litigation.

Another important point in Krafft's account is the tripartite bargaining among the German merchant, the Jewish creditors, and the *kadı*. The litigants as well as the *kadı* himself were primarily oriented towards maximizing their interests and were very much involved in individually isolated processes of negotiation. For the litigants, a way to gain advantage over their legal opponents was to win the favor of the *kadı*, and for this reason they were ready to pay him for his support. The details of the agreement between the *kadı* and Krafft are interesting in this context. According to the information presented in the memoir, there seems to be a set price for the services of the *kadı*. Indeed, Krafft was instructed by the consul to pay as much as 10 per cent of the money that he was willing to pay the Jewish creditors. We do not know how this amount was determined, but the fact that it could be subject to further negotiation is implicit in the consul's warning to Krafft that he should pretend to be poor in front of the *kadı*.

We cannot be sure whether or not the *kadı* received anything from the Jewish creditors after the settlement. The fact that an amicable settlement was neither desired nor pursued by the Jewish creditors might lead us to think that this could not be the case. Yet, it is also conceivable that the *kadı* might have claimed a share of the money that he had recovered for the creditors. After all, he had convinced them earlier that they would not be able to get any kind of compensation for their losses had he not arbitrated between them and the German merchant. Given the authority and the force reportedly demonstrated by the *kadı* in the presence of the Jewish creditors, it is indeed probable that he also extracted money from them.

Basically, it was the *kadı*'s material interests that determined the role that he played in the court and shaped his decisions. The motivation behind his actions was not too different from those of the disputing parties. He supported Krafft and forced the creditors to settle the case amicably, since it was this option that would benefit him the most. If he agreed to keep the German in jail, as the Jewish creditors had insisted, he would not be able to extract money from Krafft and the creditors. Krafft's success depended not only on his ability to neutralize the power differential but also on his skill in convincing the *kadı* that an amicable settlement best served his interests.

Interestingly we find the *kadı* in this case acting as an arbitrator rather than an adjudicator. This datum is indeed unique to Krafft's account since the role of an Ottoman *kadı* in the enactment of amicable settlements (*sulh*) has never been documented in the archival sources. In the *sicil*s, an amicable settlement is always and with no exception reported as the result of the intervention of the "believers and mediators" (*Müslimun ve muslihun*). In the trial of Krafft this explanation is not quite accurate for two reasons: First, no one else but the *kadı* intervened in the dispute. Second the way he got involved and forced an amicable settlement cannot be described as mediation. In this particular example, the *kadı* did not even let the parties come together and settle their differences by themselves in a face-to-face bargaining process. He might have guessed that this would have been impossible since the Jewish merchants did not have the slightest intention of setting the German free before they received full compensation. That is probably why he took a more hands-on approach by meeting with the parties privately and enforcing a resolution on the Jewish creditors that he thought to be the most appropriate—at least in terms of his own interests.

On the other hand, it should be emphasized that there indeed were certain legal limits to his discretion, and that is probably why he could not act as an adjudicator. For one thing, he did not have the option of enforcing a resolution through adjudication since the case had already been heard and decided earlier by the previous *kadı*.[51]

---

[51] Ahmet Akgündüz, *Mukayeseli İslam ve Osmanlı Hukuku Külliyatı* (Diyarbakır: Dicle Üniversitesi Hukuk Fakültesi Yayınları, 1986), p. 771.

Second, it was a well-established fact that Krafft was responsible for at least a portion of the losses of the Jewish creditors. Hence, it would have been impossible for the *kadı* to acquit the German through legal means and try to extract a greater amount from him. That is why the most he could do to use his judicial authority on behalf of Krafft was to threaten the creditors with transferring the case to Istanbul, where they would have been without their social networks in Tripoli and the German might have hoped to get the support of more powerful allies. An amicable settlement was, therefore, the optimal solution from the perspective of the *kadı*, as well as the German, given the legal circumstances under which he was operating.

This observation is in accordance with what we have observed in other Western accounts of Ottoman legal practice. Although *kadı*s enjoyed a significant degree of autonomy, there seemed to be certain legal boundaries that they chose not to overstep. In the memoir of Krafft, we observe the anxiety of the *kadı* as he tried to find a legal way to help the German merchant. In this sense, although his motivation to favor Krafft was entirely subjective and oriented towards the maximization of his own interests, the resolution that he pushed for was entirely legal.

Finally, we need to emphasize that the threat of sending the case to Istanbul demonstrates the variability of justice in different legal venues—a point noted previously. We understand from Krafft's account that the creditors knew that such a change would radically alter the balance of power in the adjudication process and, for this reason, they agreed to settle their dispute with Krafft amicably.

Conclusion

I will conclude by reiterating several related points that have been raised in the discussion above. For one thing, corruption was a characteristic of Ottoman judicial processes, at least during the late seventeenth and the early eighteenth centuries. Archival sources and Western accounts of judicial practice in the Ottoman Empire consistently demonstrate this fact. As emphasized earlier, this must have affected how and why disputes were brought to the court. When the litigants sought resolution in the court they were not necessarily seeking justice. And they were not always satisfied, nor did they cease to come to the court when justice was dispensed justly.

Nevertheless, this situation does not necessarily imply that Ottoman justice was totally random or unpredictable. Money was necessary, of course, but there were also other conditions to play the legal game successfully. Networking, personal connections, and the ability to choose the court in which one's case would be heard were necessary for successful litigation. And so was the ability to observe the letter, if not the spirit, of the law, since the courts tried not to violate the boundaries of the judicial system.

The findings of this chapter both support and modify the observations in chapter four. As indicated in the accounts of the Western observers of Ottoman justice, courts were susceptible to outside influences, and, naturally, those parties who combined wealth and social prominence had a greater chance to defeat their opponents. At the same time, judicial processes were complicated, and it was possible for weaker parties to gain the favor of courts if they could find allies against their opponents, if they knew how to play the legal game successfully, and if they could "afford" justice. In this sense, it is arguable that the Ottoman court had some capacity to act independently from the prevalent patterns of social, cultural, and religious domination.

CHAPTER SEVEN

INTERMISSION: *SİCİL* AS TEXT

The next chapter will continue the analysis initiated in the previous one, but this time with reference to the documents from the court records of Çankırı and Kastamonu. Before we do so, however, we need to examine the textual characteristics of the court records and understand how they depict the legal and administrative transactions in the courts. After all, our ability to make sense of the judicial processes is largely determined by the scope and nature of information in these documents. In this chapter the discussion will involve a number of separate and related issues, including record-keeping practices in the court and the potential of the court records to represent and misrepresent the court processes.

Regrettably, adequate attention has not been paid to the study of such topics in Islamic legal history. The contributions of scholars like Jeanette Wakin, Brinkley Messick, Iris Agmon, and Işık Tamdoğan-Abel, although useful for researchers who are concerned about the functions, diplomatics, and semiotics of legal documents, are true exceptions in the field.[1] This is unfortunate since the extent of our understanding of the stories told in the court records is very much dependent on our ability to make sense of how these documents were produced, what they hid and disclosed, and how they were used in the judicial processes.

As will become apparent, a number of observations and conclusions in this chapter are somewhat speculative. Nevertheless, they do reflect both my findings and the findings of others up to this point and, it may be hoped, can help to chart the course for further scholarship.

[1] Jeanette A. Wakin, *The Function of Documents in Islamic Law* (Albany: State University of New York Press, 1972); Brinkley Messick, *The Calligraphic State; Textual Domination and History in a Muslim Society* (Berkeley: University of California Press, 1993); Iris Agmon, "Gender and Welfare: The Discourse of the Family and the State in Late Ottoman Shariʿa Court Records," Unpublished Paper, Ben-Gurion University of the Negev (1999); and Işık Tamdoğan-Abel, "L'écrit comme échec de l'oral? L'oralité des engagements et des règlements à travers les registres de cadis d'Adana au XVIIIe siècle," *Revue du Monde Musulman et de la Méditerranée*, vol. 75–76 (1995), pp. 155–165.

Recording the Proceedings

We do not exactly know how disputes brought to and resolved in the Ottoman courts were recorded in the court records. *Sicil*s as well as other contemporary sources are silent about record-keeping practices in Ottoman courts, and this may be why only a few scholars have examined or even taken an interest in this issue. Since there is not much basis for the *sicil* scholars to suspect anything complicated about the preparation of these documents, many of us continue to assume that what we observe in the *sicil*s is the direct and immediate representation of the court proceedings.

Such an assumption may not be necessarily true. There is some evidence that the proceedings were not actually recorded during or even immediately after the hearings. For example, separate accounts of particular court hearings[2] do not always follow each other in the volumes where they are found.[3] Furthermore, although these entries describe the same hearing, their narratives could be quite different in stylistic terms, in terms of word choice, and in terms of particular details of the dispute in question.[4] Such differences suggest that there might have existed an intermediate stage between the actual court proceedings and their recording in the *sicil*s: It is possible that these accounts were based on earlier, less formal and less complete drafts of the proceedings that were recorded on separate ledgers or even on loose pieces of paper. According to Iris Agmon, these drafts were kept in the possession of the court personnel—most probably the scribes—and were periodically transferred to the court registers in a more formal and perhaps formulaic manner.[5]

As mentioned, there can be significant differences between alternative accounts of a particular hearing. In such cases, later accounts often provide more complete descriptions of the disputes or are more explicit about the judicial proceedings than earlier ones. This situa-

[2] Some court hearings were recorded twice or, sometimes, three times in separate entries. See, for example, KCR, vol. 34, 21–34 and 22–35; KCR, vol. 34, 31–52 and 32–53; KCR, vol. 36, 38–74 and 39–85. No reason is given for this practice of multiple recording in the court records.

[3] For example, a page and two entries separate KCR, vol. 3, 7–27 and KCR, vol. 3, 9–29; and there are 73 pages and more than 160 entries between KCR, vol. 35, 85–136 and KCR, vol. 35, 158–229.

[4] See, for example, KCR, vol. 19, 63–118 and 63–118; and KCR, vol. 36, 38–74 and 39–85.

[5] Personal communication.

tion may indicate that the subsequent account of a particular trial was produced when the initial account, presumably reflecting the imprecise information supplied by a rough draft, failed to represent the full scope of the litigation and/or of the nature of the court's judgment.

On the other hand, in those cases where we find only minor differences between the accounts of a specific hearing, the draft of the proceeding must have been transferred to the court ledger multiple times merely as a result of a scribe's carelessness. If the drafts constituted nothing more than informal and brief sketches of the actual proceedings, then they would have required some narrative reconstruction in order to be molded into formal accounts. It is conceivable that this effort would generate almost—but not exactly—identical accounts in different attempts.[6]

The hints of inaccuracy and forgetfulness that we encounter in the court records demonstrate that these accounts did not have an immediate relationship with the actual court proceedings. For example, we notice that the paternal names or the residential affiliations of some participants in the court processes are not only withheld in a number of court records but are intentionally left blank. We would not have encountered such lapses in the documents if the court records were produced at the time of the proceedings.

> The holder of this document, Ayşe bint Musa from the Topçuoğlu quarter of the town of Kastamonu, came to the noble court and filed a complaint against an Ahmed bin (*blank in the original*) from the village of (*blank in the original*) in the district of Küre . . .[7]

On other occasions, the nature of the relationship between the participants in the court process is characterized differently in various documents. For example, we find a woman who was introduced as

[6] See, for example, KCR, vol. 35, 85–136 and 158–299. In this example the entries are almost exactly identical: Whereas the name of the plaintiff is given as "Hafiz Ali Efendi bin Ahmed Efendi" in the first entry, in the second one he is introduced as "Hafiz Ali Efendi." A "*sahip olalı beri*" in the first document is written as "*sahip olduğumuzdan beri*" in the second one (both of which have the same meaning: "since the time that we have owned [the land]"). A witness who was defined as "*mefahür el-kudat*" ("the pride of the *kadı*s") in the first entry was called "*fahr el-kudat*" (same meaning) in the second one. And finally the name of one of the witnesses that we find in the first account is missing in the second one. Otherwise, these documents are identical.

[7] KCR, vol. 1, 61–142.

the virgin bride of a certain man in one document being described as the mother of his child (or children) in the next entry.[8] These observations suggest once again that the court records must have been constructed some time after the court proceedings.

Table 7.1: Dates of the Successive Entries in a Kastamonu Court Ledger (volume 39)

Dates—first 33 entries	Dates—second 33 entries	Dates—third 33 entries	Dates—fourth 33 entries
8 Safer **1154**	1 Cemazi I (CI)	24 Şevval	3 Muharrem
7 Safer	27 RII	24 Şevval	2 Muharrem
11 Safer	27 RII	12 Ramazan	6 Muharrem
2 Safer	25 RII	21 Şevval	2 Muharrem
19 Safer	21 RII	17 Şevval	8 Muharrem
23 Safer	10 CI	26 Şevval	26 Zilkaʿde
20 Safer	27 RII	24 Şevval	23 Muharrem
19 Safer	7 CI	4 Zilkaʿde	10 Muharrem
1 Rebiʿ I (RI)	9 CI	8 Zilkaʿde	26 Muharrem
20 Safer	27 CI	15 Ramazan	25 Muharrem
2 RI	17 CI	2 Zilkaʿde	27 Muharrem
4 RI	14 CI	21 Şaban	20 Muharrem
15 RI	25 RII	8 Zilkaʿde	27 Muharrem
14 RI	25 RII	7 Zilkaʿde	27 Muharrem
4 RI	25 RII	10 Zilkaʿde	20 Muharrem
22 RI	3 Cemazi II (CII)	21 Zilkaʿde	2 Safer
21 RI	8 CII	19 Zilkaʿde	26 Muharrem
20 RI	8 CII	16 Zilhicce	20 Muharrem
27 RI	25 RII	22 Zilkaʿde	8 Safer
27 RI	15 CII	21 Zilkaʿde	6 Safer
29 RI	3 CII	7 Zilkaʿde	6 Safer
1 Rebiʿ II (RII)	24 CII	8 Zilkaʿde	10 Safer
14 RI	21 CII	28 Zilkaʿde	13 Safer
2 RII	27 CII	24 Zilhicce	12 Muharrem
2 Muharrem	22 CII	25 Zilhicce	26 Muharrem
29 RII	2 Receb	24 Zilhicce	17 Safer
14 RII	20 CII	25 Zilhicce	20 Safer
14 RII	10 Receb	26 Zilhicce	13 Safer
14 RII	16 Receb	25 Zilhicce	24 Safer
18 RII	10 Şevval	27 Zilhicce	24 Safer
22 RII	9 Şevval	2 Muharrem **1155**	25 Safer
26 RII	14 Şevval	2 Muharrem	28 Safer
29 RII	22 Şevval	4 Muharrem	6 RI

[8] ÇCR, vol. 10, 26–43 and 26–44.

Finally, the loose chronological order observed in the court records (see table 7.1) supports the hypothesis that the drafts prepared by the scribes were probably not transferred to the court registers immediately, but accumulated for some time until they were recorded in the registers in no particular order. The table above provides the dates recorded for consecutive entries in a Kastamonu ledger.

Problems of Representation in the Court Records

Sicil *as Translation*

Although relatively rare, substantive differences between separate accounts of a particular court hearing raise another important issue:[9] the problem of representation. Since these accounts refer to the same court hearing, one of them obviously misrepresents the judicial process in question. This situation demonstrates that the ability of the court records to accurately portray the Ottoman court processes may indeed be limited.

As argued above, the reason for the production of the second account of a particular hearing may be that the first document inadequately represented the exact nature of the dispute and the full scope of the court's decision. If this was really the case, the production of the subsequent account proves the existence of a concern for accuracy on the part of the litigants and/or court officials. Nevertheless, the problem of representation in the court records is not restricted to the distortion of legal claims or the terms of a settlement. According to Jack Goody, the production of the written record of any kind of performance (be it judicial, ritual, or artistic) involves a "disposition of formalization," that is, an inclination on the part of the "recorder" to single out the formal aspects of the performance.[10] Goody likens this tendency to the elimination of

---

[9] One such case is related to the dispute between Mehmed Efendi bin Ebu Bekir Efendi and his stepmother, Rahime bint Elhac Bahri, over Mehmed Efendi's maternal half-brother Karakaşzade es-Seyyid Mehmed Ağa's inheritance; see KCR, vol. 19, 61–116 and 63–118. According to 61–116, the dispute was over Karakaşzade's lands. 63–118, however, indicates that the contention also involved Karakaşzade's house and his "properties" (emlak) in two separate villages, in addition to his lands.

[10] See Jack Goody, "The Construction of a Ritual Text: The Shift from Oral to Written Channels," in *The Power of the Written Tradition* (Washington and London: Smithsonian Institution Press, 2000), pp. 47–62.

"noise" from the record of the performance. "So if I were trying to reverse the process and reconstruct an actual ceremony as enacted from the written text, the script would represent a version of the whole proceedings that has been drastically cleaned up into some more orderly, less informal sequence."[11]

The *sicil*, of course, is nothing but a translation of a particular legal performance into a formal and immensely formulaic language.[12] In the process of this translation, variation is eliminated, and temporal, spatial, and improvisational characteristics of individual performances are left out. Furthermore, just as in Goody's own transcriptions of the LoDagaa funerals, the *sicil* severely discriminates against non-verbal acts, body language, or facial expressions of the performers and privileges the spoken word against other acts of communication.[13] That is why no confessions (*iʿtiraf*) or acknowledgements (*ikrar*) found in the court records could be assumed as inherently sincere. Since "it is only eyes that do not lie," as the old Turkish proverb goes, *sicil*s may be significantly misleading sources.

The misleading nature of the *sicil*s is apparent in the tension between Hans Ulrich Krafft's description of his own experiences with the legal system and how the court processes are typically described in the court records. As described in the previous chapter, we indeed learn a lot from Krafft's account of objectives and strategies of the litigants as well as the process of adjudication. Indeed for a historian of Ottoman court records, Krafft's account is a source of embarrassment since it demonstrates the limits of his or her ability to understand the nature and backgrounds of the resolutions represented in the court records. Consider, for example, the information provided in the following entry and compare it to what we know about Krafft's case:

[11] Ibid., p. 53.

[12] Al-Qattan, "Dhimmis in the Muslim Court: Documenting Justice in Ottoman Damascus 1775–1860," Unpublished Ph.D. Dissertation, Harvard University (1996), pp. 141–142. See Sally Engle Merry, "Courts as Performances: Domestic Violence Hearings in a Hawai'i Family Court," in Mindie Lazarus-Black and Susan F. Hirsch (eds.) *Contested States: Law Hegemony and Resistance* (London and N.Y. Routledge, 1994), pp. 35–58 for an approach that compares litigation to different kinds of performance.

[13] See Goody, "The Construction of a Ritual Text," p. 57.

> After it had been legally established that the estate of a deceased İbrahim from the neighborhood of Alaca Mescid in Kastamonu should be divided between his widow Fatma bint Davud, his son of legal age Mahmud and his daughter Ayşe, the aforementioned Mahmud, in his own right (*asaleten*) and an Abdurrahman bin Abdurrahman from the neighborhood of Tarakçı, acting as the agent (*vekaleten*) of the aforementioned Fatma and Ayşe (his agency being confirmed in the court by the testimonies of Mehmed bin İbrahim and Mustafa bin Elhac Hüseyin who both know the women), came to the noble court and stated in the presence of the brother of the deceased, Elhac Abdi, that: "Previously the aforementioned Elhac Abdi took some property and belongings of the late İbrahim from his estate in order to use and profit from them. When we demanded that he return these items to the estate, he denied that he had them and therefore there emerged a major contention between the two sides. Subsequently, Muslims and mediators intervened and the dispute was settled amicably in return for a payment of fifty *vukiyye*s[14] of coffee by Elhac Abdi to the heirs of the deceased.[15]

Had we found the account of the settlement between Krafft and the Jewish creditors in Tripoli court records, we would have seen that the entry would probably have been as limited as the information that we find in the example above. And had we attempted to understand the contention between the German merchant and his Jewish opponents with reference to that entry, we would have completely missed the real dynamics of the dispute resolution process, the roles played by key actors, and the strategies employed by these actors during the litigation. The official account of an amicable settlement between a German named "Hans ibn Hans"[16] and four Jews would have hidden as much as it revealed in terms of the legal and commercial relationships in sixteenth-century Tripoli.

The problems with *sicil* entries are not limited to the fact that they resist the disclosure of essential information about the processes of litigation. They also distort the roles and functions of the court officials. For example, the depiction of the activities of the *kadı* in Krafft's account could not be more contradictory than in the *sicil* entry presented above. In this entry we cannot detect the existence

[14] One *vukiyye/okka* = forty *dirhems* = 2.82 lbs.

[15] KCR, vol. 5, 121–258, entry of 21 Şaban 1104/27 April 1693.

[16] Krafft indicates in his account that his name was recorded as "Hans ibn Hans" in the court record; Krafft, p. 127.

of the *kadı* or observe his operations; it seems that record-keepers erased his presence from the document. In fact, according to the entry above—as well as in others examined during this research—the process of adjudication seems predictable and even streamlined. It almost seems that a judicial authority was unnecessary, as if all the litigants knew exactly what to do and what to say in court.

We sense the presence of court officials only indirectly and when there is something wrong or illogical with a certain aspect of the litigation process. Consider the following case:

> After it had been legally determined that the estate of the late Mehmed from the neighborhood of Cibrail in the town of Kastamonu must be divided between his wife Alime, his mother Kerime, his young son Ali, his daughter of legal age Saliha, and his young daughter Ümm Gülsüm, Ali Efendi bin Şeyh Ahmed Efendi came to the noble court and sued the aforementioned Saliha claiming that "the late Mehmed, who had passed away eight years ago, owed thirty-six *guruş* to my late father Şeyh Ahmed Efendi in relation to a coffee transaction that took place between them six [sic] years ago. Since both of the parties have passed away, I demand that the aforementioned amount be paid to me from the estate of the deceased." Since the claim of the plaintiff is contradictory in itself (*husus-u mezburda müddei-i mezburun davası tenakuz olmağla . . .*) there is no need to question the defendant on this matter, and the request of the plaintiff is rejected.[17]

It is likely that the plaintiff did not express his claim as it is presented in the account. The *kadı* or the scribe must have rephrased his statement to emphasize the inconsistency that we immediately notice in the text.[18] And it is this inconsistency that makes the presence of a judicial authority visible in the document. In this particular situation this authority apparently used his discretion to wrap up the case immediately, instead of completing the full judicial procedure, which would have involved the questioning of the defendant as well as listening to the witness testimonies. Yet, even in this rare example, we cannot understand the full extent of the *kadı*'s operations. We do not know, for example, how he questioned the plaintiff or even whether he interrogated him or not. In other words, all we can deduce from this otherwise extraordinary account is a partial image of the *kadı*'s agency in the court of Kastamonu.

---

[17] KCR, vol. 34, 21–34, entry of *evahir* Safer 1148/mid-July 1735.
[18] See the next section for a more detailed discussion of this issue.

Of course, the *kadı* of Tripoli is anything but absent in Krafft's account. On the contrary, the latitude of his judicial discretion is extensive, and he does not hesitate to use this discretion to his own advantage. In this sense, it is not the pre-established or well-known legal procedures—as insinuated in the entries above—but rather the *kadı*'s subjective preferences that shape the processes as well as the outcomes of litigation. That is why the litigants compete in Krafft's account to gain the *kadı*'s favor in order to win their cases or minimize their losses. Almost all Western accounts of Ottoman legal procedures indicate that the subjectivity, personal inclinations, material interests, and, of course, the "cunning intelligence" of the Ottoman *kadı* (as well as other court officials) are very important in the process of dispute resolution.

Voices and Screams in the Sicils

One interesting characteristic of the *sicil* is the fact that it embodies the voices of the litigants. We recognize these voices in the transitions from the passive voice ("text without an author") to first-person narrative in the document. Consider, for example, the following excerpt from an account that we have used above:

> After it had been legally determined that the estate of the late Mehmed from the neighborhood of Cibrail in the town of Kastamonu must be divided between his wife Alime, his mother Kerime, his young son Ali, his daughter of legal age Saliha, and his young daughter Ümm Gülsüm, Ali Efendi bin Şeyh Ahmed Efendi came to the noble court and sued the aforementioned Saliha claiming that "the late Mehmed, who had passed away eight years ago, owed thirty-six *guruş* to my late father Şeyh Ahmed Efendi on account of a coffee transaction that took place between them six years ago. Since both of the parties have passed away, I demand that the aforementioned amount be paid to me from the estate of the deceased."

Of course, there are no quotation marks in Arabic script, and the transition that we notice in the text is marked only by a change in the grammar. Yet this transition is definite and generates an interesting effect in the account by augmenting the feeling of proximity between the litigants and the readers of the *sicil*. As a result, we feel that the participants in the court process are speaking directly to us—to the readers—without any intermediaries. Naturally, we cannot be sure whether this was intentional or not. It is more likely that the *sicil* was designed as the textual replica of a properly conducted court process. Direct quotations from the litigants and their witnesses indicate that these people were present during the trial—as they were legally supposed to be—and they were allowed to contribute their sides of the story through appropriate means. In other words, the textual design of the *sicil* might have something to do with the demonstration of the legitimacy of the process.

In any case, although the existence of a number of distinct voices in the *sicil* demonstrates its polyglossal character,[19] we should resist the temptation to identify the quotations in the *sicils* with the actual words of the litigants. Indeed there are indications in the court records that what is reported in the *sicils* as the speech of the litigants is in fact the translation of their voices into the official language of the legal system. For example consider the following statement of a Christian woman:

> I lost my eyesight a couple of years ago, and since then I have been in no condition to serve the needs of my husband. For this reason, my husband has recently gotten married to another woman in accordance with our *unsound* customs (*ayin-i batılamız üzere*), and now I would like to get divorced from him. . . .[20]

We cannot be sure what made this woman define her own customs as false or unsound (*batıl*). It might have been her own choice to appropriate the official language of the court. Alternatively, the officials of the court may have reconstructed her speech when it was recorded in the court records. In any case, what we observe in this example is a translation of her actual thoughts, feelings, and perhaps even words into a legal statement that was acceptable according to existing legal and religious norms. In the following statement of an apprentice, Mehmed bin Mustafa, we find a more explicit example of this process of translation.

> Six months prior to the date of this document (and while I was still in his service) I was with my master the aforementioned Halil Beşe (on his farm, which is located) in the village of Aymerler. (The aforementioned Halil Beşe) intended to put some wood in a bag to take it home and I wanted to help (him, without his knowledge) to lift the

[19] Mikhail M. Bakhtin, "Discourse in the Novel," in *The Dialogic Imagination; Four Essays* (Austin: University of Texas Press, 1990), pp. 259–422.
[20] KCR, vol. 36, 26–42, entry of 20 Şaban 1151/3 December 1738.

> bag. When I tried to lift the bag, a stump of a branch ripped the bag open and entered into my right eye (through no consequence of the aforementioned Halil Beşe's actions [*mezbur Halil Beşe'nin fiilimsiz*]). Currently my right eye does not see and I demand the (necessary) compensation for my eye.[21]

The text shown here in parentheses was included to the record (between the lines), later on in a different handwriting, and the changes explicitly demonstrate some aspects and objectives of the translation process. These additions are crucial for clarifying the nature of the relationship between Mehmed and Halil Beşe: They provide the details regarding the location of the incident as well as the exact actions and intentions of the individuals. Interestingly, these additions appear to have resolved the issue of responsibility in this particular situation. By making Mehmed acknowledge—at least on paper—that he acted on his own initiative and that Halil Beşe did not do anything to cause harm to his eye, the court transformed his original speech into a statement that contradicted his request for compensation. Indeed, the court decided that "since the injury was not a consequence of Halil Beşe's actions, there is no need to pay compensation to the plaintiff."[22]

The translation of Mehmed's speech into the legal statement is an aspect of the creation of the "unitary language" observed in the court records.[23] In this process not only are certain kinds of information (time, place, and exact description of the activities) privileged over others, but, as in the examples above, the actual speech of a litigant is reconstructed in order to legitimize the decisions of the court. The language of the court incorporates the voices of the participants in such a way that they contribute to the feeling of "smooth flow" that we get from the *sicil*s. Although the *sicil*s contain the words

---

[21] KCR, vol. 38, 86–136, entry of 28 CI 1153/21 August 1740.

[22] Ibid.

[23] Bakhtin defines this unitary language as follows:

> A common unitary language is a system of linguistic norms. But these norms do not constitute an abstract imperative; they are rather the generative forces of linguistic life, forces that struggle to overcome the heteroglossia of language, forces that unite and centralize verbal-ideological thought, creating within a heteroglot national language the firm, stable linguistic nucleus of an officially recognized literary language, or else an already formed language from the pressure of growing heteroglossia.

See Bakhtin, pp. 270–271.

of the litigants, these words are "enslaved" to the unifying language of the legal.

> Unitary language constitutes the theoretical expression of the historical processes of linguistic unification and centralization, an expression of the centripetal forces of language. A unitary language is not something given but is always in essence posited—and at every moment of its linguistic life it is opposed to the realities of heteroglossia. But at the same time it makes its real presence felt as a force for overcoming this heteroglossia, imposing specific limits to it, guaranteeing a certain maximum of mutual understanding and crystal[l]izing into a real, although still relative, unity.[24]

"A real, although still relative, unity" is indeed what we encounter in the court records since the victory of legal language over the actual word, although prevalent, cannot be considered absolute. We notice in the *sicil*s that occasionally certain remarks were left "untranslated." For example, during a heated trial for assault in the court of Kastamonu, we observe the defendant screaming at the plaintiff, "You tyrant!" (*Zalimsin!*).[25] In another example from the same *sicil* volume, the plaintiff's feelings towards one of the defendants are made unusually explicit.

> The holder of this document, Mustafa Ağa bin Mehmed Ağa, who owns a farm in the village of Karasu, came to the noble court and made the statement that: "Three days prior to the date of this document, the daughter-in-law of one Ahmed bin Yahya from the village Kara Haliller, a whore (*fahişe*) by the name of Fatma bint Şaban, came to the village where my farm is located and stayed in the house of my sharecroppers (*ortakçılar*) [as a guest]. [Reportedly] she was on her way to the court to report that her father-in-law, the aforementioned Ahmed, and his sons, her husband Hüseyin and her brother-in-law İsmail, did not leave her alone and attacked her and beat her with the intention of sexual intercourse. Later on, the aforementioned Ahmed and his sons, Hüseyin and İsmail, also came to the village where my farm is located and encircled the house of my sharecroppers. They were carrying sticks and clubs with them. They cursed at my servants and then attacked and injured one of them. After this incident the

[24] Ibid., p. 270. See Lynn Mather and Barbara Yngvesson, "Language, Audience, and the Transformation of Disputes," *Law and Society Review*, no. 3–4, vol. 15 (1980–81), pp. 775–821, on the consequences of the translation of a particular dispute into the official language of law.

[25] KCR, vol. 5, 66–103, entry of 15 RI 1149/24 July 1736.

> aforementioned Fatma, Ahmed, Hüseyin, and İsmail all ran away. Now I request from the court that their reputation be investigated and their attack on my farm be recognized.[26]

The translation of the actual utterances into legal statements usually conceals the true feelings of the litigants about each other. That is why we do not find in the *sicil*s many litigants insulting each other as "whores" or screaming "You tyrant!" at one another, although this must have occurred frequently if the Ottoman courts resembled their modern counterparts even slightly. On the other hand, what these two examples of intense emotional outbursts do demonstrate is that the process of translating actual speech into legalistic formulas could occasionally be overpowered by the passionate intensity of the oral, even in the written legal text. Işık Tamdoğan-Abel insists that traces of a more personal discourse are noticeable in the court records of eighteenth-century Adana, when the documentation in question concerned the bodies and, particularly in the depositions of the females, the children of the litigants: "My only son, he was only thirteen, the pupil of my eye, the corner of my liver . . ."[27]

We cannot be absolutely sure why such statements were left untranslated in the *sicil*s. Nevertheless, it is improbable that the anguish of the mother whose sobbing Tamdoğan-Abel reports did not touch the souls of the court officers as it touches us today. Such strong emotional outbursts (because of grief, anger, or even happiness) might have occasionally cracked the professional shell of the scribe; he might have desired to report these emotions in his account but could not find the appropriate words to translate them into the legal language of the court records.

It is also probable that the language of the *sicil* occasionally reflected the feelings of the community against those individuals who were generally considered criminal, immoral, or simply "undesirable." We will see in the next chapter that the courts of Çankırı and Kastamonu generally sided with the community and turned the full force of the

---

[26] KCR, vol. 5, 68–106, entry of 25 RI 1149/3 August 1736. Fatma, Ahmed, Hüseyin, and İsmail were absent during the trial. My emphasis.

[27] See Tamdoğan-Abel, p. 157. Susan Hirsch argues that men and women appropriate different discourses and narrative strategies in the Muslim courts of Kenya. For this reason, she insists that litigants should be seen as "gendered, legal and linguistic subjects." See Susan F. Hirsch, *Pronouncing and Persevering; Gender and the Discourses of Disputing in an African Islamic Court* (Chicago: The University of Chicago Press, 1998), p. 140.

law against these "undesirable" elements. I believe that the account in which Mustafa Ağa accused Fatma of being a whore is an example of such a situation (since his witnesses reported the evil character of the defendants), and it is possible that the *sicil* entry in question simply reflected the communal feelings about Fatma.

Temporal Compression

The sense of timelessness in the court records is—at least partially—responsible for the false feeling of spontaneity in their narratives, which hides the intense strategic struggle among the participants during the court proceedings. In court records, we usually find no information about the length of litigation processes. We do not know, for example, how long it took to settle the contention between the heirs of İbrahim and his brother Elhac Abdi after the initial disagreement (see the account of the amicable settlement above that I have compared with Krafft's case). This information is critical, since we learn from Krafft's account that it is in the intervals between the different stages of the trial that the participants in the court process conducted their negotiations and designed their strategies. And it is by refusing to account for this temporal gap that the accounts conceal certain key operations and interactions of the litigants. Consider the following example:

> An order has been sent to this poor one [the *kadı* of Kastamonu], the *kadı* of the district of Göl, and the sub-governor of Kastamonu to resolve the following dispute. We met in the court of Kastamonu and received Fatma bint Abdullah—originally from the neighborhood of Karataş in Istanbul and currently staying in Kastamonu as a guest—who is the mother of the deceased minor Abdullah bin Elhac Ali. The aforementioned Fatma filed a complaint against Ahmed Beğ bin Elhac Şaban who is the chosen guardian of the orphans of the deceased Mehmed bin Mehmed bin Elhac Hüseyin from the village of Orta Bayramcı in the district of Göl, and Emine bint Mehmed, the widow of the deceased. Fatma claimed that "Mehmed bin Mehmed had no sons and his estate should have been divided between his wife Emine, his mother Kerime, his three minor daughters, and his minor nephew—my son, the aforementioned Abdullah. And although the share of my son, the late Abdullah, should have legally been transferred to me as [I am] his only heir, the aforementioned Ahmed Beğ retained my share, 1,200 *guruş*, claiming that the deceased Mehmed had left behind a son and a first-degree male heir to his inheritance with the name of Mustafa. I know that the deceased Mehmed did not have any sons,

> and I can prove this with reference to common knowledge (*tevatüren*)." Then she presented a *fetva* [the legal opinion of the local jurisconsult] to the court, stating that she could use *tevatür* to challenge the claim that the deceased had left behind a son. When questioned about the situation, Ahmed Beğ confirmed that he had retained 1,200 *guruş* from the estate of the deceased but denied that Fatma could challenge the existence of Mustafa. Indeed when Fatma was asked to demonstrate the common knowledge that she mentioned in her statement, she could not do so. Then the aforementioned Ahmed Beğ and the aforementioned Emine were asked to prove that the deceased Mehmed had indeed had a son by the name of Mustafa. Mustafa Çelebi bin Mehmed Efendi, Ahmed Beşe bin Mehmed, etc. (ten more individuals from the villages of Orta Bayramcı, Şeker, Hafife and Yazıcı, and from the town of Ilysu) all testified in the court that when Mehmed had died he did indeed leave behind a son with that name. Consequently the court ordered Fatma to restrain herself from further opposition.[28]

The feeling of time compression results from two characteristics of this document: First of all, the document does not provide any dates for the actual incidents reported in the text; we do not know, for example, when Mehmed died. Apparently, Fatma had sent a petition and asked the government to help her resolve her dispute with the heirs of Mehmed bin Mehmed. Although we can infer this information from the text, there is no way to tell when Fatma sent her petition or when the imperial order arrived in Kastamonu. All of these incidents could have taken place in the course of a couple of weeks, months, or even years.

Second, and more important, it is impossible to guess how long it took for the individual stages of the hearing to reach a conclusion. Although these stages can be identified (initial hearing of the plaintiff's claims, submission of the *fetva* to the court and the disclosure of its contents, hearing of the defendant's responses and counterclaims, documentation of the claims by the plaintiffs and the defendants, and, finally, the decision of the court), the account generates an impression that these stages followed each other rapidly and quite smoothly. Yet this picture is deceiving, as the narrative diverts our attention from the details of what must have been a very complicated and informative struggle for evidentiary documentation.

It seems that Fatma was well prepared for this hearing, as demonstrated by the *fetva* that she submitted to the court. It is not clear

[28] KCR, vol. 34, 37–63, entry of 13 R II 1148/2 September 1735.

when she acquired this *fetva*. She might have acquired it after she had sent the petition, after the arrival of the order or even possibly after the initiation of the hearing—we simply do not know. Nevertheless, the existence of the *fetva* discloses her strategy in the court. Arguably, she was planning to challenge the claim of the defendants with the help of what was then publicly known about the deceased and his familial connections. To be able to do that, she must have trusted her ability to present this public knowledge to the court.

For this reason, the statement in the document that "she could not do so" constitutes a contradiction that requires some attention. The investment of time and money in a *fetva* to validate the legitimacy of evidence she was planning to submit indicates that Fatma was confident about the existence and availability of such information. The text itself is unhelpful in explaining this contradiction. To explain why the court decided against Fatma, the text simply says: "when the plaintiff Fatma was requested to establish the existence of any public reports that would prove the validity of her denial, she could not do so." What it does not indicate is the length of time granted to Fatma to find and submit information. It is clear from a handful of *sicil* entries that litigants were not forced to document their claims immediately after they submitted their statements in court. In fact, it is frequently reported that a delay of as much as fifteen days was allowed before the court decided to rule against litigants who were unable to substantiate their allegations.[29] Therefore, it is more probable than not that Fatma was given some time to seek evidence.

The reasons that kept her from providing evidence in the allotted time are unclear. It is possible that during these fifteen or so days the defendants were able to develop counter-strategies, while Fatma was probably trying to find witnesses. The fact that the defendants were able to present twelve witnesses, including *seyyid*s, *çelebi*s, and even a "*kadı*," demonstrates that they were better connected in the local community and capable of playing the legal game effectively. Unfortunately, however, we cannot be entirely sure about this possibility, since the document conceals what really happened during the most critical interval in the process of litigation. Indeed, by compressing time, the document displays only a truncated image of the legal contention between the litigants.

[29] See, for example, KCR, vol. 1, 61.

Conclusion

In this chapter, I sought to understand the nature of the connection between the actual processes that took place in the Ottoman courts and their records as found in *sicil*s. I have argued that this connection may not be as direct or immediate as has been generally assumed in the literature. There are two reasons for this situation. First of all, there is evidence that cases were not recorded in the registers during or even immediately after the proceedings, which diminishes the reliability of the information in the court records, at least to a certain extent. Secondly, the fact that *sicil* entries were the "translations" of particular disputes into the language of the court should lead us to question the representative power of these documents and our tendency to accept them as accurate depictions of past realities.

The claims and observations presented in this chapter do not aim to discredit any attempt to make sense of the documentation in court records. Rather, they were presented to provide an evaluation of the strengths and weaknesses of the historical material that this study, in general, and the next two chapters, in particular, are based on, and to develop an awareness of the fact that the textual characteristics of these documents influence the ways in which we understand the judicial practices portrayed by them. I believe that, only after such a critical evaluation can we engage in the court records in the way that we do in chapters eight and nine.

CHAPTER EIGHT

THE COURT PROCESS II: STRATEGIES OF LITIGATION

In this chapter, I will continue to identify the evidence of litigants' familiarity with various legal strategies that could help ensure favorable outcomes in the court. The ability of the litigants to manipulate the judicial system has already been discussed to some extent in the previous chapters. I have mentioned that the litigants in Çankırı and Kastamonu could take their disputes to different *kadı*s or courts over and over, if they were not satisfied with previous decisions (chapter six). I have also cited some intriguing methods of witness recruitment as reported in Western accounts of Ottoman administration of justice. These practices demonstrate that many litigants had adequate experience in, and knowledge of, the judicial system to be able to push for their causes. This chapter will provide a more focused analysis of the legal competence of the court clients and hopefully give us an idea about their degree of control over court processes.

In the light of what we know about the limitations of the court records in representing actual court practices, it would seem unlikely that the records could provide much information about the litigants' legal knowledge and experience. A typical account that we find in the *sicil*s does not disclose much about the strategies utilized in the court since its formulaic structure frequently hides the peculiarities of individual cases. This is why a single relatively detailed Western account, such as the one by Hans Ulrich Krafft, can be so valuable in an exploration of Ottoman court processes. Nevertheless, the issue of court clients' legal competency is too important for the purposes of this study to take an agnostic approach to the material in the *sicil*s. Although the opacity of the court records limits our understanding of the legal practices that they imperfectly account for, they still constitute our main access to past realities.

This chapter is divided into two main sections. The first section explores the legal competence among individual litigants and their ability to influence the outcomes of their trials. The second section studies how the community—as a community—used the court to punish or get rid of those individuals who were generally regarded as "undesirable." Distinguishing between those litigations that took place between individuals and those that pitted the community against an individual is necessary for the purposes of this chapter since, for reasons that will be described below, the courts functioned differently in these two situations.

Strategy and Legal Competence in Disputes between Individual Litigants

Ingenuity in Action: Mastery in Legal Deception

If the ability to manipulate the judicial system is an indicator of legal competence, we can claim that certain clients of the Ottoman courts were quite proficient in the practice of law. The following example demonstrates that some litigants were indeed able to develop ingenious methods to exploit the loopholes in the system.

In an imperial order dated 1739, we find an account of a remarkable dispute between Mehmed bin Mustafa from Kastamonu and Şeyh Mustafa, the Şeyh of the Yıldız Dede lodge (*tekke*) in Istanbul.[1] This order was sent to the court of Kastamonu in response to a previous petition made by Mehmed bin Mustafa. As is typical, Mehmed's petition is summarized at the beginning of the order. According to this summary, the trusteeship (*mütevellilik*) to the assets of the endowment (*vakıf*) of İbrahim Beğ in Kastamonu had been granted to Mehmed's father, Mustafa, some seventy-five years earlier as a reward for his courage in the military expedition against Austria. Mustafa had kept the trusteeship for about forty years and then transferred it to his son Mehmed. Afterwards, Mehmed retained the trusteeship for another thirty-five years before Şeyh Mustafa claimed the position for himself. According to the petition, Şeyh Mustafa alleged that the trusteeship was to be occupied by descendants of the founder of the *vakıf* (*evladiyet üzere*). Claiming to be a descendant of the founder, Şeyh Mustafa requested that the position be transferred to him from Mehmed. The government subsequently granted this request.

Seeking to get the trusteeship back, Mehmed made it clear in his petition that Şeyh Mustafa's allegation regarding the conditions of

[1] KCR, vol. 38, 89–140, entry of 20 RII 1152/27 June 1739.

trusteeship was untrue and that Şeyh Mustafa could not produce any endowment deed (*vakfiye*) to document these conditions. Instead, Şeyh Mustafa had submitted a court order regarding a dispute over the ownership of an estate in Plovdiv (Filibe) to establish his relationship to the endowment.[2] Mehmed alleged in his petition that the contents of this order were not accurate, because false witnesses had been used in the hearing that was being reported in it. Also, Mehmed reminded the government that the same Şeyh Mustafa had previously claimed the trusteeship of the Cem Sultan endowment in Sinop deceitfully. In conclusion, Mehmed requested that the situation be investigated and that the trusteeship be returned to him.

We infer from the remainder of the imperial order that the government subsequently investigated the allegations against Şeyh Mustafa. The order confirms that Şeyh Mustafa had indeed submitted a petition to the government. In this petition, he claimed that the trusteeship of the İsmail Beğ, the İbrahim Beğ (the father of İsmail Beğ), and the İsfendiyar Beğ (a grandfather of İsmail Beğ) endowments had long been held by people who were not lineal descendants of the founder (*ecnebi*), contrary to what was stipulated in the endowment deeds. He admitted in his petition that he had lost his copies of the endowment deeds and the imperial warrants, and for this reason he could not document his claims with reference to these documents. Nevertheless he did submit a court order regarding a dispute over the proprietorship of an estate in Plovdiv, claiming that this document demonstrated the nature of his relationship to the endowments.

Next, the imperial order reveals the contents of this court order. Accordingly, Şeyh Mustafa had previously[3] sued an Ali bin Mehmed in Istanbul claiming that Ali had been occupying a house in the İsmail Beğ neighborhood of Plovdiv that belonged to the İbrahim Beğ endowment, without Şeyh Mustafa's permission. When the defendant was questioned, he acknowledged that the house belonged to the İbrahim Beğ endowment and that Şeyh Mustafa was its trustee because of his descent. As a result, the court acknowledged Şeyh Mustafa's relationship to the endowment and ruled in his favor.

---

[2] Mehmed's petition, as reported in the order, does not disclose the relevance or the contents of the court order. Also the nature of the support by Yeğen Mehmed Paşa is not clear in the document.

[3] It is not clear exactly when.

We learn from the imperial order that Şeyh Mustafa used the court order to prove his claim regarding the trusteeship. Indeed, according to the well-known precepts of Islamic law, as well as its practice in the Ottoman lands, this court order constituted adequate proof of the trusteeship of Şeyh Mustafa. Theoretically, a decision of the court could not be appealed or revoked unless it was proven that the facts that constituted the basis of that decision were inaccurate or had been misrepresented in the court. Therefore, because a court of law had acknowledged his trusteeship to the endowment of İbrahim Beğ, Şeyh Mustafa did not need an endowment deed or any warrant to prove his claim of trusteeship.[4]

Later, however, when this case was investigated in Plovdiv, it appeared that there was neither an İsmail Beğ neighborhood nor a house that belonged to the İbrahim Beğ endowment in the city. Furthermore, no one among the notables, the military, or the religious dignitaries of the town knew anybody with the name Ali bin Mehmed. In other words, the trial in Istanbul was a ruse, fabricated in order to provide legal documentation for Şeyh Mustafa in support of his current claims in Kastamonu. Of course, after this was discovered, the government ordered that Mehmed bin Mustafa should be reappointed as trustee.

We should admire here not only Şeyh Mustafa's ingenious manipulation of the system, but also the ability of Mehmed bin Mustafa to anticipate or detect Şeyh Mustafa's deceits and to protect his own interests through judicial means. The actions of both men demonstrate a significant degree of legal competence in the employment of the law for their own interests.

It is noteworthy that we do not find examples of such legal sophistication in the court records more frequently.[5] There may be

---

[4] Mohammad Hashim Kamali maintains in this context that "[t]he basic norm of *sharīʿa* on judicial decrees issued by knowledgeable judges of upright character is that they are valid and enforceable without delay. For judicial decrees are designed to settle and bring to an end disputes among people. Once a decision is properly formulated and issued the court is presumed to have fulfilled its duty. The application of this norm is also deemed to be in harmony with the need to maintain and promote public confidence in court decisions. By virtue of the same principle it may be added that Islamic public law proceeds on the assumption that justice, in order to be effective, must be swift and that justice delayed can often mean justice denied." See Mohammad Hashim Kamali, "Appellate Review and Judicial Independence in Islamic Law," in Chibli Mallat ed., *Islam and Public Law: Classical and Contemporary Studies* (Boston: Graham & Trotman Press, 1993), p. 63.

[5] This, however, does not mean that there are none. See, for example, KCR,

various reasons for this absence. On the one hand, it is likely that there were not many people in Çankırı and Kastamonu who were as educated and experienced in the practice of law as Şeyh Mustafa was. It may not be a coincidence that the only example of such legal competency appears in a case that involves a *şeyh* from Istanbul. On the other hand, it is also likely that we cannot find similar examples of judicial manipulation precisely because they were successful enough not to leave behind any traces: The evidence of our awareness of Şeyh Mustafa's operations is a result of their failure. The formulaic nature of the court records and their condensed narratives may have been instrumental in hiding such traces of legal manipulation, especially when they went unnoticed in the court.

Other Indicators of Legal Competence: Use of the Principles of "Passage of Time" (Mürur-u Zaman) *and "Choice at Puberty"* (Hiyar-ı Buluğ)

While such examples of legal ingenuity are interesting in themselves and important for demonstrating the level of legal knowledge and competence among clients of the provincial courts, they do not tell much about the level of legal proficiency among the majority of the inhabitants of Çankırı and Kastamonu. Unlike the individual examples of ingenuity, a demonstration of a more general level of proficiency requires evidence of a repeated use of certain legal principles or mechanisms in the processes of litigation. Admittedly, this is not always easy to detect, as the court records do not usually reveal the legal reasoning behind rulings. Nevertheless, in many instances we observe that specific legal prescriptions were recurrently cited or implicitly referred to by litigants.

For example, litigants in the courts of Çankırı and Kastamonu often referred to the judicial principle that disputes of some significant age should be disregarded by the courts unless it could be estab-

vol. 19, 41–79, which reports that an amicable settlement between two parties was enacted and used later in the court in order to demonstrate the validity of the accusations against one of the parties. According to the document this happened after a debtor had refused to pay his debt to the creditor in full and instead had proposed an amicable settlement in return for a payment of only a fraction of the amount that he owed. According to what the plaintiff claimed later in the court, he had agreed to settle the case amicably and had accepted twenty *guruş* from the defendant to prove that the defendant had acknowledged the validity of the accusations against him. Subsequently, two witnesses confirmed the accuracy of the plaintiff's account and the court ruled in his favor.

lished that they had been brought to the court previously or that they constituted a continuous source of contention among the opposing parties in the past (*mürur-u zaman*, "passage of time").[6] In particular, many hearings about land possession were decided in favor of the defendants since they could demonstrate that the plaintiffs had not challenged (in court or not) their possession of a particular piece of land during ten years prior to the date of the hearing. It is interesting that in some of these examples, instead of elaborating on the nature of their claims over the disputed land (or presenting their side of the story in other kinds of disputes) the defendants limited their defenses to the argument that the plaintiffs had failed to confront them on that particular issue in the past.[7]

Such indications of legal awareness were not limited to individuals from certain social and economic statuses—like the ones we observe in the disputes on land possession or property ownership. Indeed, on more than one occasion we find adolescents with no signs of social or economic status demonstrating their knowledge of law in the courts.

> Ayşe bint Mehmed, a virgin of legal age from the neighborhood of Hacı Hamza who has thus been under the supervision and guardianship of her mother, sued her present husband Hasan bin Hüseyin from the aforementioned neighborhood, stating that: "My mother Ayşe forced me to marry the aforementioned Hasan fifteen days ago. However, on the morning of the eighteenth day of Cemaziyelevvel, 1152 (August 23, 1739) I had my first menses and [therefore] reached my maturity. At that very instance I wished to break up (*firkat*) with my husband, and annulled the marriage. I request that the aforementioned Hüseyin be questioned and separation be ordered [by the court]." When Hüseyin was questioned, he confirmed the marriage but denied that the plaintiff had annulled it upon reaching her maturity. Then, the court asked

[6] According to law, different kinds of litigations were subject to different temporal limitations. For example, whereas litigations regarding the possession of state-owned land (*miri arazi*) could not be heard after ten years, the time limit to bring disputes over the ownership of private property to the court was fifteen years. See Akgündüz, *Mukayeseli İslam ve Osmanlı*, pp. 736–737.

[7] The defendants were also required to establish that the plaintiffs had been fully aware of their possession of the disputed land or their claims on the disputed property, and had the material means to challenge them in the court during this period. See, for example, KCR, vol. 1, 81; KCR vol. 1, 85; KCR, vol. 38, 18–24. Such examples are not limited to the disputes of land possession or property ownership. See, for example, KCR, vol. 12, 5a–1 and 8a–2 for disputes regarding monetary transactions and commercial arrangements.

> the aforementioned Ayşe to produce evidence to support her claim. Subsequently, a Şeyh Elhac Ali Efendi from the aforementioned neighborhood and a Molla Mustafa bin Abdullah from the neighborhood of Gökdere testified as follows: "Indeed, on the morning of the eighteenth day of Cemaziyelevvel, the plaintiff declared in our presence that at the time that she had her menses and reached her maturity, she had wished for separation and annulled the marriage into which her mother had forced her. She asked us to be witnesses to this situation." After the trustworthiness of the witnesses was investigated and their testimonies were accepted, the court asked Ayşe to take an oath that she requested the separation when she reached her maturity and that there were no legal predicaments that would nullify her decision. When she took the oath, the court ordered the break-up.[8]

In Sunni legal thought, the right of adult males and females[9] to freely choose their spouses is generally acknowledged.[10] On the other hand, a legal guardian maintains the right to marry an adolescent under his/her responsibility without seeking his/her consent.[11] Adolescents do not have the right to annul these marriages after they reach maturity if the guardians who arranged their marriages are their fathers or paternal grandfathers. However, if their guardians are people other than their fathers or grandfathers, they retain the right to annul the marriage after their maturity (*hiyar-ı buluğ*, "choice at puberty").[12] For females, the scope of this right is limited in practice. According to Abu Hanifa, for example, an adolescent girl has to declare that she wishes to separate from her husband and to annul the marriage in front of the witnesses as soon as she realizes that she is having her first menses—the indication of female maturity according to Islamic law. If she misses this historical point, she loses her right to annul the marriage.[13]

---

[8] Dated 18 CI, 1152/August 23, 1739. See KCR, vol. 38, 30–32.

[9] Adulthood was legally attained at puberty.

[10] See, Akgündüz, *Mukayeseli İslam ve Osmanlı*, pp. 151–153 and 319–320. The Maliki School is the only exception to this rule. It is generally accepted in Maliki legal thought that a father has the right to force his virgin daughter to marry whomever he chooses for her, regardless of her age. See Yushau Sadiq, "Application of the Islamic Law in Nigeria: A Case Study," *Hamdard Islamicus*, no. 2, vol. 17 (1992), pp. 55–76.

[11] Akgündüz, *Mukayeseli İslam ve Osmanlı*, p. 158; Asife Ünal, *Yahudilik'te, Hıristiyanlık'ta ve İslam'da Evlilik* (Ankara: T.C. Kültür Bakanlığı Yayınları, 1993), pp. 154–156; Gökçen Art, *Şeyhulislam Fetvalarynda Kadın ve Cinsellik* (Istanbul: Çiviyazıları, 1996), pp. 35–36.

[12] Akgündüz, *Mukayeseli İslam ve Osmanlı*, p. 159; Ünal, p. 156; Art, p. 36.

[13] Akgündüz, *Mukayeseli İslam ve Osmanlı*, p. 159; Art, p. 36.

What we observe in the case of Ayşe above is the ability of an adolescent to observe a relatively technical rule to its letter. According to the entry, on the very day of her first menses Ayşe found two prominent witnesses (a *şeyh* and a *molla*) to reveal the situation and declare her wish for annulment, and immediately after that, she took the issue directly to the court. More important for our concerns is the observation that the example of Ayşe is not unprecedented in the court records. Indeed, *sicil*s supply further examples of marriage annulments by adolescents at the time of their legal maturity,[14] which suggests that at least some other members of the community shared Ayşe's legal competence.

We realize in this particular case, once again, that court records conceal as much as they reveal. For example, while we have no insight into the sources of Ayşe's proficiency, it seems more than probable that people who were knowledgeable in law coached Ayşe. Again, we cannot be sure about the identities of these individuals; they may have included people who were officially affiliated with the court. On the other hand, the prominence of the witnesses testifying on behalf of Ayşe leads the reader to think about the possibility that they were among the ones who helped her.

If Ayşe was indeed coached in the court process, this suggests that certain mechanisms within the community facilitated the dispersal of legal knowledge among its members—something we have no chance of observing in the court records. And if this really was the case, the members of the community did not have to be particularly gifted or knowledgeable about the law in order to navigate the legal system efficiently. Rather, the ability to benefit from others' experiences and the existing support mechanisms within the community may have been adequate to obtain satisfactory results in the courts.

Legal Opinions (Fetva*s*) *as Means for Legal Manipulation*

Repeated references to certain judicial principles suggest the existence of a degree of awareness on the part of certain litigants of the contents of the law. However, our ability to generalize this awareness and competence to a greater portion of the court clients necessitates

[14] See KCR, vol. 39, 71–120 and KCR, vol. 39, 91–156 for two examples.

the detection of other strategies that were employed more frequently in the processes of litigation.

A more common example of such strategic calculation appears in the use of legal opinions (*fetva*s) issued by jurisconsults (*müftis*). As demonstrated in a previous chapter, plaintiffs and holders of military and religious titles had an advantage in the courts of Çankırı and Kastamonu, which may have led weaker parties to utilize those means that could provide them with a legal edge over their opponents. In this context, it is unfortunate that we cannot be absolutely sure about the exact effect of the *fetva*s on the courts. Yet, although the courts were not obligated to enforce the opinions suggested in the *fetva*s, it is obvious that these documents had an influence on the local courts—either because of the legal guidance they offered or because of the nature of the relationship between the local *kadı* and the local *müfti* (or both). In the court records of Çankırı and Kastamonu, we find 99 hearings during which the litigants submitted *fetva*s to the court. In 80 of these 99 cases, the courts decided in favor of those who presented the *fetva*s. In 12 cases disputes were resolved by amicable settlement. In 7 cases the courts decided in favor of those parties who had not submitted *fetva*s.

Not surprisingly, of the 12 *fetva*s submitted by villagers with no military or religious titles, 9 were submitted during trials involving individuals with military and religious titles.[15] Conversely, of the 42 *fetva*s presented by military and religious titleholders during their trials, only 3 were presented against villagers with no military and religious titles. This positive correlation between the use of *fetva*s and the prominence of the opposing litigants is supported by the fact that more than half of all the *fetva*s submitted by military and religious title-holders in their litigations were submitted against other title-holders, in spite of the fact that the total number of such litigations (in which the plaintiffs and defendants were both titleholders) constituted only about a third of all the litigations in which the titleholders were involved (either as plaintiffs or as defendants).

---

[15] And only one of these cases was decided against the villagers. I am assuming here that villagers with no military or religious titles constituted the weakest group in the court; I believe that those litigants who had these titles were among the strongest parties.

Community in Action

The findings in chapter four have indicated that resort to the court *en masse* was an effective way to guarantee a favorable outcome against anyone, regardless of his or her economic and social prominence. Apparently the inhabitants of Çankırı and Kastamonu were well aware of this fact since the members of the community frequently came together to incriminate certain individuals in the court. In my view, resort to the court *en masse* constitutes one of the most convincing indicators of the collective competency of the community in the use of the judicial process to advance its own interests. In what follows I will try to elaborate on the mechanisms of the use of the court *en masse* and the reasons related to the effectiveness of this strategy.

Mohammad Fadel argues that the Sunni legal structure was developed to attain social legitimacy through different means. In civil disputes among individual litigants, the courts were supposed to act impartially:

> [T]he judge's legitimacy, especially in cases where he was trying private disputes, was closely connected to the belief that he was neutral. . . . [He] could take no step that might result in either party's doubting the legitimacy of his decision. . . . [Hence,] the main purpose of Islamic adjectival law [i.e. evidentiary procedures] was to protect the judge's position as a neutral third party. Consequently, instead of the judge making problematic, discretionary inferences based upon circumstantial evidence, such matters were deferred, usually by means of the oath, to the parties themselves, thereby maximizing the likelihood that the parties would consent to the outcome.[16]

I have already explored the validity of these assertions in the context of early modern Anatolia. More important for our current discussion is Fadel's assessment regarding the legitimacy of the court when it was dealing with public issues. Fadel claims that in such cases, the legitimacy of the court would be based not on its professed neutrality but on the community's approval of its actions. According to Fadel, in medieval times this quest for communal approval necessitated the court's appropriation of investigative functions. Furthermore,

[16] Mohammad Fadel, "Adjudication in the Maliki Madhhab: A Study of Legal Process in Medieval Islamic Law," Unpublished Ph.D. dissertation, University of Chicago, 1995, pp. 125–126.

it necessitated the development of a separate set of evidentiary rules guiding the investigation of serious public offenses. Applicable only to violations of public rights, rights of the state, felonies, and assaults, these evidentiary rules were distinguished from the rules applied in civil disputes,

> principally by the fact that in claims such as these, the court was empowered to investigate the charges, not just hear evidence. Because the court, with respect to these claims was now involved in the production of the evidence, evidentiary standards excluding circumstantial evidence were greatly relaxed, or even non-existent, and we are very close to a system of *freie Beweiswurdigung*, where the judge is given almost a free hand in collecting and evaluating evidence.[17]

We need to emphasize that the courts of Çankırı and Kastamonu did occasionally conduct their own investigations in the kinds of cases described by Fadel.[18] More often, however, the agency of the community, rather than the agency of the court, dominated the judicial processes when cases involved serious criminal disputes, violations of public rights, or threats to local security. It seems that the courts of Çankırı and Kastamonu were easily convinced of the guilt of anyone accused by the community. In such situations members of the community volunteered information and testified against the defendants and, on various occasions, let their views regarding the appropriate punishment be known to the court.

Communal Domination in the Court: "Fomenting Corruption" and the Strategy of Substitution

As demonstrated, resort to the court *en masse* proved to be most effective against local administrative-military authorities. Nevertheless this strategy was by no means used exclusively against government officials: We observe in the court records that other individuals, ordinary people accused of disorder and disturbance, might also become its targets. The legal system allowed the community to deal with these "undesirable elements" without having to make specific accusations against them or to provide proof of the offence. Indeed, accusing someone of being a *sa'i bi'l-fesad* ("fomenter of corruption") and prompting two or more members of the community to testify

[17] Fadel, p. 185.
[18] See, for example, KCR, vol. 4, 14–42 and KCR, vol. 12, 9b–1.

that "corruption" was the defendant's "constant habit" (*ʿadet-i müstemirre*) were sufficient to incriminate that individual.[19] We see in the court records of Çankırı and Kastamonu that this procedure made it easy to punish or eliminate troublesome individuals.

Case 1

In Şevval 1110/April 1699, an Emine from the village of Ünüz claimed in the court of Çankırı that six months prior to the date of the hearing, three men from the same village had entered her house and raped her. In addition to the rape, they also beat her up after she tried to resist them. As a result of this beating she lost two teeth. She also claimed that after the rape and the beating, the defendants took some valuable garments from her house. The defendants denied these accusations in the court. And when the court asked Emine to substantiate her claims, she introduced seven witnesses from the same village,[20] who testified that they had heard the plaintiff's cries and that when they had arrived at her house to help her, they had seen the defendants leaving the house with the garments. After these testimonies, Emine asked the court to investigate the reputations of the defendants among those who knew them. Consequently, more than fifteen individuals from five different villages testified that the defendants were known to be oppressors (*zalim*) and fomenters of corruption (*saʿi bi'l-fesad*). The court ordered that the defendants be punished in proportion to their crime.[21]

According to this account, Emine was unable to establish in strictly legal terms that the defendants had raped her, since she had been alone with them during the alleged incident. The witnesses reported in their testimonies that they had heard Emine's cries and seen the defendants leaving the house with the garments. Legally, the testimonies of the witnesses were sufficient to establish that Emine had been battered and robbed by the plaintiffs. The fact, that they saw the plaintiffs leaving Emine's house with her garments and that they found Emine beaten up inside the house were adequate proof.[22]

[19] Heyd, *Studies*, pp. 195–198. Also see Ahmet Mumcu, *Osmanlı Devleti'nde Siyaseten Katl* (Ankara: Birey ve Toplum Yayınları, 1973).

[20] One of these witnesses was the *imam* (prayer leader) of the village.

[21] ÇCR, vol. 5, 68–149. The exact nature of the punishment is not specified in the document.

[22] See Akgündüz, *Mukayeseli İslam ve Osmanlı*, p. 753.

Nevertheless, according to the court record, the witnesses neither saw the act of rape nor did they submit any circumstantial evidence in their testimonies that would incriminate the defendants.[23] For this reason, the support of the community was necessary to persuade the court of the defendants' evil character and, therefore, of the plausibility of the alleged rape.

This example demonstrates that concrete factual evidence (in the form of witness testimonies) pointing to the criminal actions of certain individuals (robbery and battery in this particular situation) and the involvement of the community in support of the victims could complement each other in incriminating certain undesirable individuals. In this case, this combination was extremely effective in persuading the readers of the court records of the guilt of the defendants. Yet we have other examples in which we do not observe a similar convergence between the factual indicators and the convictions of the community.

Case 2

In 1077/1667 a Receb bin Şaban came to the court of Çankırı and claimed that two brothers, Mehmed and Mustafa, had forcefully entered his house some time ago and had stolen his property. After the defendants had denied this claim in court, the plaintiff was asked to substantiate his accusations. Instead of bringing witnesses to testify to the validity of his claims, as expected according to the prescribed evidential procedures, the plaintiff claimed that the defendants were considered "fomenters of corruption" in their own village and asked the court to investigate their reputation "from those who knew them well." According to the entry, certain unidentified members of the community described the defendants as having evil character (*su-i hal*). These individuals claimed that Mehmed and Mustafa were "not good people; they would not abstain from such actions" (*mezburlar Mehmed ve Mustafa iyi ademler değildir, bu tür ahvalden ictinab etmezler*). The court found the defendants guilty and ordered that they be punished in proportion to their crime.[24]

[23] Ibid. Also see Abdülaziz Bayındır, *İslam Muhakeme Hukuku: Osmanlı Devri Uygulaması* (Istanbul: İslami İlimler Araştırma Vakfi, 1986), pp. 144–149.

[24] ÇCR, vol. 2, 17–51. Also see Galal H. El-Nahal, *The Judicial Administration of Ottoman Egypt in the Seventeenth Century* (Minneapolis & Chicago: Bibliotheca Islamica, 1979), p. 30, for a similar example from the seventeenth-century Egyptian court records.

In this example, the defendants were explicitly accused of stealing, but it was not demonstrated in the court that they had actually committed this crime. The fact that the plaintiff did not submit any witness testimonies to substantiate his claims regarding the robbery suggests the nature of evidentiary procedures observed at that time. Apparently, the plaintiff's strategy was *exclusively* based on the reputation of the defendants. And, although the nature of the punishment is not stated in the entry, Mehmed and Mustafa were found guilty merely because members of the community could not (or would not) rule out the possibility that they were guilty. It is conceivable that Mehmed and Mustafa had looked for other individuals from their village to testify on their behalf and report on their good character. The absence of any reference to such witnesses in the entry suggests that there was a consensus within the community regarding their character. Ultimately it was this consensus that determined the outcome of the trial.

These two examples demonstrate that the courts took the defendants' reputation into account, particularly when the allegations against them could not be documented with usual evidentiary procedures. I believe that this tendency constituted the basis of what could be called a "strategy of substitution" that the community utilized against undesirable individuals in their locality. The next example from the court records of Kastamonu provides an even more explicit demonstration of this communal strategy in action.

Case 3

In Zilkaʿde 1148 / March 1736, a Hüseyin bin Mehmed and his wife Ayşe bint Mustafa were accused by the legal representative (*vekil*) of a Havva bint Ali Çelebi of stealing her money, jewelry, and belongings from her house thirteen months earlier. Since some of these items had been found in the house of the couple,[25] Havva's representative asked the court to question the defendants and punish them according to law. In their statements, Hüseyin and Ayşe claimed that those items rightfully belonged to them since they had brought them from Rumelia. They denied having stolen those items from Havva's house and that any of these items belonged to Havva. Then the court asked the representative to submit evidence to prove his

[25] I do not know how.

claims. Upon this request two witnesses appeared and stated that "we do not know whether it was the aforementioned Hüseyin and his wife Ayşe who robbed the house of the aforementioned Havva. Yet we can testify that the items that were found in the house of the defendants are among the belongings of Havva that had been stolen from her house thirteen months ago." The court ordered Hüseyin and Ayşe to return the items to Havva.

Then the legal agent (*vekil*) of two other people, Hüseyin Çelebi bin Mehmed and his wife, Atike, accused Hüseyin and Ayşe of stealing their money, jewelry, and belongings six months earlier. Again some of the stolen items had been found[26] in the house of the defendants, and the representative therefore requested that the defendants be questioned and punished according to law. Once again the defendants denied that the items found in their house belonged to Hüseyin Çelebi and his wife, Atike, and claimed that they had in fact bought them from someone else about five months before the hearing. When the court asked the representative of the plaintiffs to submit evidence to demonstrate the validity of their allegations, he brought two witnesses to the court who testified as follows: "We do not know whether it was the aforementioned Hüseyin who robbed the house of Hüseyin Çelebi and his wife, Atike. Yet we testify that the items found in his house are among the belongings of Hüseyin Çelebi and Atike, which were stolen before." After the court had compelled Hüseyin Çelebi to swear that he had neither sold nor given away the found items to other people, it ordered Hüseyin to return them to Hüseyin Çelebi.

Then, seven individuals (their names are given in the entry) from the neighborhood of Hamza Ağa came to the court and gave the following statement regarding the reputations of the defendants:

> The aforementioned Hüseyin is a troublemaker and a bandit. Previously he assaulted a woman in our neighborhood and stole her money and forcefully took her silver hair-band from her head. Also he was planning to assault some virtuous women in the aforementioned neighborhood in order to rape them (*mahalle-i mezburda bir kaç ehl-i ʿırz hatuna fiil-i şenʿi kasdıyla taʿaruz murad etmekle . . .*). He is a corrupter and a bandit, and his wife too is a troublemaker. We are not sure of their character [or, "we do not trust them"], and we would not stand surety for them (*kendilerinden emin değilizdir ve kefalet dahi etmeziz*).

[26] Again, I do not know how, or by whom.

After this statement, the two legal agents submitted the following *fetva* of İbrahim Efendi, the *müfti* of Kastamonu, to the court:

> What should be done to Amr if the stolen belongings of Zeyd are found in his possession and the witnesses testify that those items belong to Zeyd although they cannot be sure about the fact that it was Amr who committed the crime? [Also, take into consideration the fact that] some individuals report that Amr robbed Hind a year ago. The answer is that the found items should be returned to Zeyd, and Amr should be imprisoned and interrogated according to law.

The court ordered the implementation of the command of the *fetva*.[27]

The testimonies of the first two witnesses are critical for our concerns here. In these testimonies, the witnesses declared that although the items found in the house of Hüseyin and Ayşe belonged to the plaintiffs, they could not verify that the defendants had actually stolen them. For this reason they could not be punished for robbery according to law.[28] Indeed, we see at the end of the first two hearings that the defendants were only forced to return the items to their owners.[29] At this point we observe the cooperation of the community and the legal agents of the plaintiffs in incriminating the defendants through a "strategy of substitution." When the crimes attributed to the defendants could not be proven, their reputation and hearsay were presented as proof of their guilt. It is noteworthy again that no information is given in the text supporting the accuracy of these reports. Moreover, no response from the accused was requested when the inhabitants of the Halil Ağa neighborhood reported Hüseyin's encounter with the woman whose hair-band he was accused of stealing, or when they accused Hüseyin of "planning to attack" virtuous women to rape them. It is not clear whether these allegations were previously taken to the court or not.

---

[27] KCR, vol. 35, 43–60.

[28] According to what we learn from Uriel Heyd's compilation of the Ottoman criminal code, the punishment of the defendant in such a situation is dependent on his or her reputation: "If something stolen is found in a person's possession or in his house and he claims that he bought it, he shall be compelled to find the person who sold it to him. If the latter is not found and *he himself is a suspicious character* he shall be tortured unless the seller is found, brought and handed over to the cadi, or the holder of the stolen goods proves that he found them in a desolate area." See Heyd, *Studies*, p. 116. Emphasis added.

[29] This is consistent with what we see in other cases of robbery in the *sicils* of Çankırı and Kastamonu.

In this example, the defendants were not immediately convicted, as happened in the previous examples. The decision to imprison and "interrogate" the defendants indicates that a more detailed investigation of their actions was considered necessary. At the same time, it should be emphasized that the purpose behind imprisonment and interrogation is not very clear in Islamic and Ottoman law.[30] While Sunni jurists considered both practices as modes of investigation, it was not too difficult for these investigatory methods to turn into punishment.[31] As mentioned, the German merchant Hans Ulrich Krafft was kept in prison for more than three years before he was able to arrange for his release. Also, we find in an imperial order that seven janissaries were imprisoned in the fortress of Çankırı for more than three months merely as a consequence of certain legally unsubstantiated allegations regarding their corruption.[32]

Before moving on, it is important to note that the support of the community was not limited to the plaintiffs but could help those individuals who were believed to have been accused unjustly.[33]

---

[30] It is likely that this "interrogation" involved physical coercion as indicated in footnote 28. The Ottoman Criminal Code prescribed torture (*işkence*) as a legitimate form of investigation. See for example Heyd, *Studies*, pp. 106 and 116–119.

[31] In regard to how Maliki jurists saw beating, Fadel claims that, "[i]t seems that the distinction between the evidentiary function of the beating and its disciplinary function came to be entirely forgotten, or at the very least, its function as punishment rapidly came to prevail over its function as a means of fact-finding." The same could be said for imprisonment: "Al-Tarablusi noted that if a man accused another who is well known for theft of having stolen his merchandise, the accused was to be arrested and imprisoned indefinitely. Imprisonment at this particular time is justified solely because of the accused's being suspicious and well-known for theft; therefore, the public must be protected against a defendant deemed to be a threat to the public.... Thus, the primary justification given for this procedure was disciplinary, while the hope that he might confess under the pressure of incarceration was only secondary and was implied." According to Fadel, many other Sunni jurists share this perception of imprisonment. See Fadel, p. 193.

[32] These janissaries had previously sent a petition to the central government and reported that their guilt had not been proven in the court since no one had testified against them. They requested their immediate release from the prison. The order is dated CI 1154/June 1741. CCR, vol. 13, 37–64.

[33] Consider the following example: In CI of 1115/September 1703, a Mustafa bin Mehmed from the village of İçemezoğlu came to the court in Kastamonu and accused Mehmed bin Mustafa and Mehmed bin Ömer from the village of Kızoğlu of assaulting his wife, Saime bint Mehmed, with the intention of rape, and stabbing her with a knife. Mustafa asked the court to question the defendants and investigate their reputations (*su'al olunup takrirleri tahrir ve ahvalleri tefahhus olunmak matlubumdur*). After the defendants denied the allegations, the court asked the plaintiff to submit evidence to prove his allegations. The plaintiff asked for time from the court

Unfortunately, not much has been written in the literature about what I call the "strategy of substitution." Yet, Uriel Heyd's description of the differences between strictly sharia-based adjudication and what he calls "punishment *siyaseten*"[34] (discretionary punishment) seems to be relevant here. According to Heyd, "punishment *siyaseten* was to be inflicted for various crimes not covered by the *shari*ʿ*a* and for many offences which could not be proved in accordance with *shari*ʿ*a*'s strict rules of criminal procedure."[35] Theoretically, only the sultan and his deputy, the grand vizier, could inflict this form of punishment, although, it is known that governors and other high military executives used to usurp this authority in practice.[36] Heyd claims that in the Ottoman Empire this form of punishment was recognized by the judicial establishment as a legitimate mechanism to deal with habitual criminals who were considered as "fomenters of corruption." In order to punish those who were considered to be "fomenters of corruption in the world,"

> the Ottoman *şeyhülislams* and other *müftis* left wide discretion to the Sultan as 'Padisah of Islam' (and hence *veli ül-emir*) and 'fountain-head of the order (or 'of the reform') of the world' (*sebeb-i nizam*, or *islah-ı* ʿ*alem*). To protect the public interest (*maslahat*) or the people (*siyaneten li'l-*ʿ*ibad*), to preserve public order (*nizam-i memleket* or *emn-i bilad*), and to give a deterrent example to others (ʿ*ibreten li's-sa'irin*), he may order the execution of such offenders 'as an administrative punishment' (*siyaseten*) or within the framework of his discretionary powers (*ta*ʿ*ziren*).[37]

to bring evidence in support of his claims, but he could not submit any evidence by the end of the period granted by the court. He also refused to take an oath. Then the court investigated the reputations of the defendants among the inhabitants of the village of Kızoğlu. The people of the village stated that "the aforementioned are not trouble-makers. We have not heard or seen them committing such crimes until this time." The court then ordered the plaintiff to stop making false accusations against the defendants. See KCR, vol. 12, 9b–1.

[34] The term *siyaset* had a variety of meanings in Ottoman Turkish. It could mean government, political administration, or even diplomacy. In the realm of law, however, this term referred specifically to the "extra-canonical [judicial] authority of the ruler," who had "the right to inflict much wider and more severe punishment on criminals than was possible under the limited and rigid rules of *shari*ʿ*a* penal law and criminal procedure." See Heyd, *Studies*, p. 199.

[35] Ibid., p. 193.

[36] Ibid., pp. 192–193.

[37] Ibid., p. 196. Baber Johansen argues in a recent article that it was first during the Mamluk period that Sunni jurists began to incorporate what he calls the doctrine of "siyāsa sharʿiyya" into the legal corpus. See his "Signs as Evidence: The Doctrine of Ibn Taymiyya (1263–1328) and Ibn Qayyim al-Jawziyya (d. 1351) on Proof," *Islamic Law and Society* vol. 9 (2002), pp. 168–193.

In this sense, the logic behind the discretionary punishment does not seem to be very different from the "strategy of substitution" in the examples above. In all of these cases, the community was able to inflict punishment upon certain undesirable individuals or groups, in spite of the fact that their guilt could not be established in accordance with the strict evidentiary standards that the courts were expected to observe in less serious contentions. The principles and rationale that constituted the basis of the sultan's "discretionary punishment" also allowed the community to punish or eliminate these individuals.

In a recent article, Eyal Ginio offers a description of *saʿi bi'l-fesad* adjudication in eighteenth-century Salonica:

> The adjudication of *saʿi bi'l-fesad* was conducted in two stages. First, the accused was convicted for the specific offense he had committed. His trial was conducted in the *Şeriat* court by the *kadı* or the *naip* [sic] and his culpability needed to be established by two eye-witnesses. In the first stage, the plaintiffs were the victim's heirs, since Islamic law regard [sic] homicide as essentially private law. In the second stage the convicted culprit was brought to a second trial in order to determine whether he was a habitual murderous criminal and thus liable for the fixed punishment (*hadd*) prescribed in the Qur'an for highway robbery. In such a case, the state, through its local agents, stepped in and took the plaintiff's role, since being *saʿi bi'l-fesad*—highway robbery in its original meaning—was regarded as a crime against religion. To do so, a long line of culprit's neighbors were examined (*istifsar*), so as to determine the criminal's character and habits.[38]

In his work, Ginio identifies two different stages of adjudication and implies that the laws applied in these stages ("private" law versus "public" law) as well as the enforcers of law (*kadı* versus governor) and the locations of adjudication (court versus governor's mansion) were different. Accordingly, it was not possible to substitute one kind of evidence for another.

I should mention that this description of *saʿi bi'l-fesad* adjudication is at variance with my understanding of it. Perhaps there was indeed such a distinction between "proper law" and what we may call "public justice" in Salonica. In Çankırı and Kastamonu, however, I did not observe such a clear-cut separation. As can be observed in all

[38] Eyal Ginio, "The Administration of Criminal Justice in Ottoman Selanik (Salonica) during the Eighteenth Century," *Turcica*, vol. 30 (1998), p. 202.

the examples above, the functions of the *kadıs* in Çankırı and Kastamonu were not limited to the enforcement of the sharia "in its pure form." Quite the contrary, they frequently heard testimonies about the corruption and evil character of the defendants and took these testimonies into consideration in their decisions. As we know, the "Ottoman Criminal Code" was an amalgamation of the Sunni legal tradition *and* state regulations, and *kadıs* were obligated to enforce all dictates of this code regardless of their origins.[39]

Unfortunately, the court records do not generally disclose the kinds of punishments inflicted on guilty parties. Yet we also know that the court could in fact enforce "non-*shar'i*" decisions, when necessary.[40] Furthermore, in many examples of *sa'i bi'l-fesad*, the registries do not even mention the presence of military authorities in the proceedings, although when the governor or the sub-governor attended the hearings or when the disputes were resolved in their residences, these details were invariably reported.

It is true that the governors and the members of the local military were present in many trials against *sa'i bi'l-fesad*. It is also true that in almost all of these cases, allegations regarding the evil character of the defendants and their "corruption" followed the reports and testimonies of specific acts of criminality. Furthermore, an example in chapter nine will demonstrate that there could be separate legal hearings of a particular dispute in the "court of the *kadi*" and in the residence of the governor. Nevertheless, none of these observations adequately demonstrates the existence of two separate stages of adjudication in which different kinds of law were enforced.[41]

---

[39] Colin Imber, *Ebu's-Su'ud; The Islamic Legal Tradition* (Stanford: Stanford University Press, 1997), pp. 24–65.

[40] Imprisonment and "interrogation" of the suspect constitute one such originally non-*shar'i* measure. According to Johansen, some Sunni jurists began to consider judicial torture as a legitimate means of investigation during the thirteenth and fourteenth centuries. See his, "Signs of Evidence," passim.

[41] In all of the examples that we find in Ginio's article, the defendants' guilt was demonstrated by the eyewitness testimonies before their reputations was investigated. Hence, in none of these cases was there a need for a strategy of substitution. The allegations regarding the evil character of the defendants and their corruption were reported presumably in order to increase the punishment inflicted on them.

Communal Domination in the Court: Other Instances

The examples of the legal initiative of the community are not limited to cases of *sa'i bi'l-fesad*. For various reasons, it may have been difficult to accuse someone of being a "fomenter of corruption" in specific occasions; yet this did not prevent the community from punishing or eliminating those individuals who were deemed undesirable through a judicial process. Indeed some examples in the court records demonstrate the community's remarkable ability to adjust and produce evidence for those kinds of allegations that were very difficult to prove in the court.

Case 5

In 1106/1695, a Kerime from a village of Çankırı came to the court and claimed that ʿAvz bin Abdullah, a slave (*ʿabd-ı memlük*) from the same village, had attempted to rape her in a barn three days prior to the trial. According to her statement in the court, she managed to escape from ʿAvz by running out of the barn while crying for help and locking the barn doors on him. After ʿAvz denied these allegations in the court, the plaintiff was asked to submit evidence. Two inhabitants of the same village testified that they had heard Kerime's cries and saw her locking the doors of the barn. They also declared that they had seen ʿAvz opening the lock from inside the barn with his knife and leaving the area. Subsequently, four other inhabitants of the village testified that ʿAvz had previously confessed his guilt in their presence. The court accepted these testimonies and ruled in favor of the plaintiff.[42]

This case is interesting for our purposes in this chapter: The testimonies of the first two witnesses, although supportive of the plaintiff's claims, were not sufficient to convict the defendant according to law, since the witnesses had not actually seen ʿAvz attempting to rape Kerime. In the absence of eyewitnesses to an alleged crime, the only way to establish the guilt of the defendant was to secure a confession. And since the defendant denied the accusations in the court, the testimonies of the last four witnesses were indispensable for his conviction.

It is these testimonies and their capacity to make the conviction judicially appropriate that draw our attention to this case. The con-

[42] ÇCR, vol. 4, 5–22.

ditions in which the four individuals witnessed ʿAvz's confession are unclear. And even if we disregard the possibility that they were lying, we cannot be sure that the confession was not taken by force before the court. Since we cannot explain why ʿAvz would willingly confess his crime to people who could use it against him in the court, fairness of the process of adjudication is called into question. Interestingly, the *kadı*, who was supposedly the person most knowledgeable about strategies of legal manipulation, did not seem to be irritated by these details. Thus, although the process of litigation seems to be perfectly (perhaps too perfectly) in order, we sense, once again, a collaboration between Kerime, the village community, and the court against the defendant.

Interestingly, this example is somewhat similar to the case of Emine discussed above. In fact, some of the facts in these two cases are remarkably alike. In both cases the plaintiffs claimed they had been sexually assaulted. They both were alone with their assailants, and nobody saw what had actually happened during the incident. Furthermore, in both cases the community intervened on behalf of the women, and the assailants were found guilty as a result. There is, however, one significant difference between these incidents. In the case of Emine, the defendants were accused of being "fomenters of corruption." In the case of Kerime, ʿAvz reportedly had confessed his crime to other people and been convicted as a result of their testimony. We may wonder about the reasons for this variation between these cases in spite of the fact that many details are so similar.[43]

Accusing ʿAvz of being a "fomenter of corruption" would have eased the evidentiary requirements and saved the witnesses from the burden of (falsely?) testifying against him.[44] It is, of course, possible that the differences between the reputations and personal histories of ʿAvz and Emine's assailants were responsible for this distinction between the two cases; perhaps ʿAvz was not really considered an instigator of evil and corruption in his village. On the other hand,

[43] Here I disregard the possibilities that the four individuals who testified against ʿAvz were not lying and that ʿAvz was not subjected to any kind of physical or psychological pressure to give that confession.

[44] False testimony was severely punishable according to law; see Bayındır, pp. 192–197. Since the accusation of being a "fomenter of corruption" was based on the character evaluations of the defendants rather than on specific incidents or criminal act, it would have been safer and easier to incriminate someone by accusing him or her of being a "fomenter of corruption."

if we believe that accusing someone of being a "fomenter of corruption" was a means to establish guilt through a legal shortcut, there might be other reasons for this difference.

Although we cannot really know the reasons, it is possible that ʿAvz's status as a slave was responsible for this variation. A careful study of primary and secondary sources on Ottoman and Islamic penal codes demonstrates that there was no regulation that determined how to allocate the responsibility for fomenting corruption or conducting highway robbery between the slaves their owners. Nor were there any specific rule that sanctioned the punishment of slaves for such actions.[45] It was perhaps the inability of the community to accuse ʿAvz of being a *saʿi bi'l-fesad* that led them to take other measures to secure his conviction. Here again we witness the resourcefulness of the community in manipulating the court in support of the communal interest even when it encountered legal restrictions.

On other occasions, when signs of "corruption" could conceivably be found only in the private realms of the defendant, we find the use of false witness testimony replacing public reports or hearsay (*tevatür*) regarding the characters and actions of the defendants in the adjudication of "corrupt" individuals.

Case 6

In Receb 1109/January 1698, for example, Şeyh Mehmed bin Abdullah, Osman bin Mehmed and Mehmed bin İsmail were brought to court by the inhabitants of their village and were accused of being *kızılbaş*, conducting heretical rituals in their houses and having sexual intercourse with each others' wives. After the defendants denied these claims in the court, four inhabitants of the village testified

---

[45] A slave's criminal responsibility is defined only for specific crimes, and fomenting corruption and highway robbery are not one of them. In the Ottoman Criminal Codes these crimes involve fornication, intentional bodily harm, defamation, use of alcohol and foul language. The punishments of these crimes for the slaves were half of what were inflicted on free men. See R. Brunschvig, "ʿAbd," *EI*[2], vol. 1, pp. 26–31; Ahmet Akgündüz, *İslam Hukukunda Kölelik—Cariyelik Müessesesi ve Osmanlı'da Harem* (Istanbul: Osmanlı Araştırmaları Vakfi Yayınları, 1995); Heyd, *Studies*, 54–132; Matthew Lippman, Sean McConville and Mordechai Yerushalmi, *Islamic Criminal Law and Procedure: An Introduction* (New York: Praeger, 1988), pp. 42, 60; Bernard Lewis, *Race and Slavery in the Middle East: An Historical Enquiry* (Oxford: Oxford University Press, 1990), pp. 3–16; Murray Gordon, *Slavery in the Arab World* (New York: New Amsterdam Press, 1989), pp. 37–38.

against the plaintiffs.[46] According to their testimony, the plaintiffs and their wives had met in Osman's house one night, where they drank wine and had anal intercourse with each other's wives according to the ritual of the heretics (*firak-ı dallenin ʿayini üzere . . . birbirinin ʿavredine ʿaksine fiʿil-i şeniʿ kastederken* . . .). Interestingly, the *kadı* accepted the testimonies of the witnesses only after making them swear that they had actually seen what they had accused the defendants of doing. It is obvious from the account that the court decided to punish the defendants; it is not clear, however, what kind of punishment was inflicted on them.

Before analyzing the legal aspects of this case, it should be emphasized that the truthfulness of the witness testimonies is extremely dubious. Admittedly, no one can be sure what these witnesses had actually seen in the house of Osman or if they had seen anything at all. Nevertheless even if they had seen something, their representation of what they witnessed was probably inaccurate given what we know about Alevi and mainstream Shiʿite religious practices today.

Leslie Peirce demonstrates in her work on two sixteenth-century Antep court records that the term *kızılbaş* loosely stood for "all that deviated from what was imagined to be normative communal behavior, for everything that the concerned neighbors did not want to be thought to be."[47] According to Peirce, these deviations included perverse or illicit sexual activities, disapproved religious tendencies, and, therefore, political or ideological dissent against Ottoman sovereignty, as well as pro-Safavid inclinations.[48] In the context of late seventeenth-century Çankırı, this term probably did not imply pro-Safavid partisanship anymore. Nevertheless, this case demonstrates that it continued to imply religious and sexual deviation.

If the witnesses had really seen anything unusual in house of Osman, it was probably a *cemʿ* ceremony that was and still is common among the Alevi communities of Anatolia.[49] Although this

[46] ÇCR, vol. 5, 27–43. Two of these witnesses carried the title "seyyid" in their names, indicating that they were from the lineage of the Prophet Muhammad.

[47] Leslie Peirce, *Making Justice: Women, Law, and Morality in an Ottoman Court* (Berkeley: University of California Press, forthcoming), p. 323.

[48] Ibid., p. 322.

[49] *Cemʿ* ceremonies involve singing, dancing, chanting, and praying under the direction and guidance of elder religious figures. These ceremonies also include sessions of communal dispute resolution during which elders listen to the disputes

ceremony does not involve any kind of sexual activity or symbolism, the violation of gender segregation norms does serve as a pretext for contempt among certain Sunni groups. Indeed we know that the *cem*ʿ ceremony has occasionally been identified with the practice of "blowing the candle out" (*mum söndü/mum söndürme*), after which the Alevis allegedly come together and have intercourse with other people in the room in the dark. Many Sunni sources imply that during such encounters family members and relatives end up having intercourse with each other.[50]

Given the information presented in the document, it is unlikely that these four witnesses saw anything. The document does not reveal anything about how these people were able to witness what they claimed to have witnessed. Given the hostile social environment in which they were living, we assume that the defendants would have been very cautious in their actions, especially if they had actually been committing such crimes. The document is suspiciously vague about the conditions in which the witnesses had observed the activities of the defendants.

From a legal point of view, this case resembles the examples of *saʿi bi'l-fesad* adjudication that we have seen before, since it involves the trial of those who were regarded as "perverse" and "corrupt" within their community. It is curious that the defendants were not made the subject of *saʿi bi'l-fesad* adjudication, which would have made their incrimination much easier. Although there is no way to be sure about the reasons for this situation, the specific nature of the accusation might have played a role in determining the nature of the evidence. The fact that the evidence for the defendants' alleged *kızılbaş* identities—ritualistic ceremonies and their alleged sexual perversity, both of which allegedly took place in the privacy of their homes—could not be corroborated convincingly by the community might have excluded the *saʿi bi'l-fesad* adjudication from being used to convict them. This would have been the case especially if the *kadı* were an unusually suspicious and inquisitory type, as seems to have been true here. The fact that he urged the witnesses to take oaths

among individuals and offer suggestions about how to resolve these disputes. See Cemal Şener, *Alevi Törenleri* (Istanbul: Anadolu Matbaası, 1991), p. 44.

[50] See Baki Öz, *Aleviliğe Iftiralara Cevaplar* (Istanbul: Can Yayınları, 1996); Hıdır Yıldırım, *Alevi Din ve Ahlak Kültürü* (Istanbul: Yıldırım Yayıncılık, 1999); Tarık Mümtaz Sözengil, *Tarih Boyunca Alevilik* (Istanbul: Çözüm Yayıncılık, 1991).

to demonstrate the trustworthiness of their testimonies, not a common practice in this period, suggests that he was suspicious of the accuracy of the accusations.[51]

Yet, despite the *kadı*'s skepticism and the unavailability of *sa'i bi'l-fesad* adjudication as a short-cut, the opponents of the defendants successfully carried out their accusations in judicial terms. After all, there were four eyewitnesses to the acts of illicit intercourse as well as the defendants' *kızılbaş* affiliations, and this was adequate to obtain a verdict against the defendants. The fact that the defendants could not secure support from any inhabitants of their own village, although some of the accusations were obviously unfounded, proves that the community had already abandoned them. In other words, the adjudication process only formalized what had already been decided among the members of the community.

Conclusion

In 1064/1654 two individuals from the neighborhood of Alaca Mescid summoned one Hüseyin to court and alleged that he had previously fled to Çankırı from a military campaign. Since then, he had been secretly entering houses in different neighborhoods and stealing the property of the townspeople. Hüseyin denied these claims, and then the court asked the plaintiffs to substantiate their accusations. The plaintiffs presented two witnesses to the court who confirmed the validity of the charges. They also added that they found Hüseyin "in his bed naked" (*Hüseyin döşeğinde donsız bulunmağın*) when they went to his house to take him to the court. The witnesses also claimed that the defendant had confessed in their presence that he was a thief and a murderer.

Afterwards, three inhabitants of the village of Alagediz also testified and claimed that Hüseyin was a thief, a highway robber, and a fomenter of corruption who should be put to silence [killed]" (*Hüseyin sarik, ve kutta'-i tarik* [sic] *ve sa'i bi'l-fesad ve aramesi lazımdır deyu . . .*). Subsequently, another witness from Çankırı stated that Hüseyin was a

[51] According to what I observe in the Çankırı and Kastamonu court records, witness testimonies were never subjected to verification through oath-taking, although the *kadı* usually made a separate investigation regarding the reputation and trustworthiness of the witnesses.

thief, a fomenter of corruption, and a *kızılbaş*. Finally, the majority (*cemm-i gafir ve cemʿi kesir*) of the notables of Çankırı (*aʿyan-ı vilayet*) testified that the defendant was a highway robber, a thief, a fomenter of corruption, and a follower of ʿAli, and for these reasons he should be put to silence. According to the record of the case, the court sentenced Hüseyin to death.[52]

This case provides an impressive demonstration of the litigation strategies discussed in the second part of this chapter. The case is in fact unique in the sense that we observe all these schemes being utilized in combination with each other. According to this entry, Hüseyin was accused of being a deserter, a thief, a murderer, a fomenter of corruption, a highway robber, and a *kızılbaş*. The claim that he was found naked in his bed is an important detail that also raised suspicions about Hüseyin's illicit or inappropriate sexual activities and further demonstrated his immoral character. These accusations were legally "established" in the court *both* by witnesses who reported the accuracy of specific allegations against the defendant *and* by the community's negative assessment of Hüseyin's character and deeds. Apparently, Hüseyin was not well liked in Çankırı; any one of these accusations, regardless of whether it was confirmed directly by witness testimonies or indirectly by communal hearsay, would have been sufficient to have him executed. The people of Çankırı seem to have done their best and taken extra measures to get rid of him for good.

On the other hand, the account of Hüseyin's trial also demonstrates more explicitly than previous examples the strong connection between the will of the community and the judicial process. Indeed, the statement made by the members of the community regarding the necessity of his execution ("he should be put to silence") is something we rarely observe in other entries, where the *kadi*'s role as adjudicator and the witnesses' role as informers remain quite separate from each other. Usually, the role of the witnesses was limited to confirming or refuting the claims of the litigants. In Hüseyin's case, however, the *kadı*, by allowing the community to interfere with his realm of authority—and sanctioning their voices by recording them in the register—seems to have accepted their lead and acknowledged the prominence of their will as clearly as possible.[53]

---

[52] ÇCR, vol. 1, 46–72.

[53] I have located only four other examples in which such explicit statements

This finding confirms my suspicions about the nature of the relationship between the provincial court and the local community. It seems clear that the community was able to use the courts against individuals considered evil, harmful, or immoral. The legal system provided them with the means to do so: *Saʿi bi'l-fesad* adjudication and the ability of the community to organize and submit both the plaintiffs and witnesses among its members made legal manipulation relatively easy.

For individual litigants, the ability to control the court and influence its decisions was clearly more limited. The courts were expected to operate in a more neutral way—or, at least, to project that image—in civil cases between individuals than in the litigation of communal matters; that is why we do not observe any easing of the evidentiary standards in such cases. Yet, individual litigants did not completely lack the means or knowledge to have an effect on the processes of litigation. This chapter has demonstrated that these parties were competent enough to execute a variety of litigation strategies successfully in the courts of Çankırı and Kastamonu. I have also suggested that the nature of these strategies may have varied according to the litigants who implemented them. *Fetva*, for example, was a particularly popular device among the villagers against holders of military and religious titles. This observation confirms the claim made in chapter six that despite the tendency of the court decisions to reflect the socio-economic balance of power, weaker parties were not altogether helpless in terms of influencing the court processes.

regarding the appropriate legal decision can be "heard" from the witnesses. However, none of these four disputes is criminal in nature. See KCR, vol. 3, 109–4; KCR, vol. 35, 55–85; KCR, vol. 38, 37–43 and 125–197.

CHAPTER NINE

ALTERNATIVE SITES FOR DISPUTE RESOLUTION

From the perspective of the inhabitants of Çankırı and Kastamonu, there were a variety of reasons to avoid the court for dispute resolution. It is probable that the costs of litigation and discrimination against poorer, weaker, and less influential litigants discouraged some inhabitants of Çankırı and Kastamonu from bringing their disputes to the local courts. In addition, the existence of alternative sites for dispute resolution may have further discouraged interaction with the courts whenever possible. In this chapter I will present my observations on these sites and examine their impact on the operations of the courts.

The subject of alternative sites for dispute resolution is one of the least studied topics in Ottoman legal history. This is hardly surprising since we have few primary sources that demonstrate how disputes were resolved when they were settled outside the courtroom. Ironically, we learn most about these sites from the court records, which illustrates the fact that there was some degree of interaction between the courts and other venues at the local level. Although this interaction may have complicated the dispute resolution process, it seems that some litigants were especially skilled in employing judicial and extra-judicial mechanisms of dispute resolution simultaneously—and in combination with each other—to obtain favorable outcomes.

Official Alternatives to Local Courts

Attempts to Involve Imperial and Provincial Centers in Local Disputes

The inhabitants of Çankırı and Kastamonu were not hesitant about sending complaints to the centers of imperial and provincial government, which indicates that local courts were not considered to be the sole arenas for dispute resolution. Indeed, as the court records demonstrate, what seem to be some of the most straightforward and uncontroversial judicial issues were occasionally taken to the central government or provincial headquarters in Kütahya for resolution. For example, in 1144/1731, the court of Çankırı was ordered by the government to hear and resolve a dispute pertaining to a marriage between a "virgin of legal age" (*bikr-i baliğa*), Ayşe, and her fiancé Mustafa. According to what Mustafa reported to Istanbul, her father had previously promised her hand to him while she had been still under legal age. However, the father had died before the wedding, and the girl, now of legal age, was refusing to marry Mustafa under the influence of her grandfather and foster father.[1] We do not know how the court resolved this case, but given what we know about Ottoman law, we can assume that the court must have ruled in favor of Ayşe.[2] What makes this relatively uncomplicated case interesting for us is Mustafa's decision to take it to the central government instead of the local court.

In another imperial order, the government demanded that the local authorities as well as the *kadı* of Çankırı hear and resolve a dispute between a certain Ali and a Sarı Hüseyin. According to what was stated in the imperial order, Ali had appealed to Istanbul and claimed that Sarı Hüseyin had stolen his belongings while passing through his village.[3] Again it is not clear why Ali chose to appeal to the central government rather than the local court. Nor do we know how this dispute was resolved in the court of Çankırı. Nevertheless, this example, like the previous one, indicates that for many people, local court was not the only option to resolve their contentions.

Most of the examples that are found in the *sicil*s of Çankırı and Kastamonu were re-directed to the local courts for resolution. Yet this does not necessarily indicate that no contentions were resolved in the center. After all, we may assume that litigants who sent petitions to the government and reported their disputes would not have done so if they knew that their petitions would be returned to the local courts. And even when the central government did re-direct these cases back to the local courts for resolution, it frequently sent its agents to supervise the proceedings. Since the presence of these

[1] See ÇCR, vol. 8, 115–197; also see ÇCR, vol. 9, 18–27 for a similar example.
[2] See Akgündüz, *Mukayeseli İslam ve Osmanlı*, pp. 156–163.
[3] See ÇCR, vol. 11, 54–85 and 54–86.

agents must have affected the judicial process and modified the power balance in the court, it may have satisfied the petitioners.

Military-Administrative Authorities as Partners to and Rivals of Provincial Courts

We know that military-administrative authorities played important roles in judicial processes. Certain cases were heard by the governor in his own palace while the *kadı* and some other members of the court were also present. In the case of Çankırı, the accounts of these hearings indicate that these were almost always criminal cases and usually involved rape or attempted rape. Consider the following entry:

> A beardless youth (*şabb-ı emred*) by the name of Mustafa bin Elhac Mehmed from the neighborhood of Hoca Elvan in the town of Kengiri came to the noble court and sued Mustafa bin Mehmed, Hasan bin Mahmud Kethüda, and İbrahim bin Solak Ali from the neighborhood of Alaca Mescid and Ahmed bin Ahmed from the aforementioned Hoca Elvan, claiming that: "On the night of the thirteenth day of Rebiʿülahir, I left my house to check on our horse in the village of Balınedik (?). On the way, the defendants—who are currently present in the court—and the stepbrother of the aforementioned İbrahim, Ahmed—who is currently absent—caught me in the vicinity of the village of Aynaç. They beat me up, and each and every one of them raped me. I demand that the defendants be interrogated and what is required according to the holy law be executed." When questioned, the aforementioned Mustafa, Hasan, İbrahim, and Ahmed all confessed that they went after and caught the plaintiff at the time and the place that he mentioned. Subsequently, Mustafa acknowledged that he was the first to rape the plaintiff. Then Hasan, İbrahim, and Ahmed all confirmed that they too had raped him. Afterwards all four of them stated three times in the noble court that the other Ahmed, who was absent at the time of the legal proceeding, also had raped the plaintiff.
>
> Next, the defendants were taken to the court that was set up in the presence of the governor of Kengiri, his excellency Can Arslan Paşazade Hüseyin Paşa, with the participation of the religious scholars (*ʿulemaʾ*), the righteous people (*sulehaʾ*), the notables of the sub-province, and other impartial Muslims. Here, the plaintiff re-stated his accusations and the defendants confessed once again without being subjected to any external pressure or coercion. Subsequently, the plaintiff presented a legal opinion (*fetva*) from the jurisconsult (*müfti*) of Kengiri in which it was stated that it is legally legitimate to execute Zeyd, if he rapes a minor, Amr, and it is also demonstrated that Zeyd is a "fomenter of corruption" (*saʿi biʾl fesad*). Then the plaintiff Mustafa asked the

> court to investigate the reputation of the defendants from those who knew them well, and administer the punishment that corresponds to their crimes. Prayer leader (*imam*) Abdullah Halife, Hacı Musa bin Hacı Musa, etc. [more than twenty names, some from the neighborhood of Alaca Mescid and some from the notables of Çankırı] all testified in the court that sodomy (*livata*) is a common habit (*ʿadet-i müstemirreleri*) of the defendants. The court has decided to execute the punishment stated in the *fetva*.[4]

This example, like many others in the *sicil*s of Çankırı and Kastamonu, demonstrates that the governor (or the sub-governor) could participate in the process of adjudication, although, unfortunately, none of these documents discloses any information regarding the exact role they played in the court. Secondary sources indicate that it was a responsibility of the high military-administrative authorities to supervise criminal cases in the provinces.[5] Nevertheless, the variety of cases heard in the palace of the governor or the sub-governor was definitely not limited to criminal disputes in Kastamonu, as was the situation in Çankırı. In addition to cases of rape, murder, and robbery, the governor or the lieutenant governor of Kastamonu also heard disputes over inheritance, property, debt, and land usage.[6]

---

[4] ÇCR, vol. 6, 142–242, entry of 14 Rebiʿülahir 1125/10 May 1713.

[5] İsmail Hakkı Uzunçarşılı describes some situations in which the provincial governor shared some judicial authority with the *kadı*, especially in criminal cases. He claims that the governor had the right to review the legal decisions of the *kadı* before the execution of the punishment, which remained strictly within the boundaries of his authority; see his, *İlmiye Teşkilatı*, p. 110; Although Uzunçarşılı cites no source for this statement, Mouradgea D'Ohsson, who was among the most knowledgeable and perceptive non-Ottoman observers of Ottoman justice, makes a similar statement in his eighteenth-century account: "Les jugements qui condamnent à la mort ou à de moindres peines afflictives, peuvent être revus par des agents de la force publique, notamment par les Gouverneurs de province. Cet examen se fait légèrement, et il arrive qu'en considération de quelque circonstance atténuante, la peine capitale est commuée en celle des travaux forcés ou d'un simple emprisonnement. Mais ces fonctionaires agissent quelquefois en sens inverse; s'ils estiment que la sentence n'est pas assez rigoureuse, ils l'aggravent de leur chef." See D'Ohsson, vol. 6, p. 209. Also see, Heyd, *Studies*, pp. 220–221.

[6] The legal compilation (*kanunname*) prepared by Abdurrahman Paşa (1087/1676–7) indicates that "the governors (*sancakbeyleri*) are obliged to hear legal cases (*sancaklarında daʿva dinleyüp*) and execute the orders of the sharia." Interestingly, this source does not even attempt to make any distinctions between the types of cases that could be heard by the governors and the *kadı*s. Abdurrahman Paşa describes the duties of the *kadı* as the execution of the orders of sharia as interpreted by the leading imams of the Hanefi school, recording entries and contacts in the *sicil*, dividing estates between heirs, protecting the property of orphans and absentees, appointing or dismissing legal guardians, etc. See "Tevkiʿi Abdurrahman Paşa Kanunnamesi," p. 528.

In addition to the cases of judicial cooperation, the court records also indicate that some individuals preferred to take their complaints and disputes to the governor and other military officials in their vicinity rather than to the court, who heard and resolved these cases independently.[7] These authorities collected fines from the "guilty" parties and jailed them for considerable periods of time without having to establish their guilt in the court; in at least one such case, the punishment was not compatible with recognized legal procedures.[8] Not surprisingly, the tendency of the governor and other members of the military to administer justice independently generated some rivalry.[9] The following example is from Kastamonu *sicil*s:

> A Seyyid Hasan Çelebi bin Ahmed from the village of Ancugez (?) in the district of Devrekani came to the noble court and claimed the following in the presence of Salih Beşe bin Halil from the village of Çıtak: "Two years ago I threatened to have the plaintiff reprimanded [in the court] (. . . *muʾahaze etdirdeyüm deyu tehdid etdiğimde* . . .) because he had been cutting trees on my mountain, which is located in the vicinity of my village. In response, he went to the lieutenant governor of Kastamonu and complained against me falsely. Subsequently, the lieutenant governor sent one of his agents to my village; he jailed me, put me in chains, tormented (. . . *taʿciz* . . .) me for three days, and seized my sixty *guruş* unjustly. He did all of these things without any ruling by the court. Now I demand these sixty *guruş* back from Salih Beşe in conformity with the noble *fetva* that I have acquired. I request that the aforementioned Salih Beşe be interrogated and the money be returned to me."[10]

Salih Beşe subsequently confirmed the validity of Seyyid Hasan Çelebi's claims and was ordered by the court to return the money that had been extracted from him.

---

[7] See for example KCR, vol. 5, 139–299 and 143–306; KCR, vol. 36, 39–65; KCR, vol. 38, 85–134, and KCR, vol. 39, 13–16.

[8] See, for example, KCR, vol. 37, 47–153. The governor of Kastamonu sent an agent (*mübaşir*) to a village to bring someone to his presence in relation to a financial dispute that had been previously brought to him, but the villager was able to escape from being taken to Kastamonu by paying a substantial fine (115 *guruş*) to the agent on the spot.

[9] See, for example, CA 4733, which contains the response of the government to a petition of the *kadı* of Kayseri. It was made clear in this order that "the military administrators should not interfere with the issues of imprisonment and release [from prisons] since such decisions [are supposed to] belong to the *kadı*s." Dated Muharrem 1195/January 1781.

[10] KCR, vol. 39, 13–16, entry of 23 Safer, 1154/10 March 1741.

This document is interesting for various reasons. On the one hand, it indicates once again that the military-administrative authorities had a tendency to interfere in local cases and enforce fines and punishments independently of the courts. On the other hand, it also demonstrates that the lieutenant governor and the local court were indeed considered alternate sites for dispute resolution. When Hasan Çelebi threatened to take his opponent to the court, the latter responded by seeking the intervention of the lieutenant governor.[11] It is also noteworthy that in his statement Hasan Çelebi described the actions of the agent as being unjust since the court had not ordained them.

The document does not indicate who collected the sixty *guruş* belonging to Seyyid Hasan Çelebi. The fact that this amount was claimed from Salih Beşe does not indicate that it had been transferred to him by the agent of the lieutenant governor, but it might demonstrate the incapacity of the court to force the military authorities or their agents to return what had been forcibly and illegally taken by them. Money could in fact be the reason the lieutenant governor had chosen to interfere with and "settle" the dispute himself. On the other hand, the fact that the complaint against Salih Beşe and the lieutenant governor was brought to the court two years after the incident may also be indicative of the influence of military authorities. It was only after the appointment of a new lieutenant governor that Seyyid Hasan Çelebi dared to take his complaint to the court.

In another example, the legal agent of İne bint Şaban sued Menend bint Hasan in the court.[12] According to the statement of İne's representative, there had been a dispute between İne and her brother's wife, Menend, over property inherited from İne's father (Menend's father-in-law), Şaban, and İne's brother (Menend's husband), Şaban (sic). The representative also stated that this dispute had later been settled amicably "five years prior to the day of the hearing" with the agreement to transfer a barn and a cow from Menend to İne. Later on, the representative claimed, during an inspection (*teftiş*) of Kastamonu by a Paşa—whose identity is unclear in the document—Menend had "threatened and scared" İne with having her "reprimanded by the Paşa" (. . . *seni Paşa'ya mu'ahaze etdirdirum deyu* . . .) and

[11] The fact that Salih Beşe was a member of the military class might have played a role in this decision.

[12] KCR, vol. 5, 143–306, entry of 22 Zilkaʿde 1104/25 July 1693.

had seized the cow from her. The agent demanded that Menend be questioned and the cow be returned to İne. When she was questioned, Menend acknowledged that the cow was in her possession but denied the existence of a previous amicable settlement. Nevertheless, two witnesses subsequently confirmed the accuracy of the representative's claims, and the court ordered Menend to return the cow to İne.

This case is another example of the ways military authorities and the local courts might differ in the administration of justice and how different venues for dispute resolution were used by the litigants to their advantage. The discretion of the Paşa constituted a real alternative to the court, which, at the very least, prolonged the processes of contention. Unfortunately, it is not clear why İne was convinced that Menend would have been able to gain the support of the Paşa, had she tried to do so. Although her case certainly seems very strong in the document, İne agreed to transfer the cow to Menend as a result of the latter's threat. İne probably knew something that we do not find in the document, something that would have played an important role in the decision of the Paşa. It is arguable that this unspecified factor was not of a legal nature since it is not mentioned in the document. In this sense, we may be talking about some sort of personal relationship between Menend and a member of the Paşa's retinue.

The responsibilities of the ranking military-administrative authorities regarding the administration of justice remain unclear, at least theoretically, in the primary and secondary sources. On a different note, however, the responsibilities of certain local functionaries did include the hearing and, if possible, the resolution of cases among the members of the groups they were affiliated with. For example, in warrants given to the commander of the provincial janissaries (sing. *kethüdayeri*), it is clearly stated that he is responsible for hearing and settling "the fights, contentions, and disagreements" among the soldiers under his command according to law.[13] Also, someone

[13] See KCR, vol. 39, 243–244 for an example of such a diploma. In ÇCR, vol. 5, 29–63 and ÇCR, vol. 7, 24–48 (two imperial orders), it is ordered that the governors, lieutenant governors, and even the *kadı*s should not interfere with the legal actions and responsibilities of the *kethüdayeri*s in Çankırı. Apparently, these orders were sent in response to the complaints of the members of local cavalry units in Çankırı.

in Kastamonu with the title "chief of the *ʿulema*" (*reʾis el-ʿulemaʾ*) heard and resolved contentions among members of the *ʿilmiyye* class. This person reportedly had fined and jailed certain members of the *ʿilmiyye*.[14]

Unofficial Sites for Dispute Resolution

More interestingly perhaps, we can infer from the court records that the local community provided independent mechanisms for dispute resolution.[15] There are rare, indirect, but informative traces of these mechanisms in the court records. For example, in 1715 the inhabitants of two villages in Çankırı selected four representatives (two from each village) to meet, discuss, and resolve a tax dispute between these villages. The entry does not indicate how this dispute was resolved, but the fact that these villages were able to resolve their disagreements without any help from legal and military officials is unprecedented in the court records under study and are, therefore, remarkable.[16]

On the other hand, it is probable that unofficial forms of dispute resolution were utilized more frequently in different kinds of disagreements. Consider the following example:

> An Emine bint Davud Halifezade [Mehmed Halife] came to the noble court and stated in the presence of her father, Mehmed Halife: "Although I did not do anything wrong in the service of my father and there was no reason for him to punish me, he beat me severely five days ago in the village of Has. Because I could not withstand this beating, I subsequently went to the house of the village imam, Ali Halife, who is also a relative of ours. He took me to the house of my uncle Mustafa and I stayed there for a few days as a guest. Consequently, certain

[14] KCR, vol. 5, 58–104 and 96–179. See Mehmet Zeki Pakalın, *Osmanlı Tarih Deyimleri Sözlüğü* (Istanbul: Milli Eğitim Basımevi, 1972), vol. 3, p. 27, for the definition of *reʾis ul-ʿulemaʾ*.

[15] There are not many studies on informal mechanisms of dispute resolution in Anatolia. To my knowledge, June Starr's work on patterns of dispute settlement among the inhabitants of Bodrum is the only example of such an orientation thus far; see her *Dispute and Settlement in Rural Turkey: An Ethnography of Law* (Leiden: E.J. Brill, 1978). İsmail Metin's book on the "peoples' courts" among the Alevis of Çamşıh (in Sivas) provides interesting comparisons to Starr's findings, although this work is not an academic study by any standard; see İsmail Metin, *Alevilerde Halk Mahkemeleri* (Istanbul: Alev Yayınevi, 1995). The ritualism and well-ordered routines of dispute resolution among the Alevis contrast markedly with Starr's observations in Bodrum.

[16] ÇCR, vol. 6, 138–230.

> talebearers (*gammazlar*) began to make up false stories and even alleged to the lieutenant governor that I had run away from my father's house. As a result, the lieutenant governor sent his adjutant (*subaşısını*)[17] to investigate these allegations. Now I request from the court that my reputation (*keyfiyet-i ahvalim*) be investigated among those who know me and that my father be counseled not to beat me without any reason." When the aforementioned Mehmed Halife was questioned about the situation, he confirmed the statement of the aforementioned Emine as follows: "I do not have anybody to attend to my needs other than my daughter, the aforementioned Emine. After I had beaten her because of a fault in her service, she went to the house of Imam Ali Halife, who subsequently took her to her uncle's house. She stayed there for a few days."
>
> When the reputation of the aforementioned Emine was investigated among those who knew her, the aforementioned Imam Ali Halife bin Mustafa and Mehmed bin Mustafa and [seven other names] all stated in the court that "the aforementioned Emine is a respectable and virtuous girl, and she never associates with those people with whom she is prohibited to associate. She went to her uncle's house and stayed there for a few days because she could not stand her father's beatings. Nevertheless, certain malicious people (*ashab-ı ʿağraz*) falsely alleged that she had run away from her father's house, and the lieutenant governor sent his agent to inquire about the claims. She is a good girl, and she did not run away from her father's house." As a result of this statement, the court counseled the aforementioned Mehmed Ağa not to beat his daughter without any legitimate reason.[18]

There are many interesting points in this document. First, the statements of Emine, Imam Ali Halife, and other members of the community indicate that the incident was never meant to be taken to the court or brought to the attention of the lieutenant governor. Instead, they tried to resolve it among themselves.[19] The fact that

[17] It is interesting that the text identifies the *subaşı* as an officer under the command of the lieutenant governor. According to Heyd and Jennings, the term *subaşı* refers to the chief of the local police force, who worked under the direct command of the *kadı*. See Heyd, *Studies*, p. 339, and Jennings, "*Kadı*, Court, and Legal Procedure," pp. 149–150.

[18] KCR, vol. 34, 57–95, entry of 8 CII 1148/26 October 1735.

[19] Unfortunately, our knowledge on communal mechanisms of dispute resolution in pre-modern Ottoman Anatolia is limited. Luckily, however, there are increasing numbers of anthropological studies on potentially relevant topics. For example, Susan Hirsch shows in her study on marital disputes among the Muslims of modern Kenya that before a conflict is taken to the court of the *kadı*, resolution is attempted in the communal arena. She argues that if the spouses themselves cannot solve a marital conflict, they take their problems first to family elders. If the family elders fail to resolve the conflict, couples go to people whose skills in dispute resolution are

we do not find many such disputes among kin in the court records indicates that they were usually resolved outside the court.[20]

The role of Imam Ali Halife is critical in this context. After the beating, it was to his house that Emine went and it was he who took steps to resolve the problem between the girl and her father. The choice of taking the girl to her uncle's house instead of sending her back to her father was no doubt intended to protect the girl from her father's anger without hurting her reputation, and to give the father time to calm down. In this sense, the imam tried to contain the crisis and played perhaps the most important role in the process of dispute management.[21]

In their statements, Emine, Imam Ahmed Halife, and other participants in the hearing sound upset about the fact that this incident was brought to the attention of the lieutenant governor and the court. The arrival of the lieutenant governor's agent in the village may have generated some concern among the villagers because they—at the very least—had to feed and accommodate him for the duration of the legal process. Perhaps more important, by misrepresenting Emine's actions and character, "people of malice" and "talebearers" changed the forum in which a dispute between the family members would have to be handled. These people interfered with the

---

recognized in the community. Hirsch claims that Muslim women in Kenya are especially likely to relate their domestic problems to practitioners of spiritual medicine. Men, on the other hand, are more likely to turn to local religious leaders such as imams. It is only when disputes cannot be resolved in these platforms that people take them to the court. See Hirsch, *Pronouncing and Persevering*, pp. 92–93.

[20] Judith Tucker agrees that a variety of marital and family-related disputes were not resolved in legal venues. For example, she claims that spousal violence was not considered a legal issue among the prominent jurists of the seventeenth and eighteenth centuries. Furthermore she argues that the court of eighteenth-century Damascus "was not the venue for the trial of fornication (*zina'*) or other sexual offenses;" they were handled by families. Although what Tucker argues about the handling of sexual crimes in Damascus is not necessarily valid for Çankırı and Kastamonu, the distinction that she implicitly makes between judicial and non-judicial sites for dispute resolution is a valid one. See Judith Tucker, *In the House of the Law; Gender and Islamic Law in Ottoman Syria and Palestine* (Berkeley: University of California Press, 1998), p. 65 and pp. 175–176.

[21] It is not surprising to find individuals who were knowledgeable in religious and legal matters playing important roles in the processes of dispute resolution. Indeed there is evidence that certain influential people with considerable religious and legal learning could overshadow the *kadı* in a particular locality. For example, in CZ 756, we find a petition against the jurisconsult (*müfti*) of Beyşehri, who was accused of "establishing an [alternative] court and resolving disputes among the inhabitants of the district." Dated Receb 1197/June 1783.

community's conflict resolution mechanisms and undermined the unofficial influence and authority of the village notables.

The relationship that Imam Ahmed Halife and other witnesses established between Emine's character and the appropriate platform of resolution is noteworthy. Because Emine was a "respectable and virtuous girl," it was only proper that her case be handled outside the courtroom. In this sense, the court constituted a site only for those people who were known to have "evil characters." I believe it is for this reason that there is only one marital dispute in the twenty-five volumes of the court records examined for this study.[22]

In 1102/1691, a Halime bint Elhac Mehmed came to the court of Kastamonu and complained about the beatings by her husband, Hüseyin bin Mehmed. She asked the court to question her husband, investigate his reputation, and order him to stop torturing her. When questioned, Hüseyin acknowledged his beatings. Then the court investigated Hüseyin's reputation among those who knew him well. Witnesses testified in court that "the aforementioned Hüseyin severely beats, abuses, and torments the aforementioned Halime. He is a troublemaker and never minds his own business (. . . *kendi halinde değildir* . . .). We, as the inhabitants of his neighborhood, do not accept any responsibility for his actions and do not stand in surety for him. Also, he deceitfully claims that he is a janissary." The court forced Hüseyin to publicly declare that he was not a janissary and warned him to treat his wife well.[23]

Here again, in a type of dispute that was usually resolved outside the courtroom, the character of the defendant and his reputation among the members of the community was critical for the court process. It is conceivable that Halime had previously sought the assistance of certain influential members of the community to protect herself from the beatings and to convince Hüseyin to treat her better—something that we saw Emine doing in the previous example. If so, then Hüseyin's unwillingness to respond to mediation by members of the community or their refusal to interfere by mediating between Halime and Hüseyin would explain the appearance of this case in the Kastamonu court records.

[22] Here I am excluding property-related and monetary disputes between spouses, as well as disagreements pertaining to the terms of the marriage contracts.

[23] KCR, vol. 4, 10–30.

We learn from İsmail Metin that among the Alevis of Çamşıh, such a refusal to mediate indicates the guilty party's alienation from the community.[24] The statement that the witnesses would not accept any responsibility for the defendant's actions and stand surety for his character suggests that Hüseyin was indeed ostracized. And since he was not considered to be a true member of the community, he and his wife could not benefit from the communal mechanisms for dispute resolution, although these mechanisms probably constituted the usual means for the resolution of marital and familial conflicts.

Of course, communal mechanisms for dispute resolution were not limited to marital and familial disputes. In fact, they occasionally determined the outcomes of disputes that had more serious legal ramifications than conflicts between husbands and wives. Take the case between Emine and "Kara Yılan" Mehmed:

> The court of law (*meclis-i şer'i*) was assembled in the exalted council (*meclis-i 'ali*) of the governor of Kastamonu, his excellency Ahmed Paşa, and heard the complaint of Emine bint Himmet from the neighborhood of Halife in Kastamonu. The aforementioned Emine claimed in the presence of Mehmed bin Receb, who is also known as Kara Yılan ["black snake" in Turkish], from the town of Zile, that "Bolükbaşı[25] [Delikarı oğlu] Hacı Mehmed had sent my husband, Nasuh bin Mehmed, to the village of Bayındır to collect the tax of *sürsat* for him seven days ago. When the aforementioned Nasuh reached the village, he decided to spend the night in the room of a Şaban bin Mustafa, the steward (*kethüda*) of the village. During the same night the aforementioned Mehmed stabbed the aforementioned Nasuh with a knife and wounded him. The aforementioned Nasuh died five days after he returned to his house. I demand that the defendant be interrogated and what is required according to the holy law be executed." When the aforementioned Mehmed was questioned, he claimed that "I had earlier arrived at the house of Şaban to get some straw. It was late and I decided to spend the night there. When I was sleeping, the

[24] Metin implies that "trial" by the members of the community (called *görgü cem'i* among the Alevis) and punishment of the guilty parties have therapeutic purposes. Once the guilty parties "pay their debts" to the community by willingly participating in a communal "trial," accepting the punishment decided there, and fulfilling the conditions of this punishment, they rehabilitate their relationship with the community; they become "as pure as a new-born baby." On the other hand, if the community refuses to try and punish them, or to help them to resolve their contentions with their opponents through mediation, a chance for rehabilitation is denied to them. In such situations, the guilty parties have no option other than leaving their villages or neighborhoods. See Metin, pp. 219–231 and *passim*.

[25] An officer commanding a unit of janissaries.

> aforementioned attacked me with the intention of rape. I could only save myself by stabbing him twice." The confession of the defendant was recorded in the *sicil*.[26]

Two days after this initial hearing, Emine re-appeared in front of the court and claimed that bandits had killed her husband on his way from the village of Bayındır to Kastamonu, and that no one else was responsible for his death.[27]

Emine's earlier claim that Mehmed had confessed his responsibility for the death of Nasuh during the first hearing suggests that Emine's statement in the second hearing is deceptive. And the fact that Emine retracted her earlier allegations in the second hearing to absolve all the third parties—other than the two anonymous bandits—of responsibility for Nasuh's death suggests there was some kind of agreement between the litigants after the first hearing.[28] The fact that Mehmed had been trying to protect himself and his honor when he stabbed Nasuh must have played an important role in this process. It is plausible that there was considerable social pressure on Emine to withdraw her allegations and probably shift the dispute from the public arena of the court to the private arena of communal mediation. Unfortunately we have no way of knowing what happened on this new level.

We cannot be certain that the *kadı* or other members of the court did not play a role in what happened in the second hearing. As we have seen previously, the *kadı* exercised influence on the litigants to persuade them to accept various resolutions. On the other hand, if the *kadı* wanted to help Mehmed, he could have easily done so by acquitting him without forcing Emine to change her statement, since

---

[26] KCR, vol. 3, 134–69 entry of 2 Safer 1096/8 January 1685.

[27] KCR, vol. 3, 136–76. According to her statement in the second hearing, Nasuh had cried for help after the bandits had stabbed him. Reportedly, the steward of the village of Bayındır had heard his cries and taken him to his house where he had stayed for two nights before he was taken to his own house in Kastamonu. This story fits quite well with specific factual details of the incident as presented in the first hearing. In the first hearing Emine claimed that the stabbing happened in the house of the steward and that Nasuh stayed there for some time before leaving for his house. In the second hearing Emine was conceivably trying to explain a well-known factual detail—Nasuh's presence in the house of the village steward after the stabbing—without holding anybody, including the steward, responsible for the death of her husband.

[28] Emine also stated that the bandits had attacked her husband while he was on his way to Kastamonu. This is an important detail because as the attack took place on a public road no one could be held legally responsible for it.

Mehmed was merely protecting himself from Nasuh. For this reason, the removal of this case from the court (presumably to communal arenas of dispute resolution) was probably the result of a communal and non-judicial decision-making process.[29]

Ambiguous Settlements

The interaction between judicial and non-judicial realms of dispute resolution is demonstrated more explicitly in accounts of what may be called "ambiguous amicable settlements." This term refers to settlements enacted by opposing parties (with the intervention of the mediators) *after* a dispute was brought to the court and resolved in favor of a particular party. Consider the following examples:

Case 1

Sometime during the first ten days of Rebiʿülevvel 1092 (end of March, 1681), a virgin of legal age, Emine, claimed in the court that the trustee (*mütevelli*) of the cash endowment (*vakıf*) that covered the *ʿavarız* expenses of the Hoca Elvan neighborhood, Molla Mehmed bin Mustafa, had sold a house belonging to her father, İsmail, to a man named İskender after İsmail's death fifteen years ago. Emine claimed that she should have inherited that house and asked the court to enforce what was legally necessary. In response, Molla Mehmed claimed that the late İsmail had owed thirty *guruş* to the endowment, and he, as the trustee of the endowment, had to seize the house legally after his death and sell it to İskender to reclaim this amount for the endowment. He demonstrated the validity of this statement with the help of two witnesses who confirmed what he had said in the court, verbatim.[30]

Thus, the trustee seems to have legally established his innocence since neither the plaintiff nor the *kadı* challenged the testimonies of his witnesses. Yet, an entry on the following page indicates that the dispute continued even though it had been legally resolved in the court. According to this second entry, which bears the same date as

---

[29] See KCR, vol. 4, 18–52, for another example of the plaintiff's withdrawal (*feragat*) from a murder trial. No reasons are given in the document regarding the reasons for the plaintiff's withdrawal from the trial.

[30] ÇCR, vol. 3, 37–51.

the previous one, the parties came to the court once again and declared that they had decided to settle the case amicably in return for a payment of four *guruş* to Emine, the plaintiff, by İskender, the new owner of the house.[31]

Case 2

In a registry dated February 17th, 1737 (16 Şevval 1149), a brother of Ömer bin Ali from Kütahya made the following statement in the presence of Ahmed Ağa bin Osman and his servant Mustafa from Çankırı:

> Six months ago, Ahmed Ağa and his servant Mustafa assaulted my brother with a sword and injured him in a location called Tacirler, close to the district of Haymana. My brother died because of this injury ten days after the incident. When I took the case to the court, the aforementioned Ahmed Ağa and Mustafa denied my accusations. I was unable to substantiate my claims in the court and subsequently there emerged a great deal of quarreling and serious hostility (*münaza-ʿat-ı kesire ve muhasamat-ı kebire*) between the defendants and me. Then reconcilers and believers (*muslihun ve Müslimun*) intervened and encouraged us to settle the dispute amicably. I have been given a Qurʾan, a sword, a horse, and ten *guruş* as the price of the settlement and accepted the settlement that acknowledged (or "that is based on") the denial of the defendants (*ʿan inkar inşaʾ-yı ʿakd-ı sulh*).[32]

In both of the examples above, the dispute resolution did not come to an end at the completion of the court process. And although the plaintiffs were not able to substantiate their accusations in the court, they were able to obtain more favorable outcomes, presumably through informal channels. We do not have much information about the desire to resettle disputes that had already been heard in the court.[33] A statistical analysis of such ambiguous settlements may be instructive in defining the limits of the court's role in the processes of dispute resolution.

---

[31] ÇCR, vol. 3, 38–53.

[32] ÇCR, vol. 11, 51–80. One interesting detail in this example is revealing about the objectives of these kinds of settlements. As is stated in the entry, the settlement did not imply that the defendants were guilty or that they were willing to pay the price of settlement as compensation. Rather, the agreement explicitly acknowledges the innocence of the defendants, and the amount paid by them probably served the function of reconciliation.

[33] The only scholar who recognizes the existence of such a practice is Uriel Heyd. Yet his discussion of it is extremely brief (six lines) and limited to criminal disputes.

In the twenty-five volumes of Çankırı and Kastamonu court records that I studied, there are 140 amicable settlement entries; 23 of these could be considered ambiguous settlements. According to my calculations, 93 of the 140 amicable settlements (67 per cent) were enacted between people of similar social and economic status as well as similar places of residence.[34] On the other hand, 16 of the 23 ambiguous settlements (70 per cent) were enacted between people of different social and economic standing. More interestingly perhaps, in 12 of these 16 settlements (75 per cent), the court had previously decided in favor of the more prominent parties.[35] This finding suggests that informal communal mechanisms for dispute resolution were oriented towards correcting biases in the legal system that favored the rich, the influential, and the prominent. In other words, when court decisions did not appease the disputants and satisfy public expectations of justice, communal mediation might force the triumphant parties to make certain concessions. The examples of ambiguous settlements indicate that the court process was only one step in the dispute resolution process in Çankırı and Kastamonu.[36]

"Going to Court" as a Phase of Dispute Resolution

The existence of alternative settings for dispute resolution must have allowed litigants to develop creative strategies to obtain favorable results. For example, on specific occasions "going to court" may have

He claims that, "it might happen . . . that a person paid damages even though the plaintiff had been denied by the *sharīʿa*. In this case the accused was probably afraid that he might be tortured to force him to confess or be punished by the secular authorities in accordance with the *kanun* or the Sultan's order." See Heyd, *Studies*, p. 249.

[34] For the purposes of this analysis, I have separated the title-holders (military and religious, regardless of their residential affiliations) and *aʿyan*, townspeople with no titles, and villagers with no titles from each other.

[35] Another major difference between these two sets is observed in the numbers of settlements enacted between relatives. Whereas 57 of the 140 amicable settlements (41 per cent) in the *sicil*s were enacted between close or distant relatives, only 6 of the 23 ambiguous settlements (26 per cent) were enacted among the relatives.

[36] See ÇCR, vol. 5, 2–3; KCR, vol. 3, 118–30; KCR, vol. 5, 110–225, 114–237; KCR, vol. 12, 4b–1 and 10b–2; KCR, vol. 35, 108–163; KCR, vol. 36, 16–23; KCR, vol. 37, 12–5, 28–30, 43–56; KCR, vol. 39, 61–100, 64–106, 70–118, 87–148 for other examples of ambiguous settlements.

been a tactical maneuver rather than a direct means to attain a resolution. In particular circumstances, stronger parties may have been willing to initiate the adjudication process, not to seek legal resolution but to threaten their opponents and to pressure them to make concessions, or to settle their disputes in a particular way.[37] Once the opposing party acknowledged the threat of legal intervention and agreed to modify his or her terms of negotiation, it was not necessary to pursue the legal process further in the court.[38] We find similar strategies in different societies. Philip Huang, for example, argues in the context of Qing China that:

> [the] filing of a plaint intensified the efforts of community or kin mediators for an out-of-court resolution of the dispute. A court summons only increased the pressures, especially when accompanied by some strong comment from the magistrate. A plaintiff or defendant would for good reasons take the magistrate's remarks as a preliminary indication of how a court judgment would go. One or the other might therefore become more conciliatory, thus preparing the way for an informal settlement.[39]

Once again, however, the court documents do not disclose the informal dealings that may have taken place simultaneously with court hearings. We need to keep in mind that these entries were recorded only after the completion of the adjudication process. In other words, the "after-the-fact" quality of the court records omits those disputes that were initially taken to the court but were later pursued to their

[37] This would be very similar to what we saw Menend doing above, when she was threatening her opponent İne with reporting her to the Paşa.

[38] From this perspective, it is even conceivable that ambiguous settlements constituted a second phase of such a process. It seems possible that when the contentions could not initially be resolved through informal, face-to-face resolution techniques, stronger parties took them to legal platforms where they had a greater chance of obtaining favorable legal resolutions. In the third phase of the resolution process, stronger parties used these legal decisions to force their opponents to agree with those conditions that they had objected to at the beginning. It is noteworthy in this context that Işık Tamdoğan-Abel's interpretation of the differences between oral and written contracts in Ottoman legal system supports this hypothesis. Since the written legal documents represent a "failure" of oral agreements, processes of legal resolution should precede direct and (legally) unmediated attempts of reconciliation. See Tamdoğan-Abel, pp. 155–165.

[39] Philip Huang, *Civil Justice in China; Representation and Practice in the Qing* (Stanford: Stanford University Press, 1996), p. 119. Also see Sally E. Merry, "Going to Court: Strategies of Dispute Management in an American Urban Neighborhood," *Law and Society Review*, 13 (1979), pp. 891–926, for similar uses of the court in a radically different social setting.

conclusion in another setting. If litigants abandoned their court cases at any stage during litigation, or a *kadı* refused to hear and adjudicate a dispute, these cases would not be recorded.

Thus litigants must have had plenty of opportunities to withdraw their cases before they were decided in the court. This was so because the *process* of adjudication consisted of numerous stages, which could, and usually did, take days or weeks to conclude.[40] In other words, it is likely that during litigation, opposing parties also explored other avenues for resolution, and when they succeeded in finding one that provided a more satisfactory outcome than the court process, they ended the court process.

Conclusion

According to the court records and other archival documents, litigants did not lack alternatives to local courts for dispute resolution. On the one hand, it seems clear that the inhabitants of Çankırı and Kastamonu frequently took their cases to the central government or the military administrators in their locality instead of the courts. There is also evidence that certain individuals were successful in utilizing the courts and the local military-administrative authorities against each other, as their judgments varied significantly in particular

[40] Once the plaintiff brought his/her case to the court, the *kadı* always ordered the accused to be present during the trial in order to defend himself/herself. This insistence occasionally required the *kadı* to send someone to a distant village to summon the accused and to wait until his/her arrival. In the next stage, the plaintiff repeated his/her claims in the presence of the defendant, and the defendant was asked to respond to the accusations. If he/she denied the claims of the plaintiff without presenting an alternative interpretation of the dispute or without making a counter-accusation against the plaintiff, the plaintiff was ordered to provide evidence for his or her claims. This usually required that the plaintiff find at least two witnesses to support his/her accusations. On the other hand, if the defendant denied the claims of the plaintiff by presenting an alternative version of the dispute, then it was he/she who was supposed to find witnesses. According to the accounts in the court records, the *kadı* gave a certain period to the parties to summon their witnesses to the court. In most cases this period was limited to three days, but it could also be longer, depending on the whereabouts of the witnesses. Also, if any of the parties objected to the accountability of the witnesses for any reason, he/she needed to provide evidence for the credibility of his/her objections, and this further prolonged the adjudication process. Finally, the court had to make its own investigation of the accountability of the witnesses, which probably took considerable time.

cases. The courts and the offices of the local authorities not only constituted alternative sites for dispute resolution, but they also administered alternative, and, therefore, divergent justices.

On the other hand, the community had its own, informal mechanisms of resolution. Although we do not know much about them, the under-representation of certain kinds of disputes in the court records indicates that these mechanisms were used frequently by members of the community, especially to resolve marital disputes (other than those pertaining to money and property). We have also seen that these mechanisms were employed in other kinds of disputes. Indeed, the cases of "ambiguous settlements" demonstrate that there was a significant degree of interaction between the justice of the court and the communal mechanisms of dispute resolution.

Finally, the existence of alternative official and unofficial sites for dispute resolution and the interaction between them appears to have stimulated the creativity of the litigants and enriched their arsenal of resolution strategies.

CHAPTER TEN

IN PLACE OF A CONCLUSION: MODELS AND TAXONOMIES

Since the early 1960s, dispute resolution has been a major topic of interest for many scholars in the field of ethnography. Thanks to the contributions of these ethnographers, we now possess a rich literature that provides alternative depictions of judicial practice and dispute management in different societies. Characteristically, these depictions are oriented towards defining the basic operative principles of such processes and identifying their individual stages. Despite the epistemological problems that haunt many of these studies[1] and the fact that they ignore historical change, we find in them sophisticated analyses of social, political, and legal phenomena. Ethnographic studies of dispute resolution constitute a body of literature that we can learn from and compare our own observations to.

These studies are relevant also because the two models of dispute resolution developed in them correspond to the ways many students of Islamic law characterize operations of the law courts and their ties with the sociopolitical setting. To be sure, the contributions made by Islamic law scholars are not as taxonomically oriented as most ethnographic examinations of dispute resolution are. Indeed, these scholars seem less concerned with producing and/or testing the validity of specific theoretical abstractions. Nor is the correspondence in question intentional: Almost no student of Islamic law has chosen to deal with a particular ethnographic model of dispute resolution in any explicit way. Nevertheless, the connection between the two ethnographic models that will be introduced shortly and the existing depictions of Islamic legal practice is real, and this chapter will explore this link to understand the differences among various approaches to judicial practice within Islamic legal scholarship. Categorical distinctions between the two models of dispute resolution, as articulated

[1] On the problems of ethnographic representation of the "other," see James Clifford, *The Predicament of Culture, Twentieth-Century Ethnography, Literature, and Art* (Cambridge: Harvard University Press, 1986).

over a period of three decades by different ethnographers, will shed light on the inherent disagreements between those depictions of Islamic judicial practice that these models correspond to. Later, and in light of this discussion, I will also attempt to interpret what is known about the Ottoman courts and the ways in which they resolved the disputes brought to them. In particular, I will explore how well the Ottoman judicial practice fit the main characteristics of the ethnographic models of dispute resolution discussed in this chapter.

This chapter shall ignore the temporal and geographical variations among different Ottoman courts for the sake of constructing an interdisciplinary framework that can help us understand the general characteristics of Ottoman judicial practices in a comparative perspective. I have demonstrated in previous chapters that such variations could be significant. Nevertheless, it can be also argued that the courts of Çankırı and Kastamonu were more alike than different in their operations. And although this argument may not have much relevance for those of us who are interested in the "micro-analysis" of Ottoman court processes, it is a necessary one for the purposes of this chapter, which will be dealing with essentially a-historical entities—models and taxonomies.

Court Model versus Bargain Model

In the literature on dispute resolution, researchers have developed two models of conflict management[2] as reference points for their own observations of actual situations. Richard Abel describes the main objective of the first model as the enforcement of the "rule of law," which denotes an orientation toward applying a set of preexisting rules and norms by a third party—the judge—to resolve disputes. The second model, on the other hand, is based on the idea of negotiation between opposing parties as they engage in direct, dyadic contentions with each other.[3] An elaborate description of the

---

[2] Sally Engle Merry calls these "court systems"; see her "Going to Court," pp. 891–926.

[3] Richard Abel, "A Comparative Theory of Dispute Resolutions in Society," *Law and Society Review*, vol. 8 (1974), pp. 217–247. Although the second model is not as rule-oriented as the first one, conforming to certain social and cultural conventions is also critical for its legitimacy; see Phillip Gulliver, *Disputes and Negotiations: A Cross-Cultural Perspective* (New York: Academic Press, 1979), p. 75.

distinctions between these models is presented in Laura Nader's studies on Zapotec dispute resolution methods.[4] With reference to previous studies by Bernard Cohn and Vilhelm Aubert, she calls the first of these models the "Court Model" and the second one the "Bargain Model," and lists the differences between them as follows:

Table 10.1: Models of Conflict Management According to Nader

Court Model	Bargain Model
1. Triadic in nature (adjudication)	1. Dyadic in nature (mediation)
2. Coercive power part of the resolution process	2. Absence of coercive power in the resolution process
3. Application of highly regarded norms and values in the resolution process	3. Pursuit of the interests of the opposing parties
4. Establishment of past facts (guilt)	4. Not necessary to establish past facts
5. Retroactively oriented reasoning	5. Prospectively oriented reasoning
6. Legal experts participate in the resolution process	6. No legal experts in the resolution process
7. Conclusion is a verdict	7. Conclusion is an agreement
8. Purely distributive decisions	8. Distributive/generative decision
9. Either/or decision (zero-sum game: win or lose)	9. Compromise (give a little, get a little)
10. Reaffirmation of previous legal cases	10. No necessary implication concerning validity
11. Affinity to legal scholarship	11. Affinity to utilitarian thinking

Before we proceed, some warnings are in order. First of all, these models are hypothetical, which means that they should not be expected to accurately depict real-life situations in any particular society; in fact, it is often difficult to identify all eleven criteria listed above in actual processes of dispute resolution. Secondly, these models are not designed to signify particular stages of socio-economic development.[5] Finally, the distinction being made here between the two models is not a matter of formal, more institutionalized processes as opposed to informal, weakly institutionalized ones. Indeed, whereas some kinds

[4] Laura Nader, "Styles of Court Procedure: To Make the Balance" in Laura Nader ed., *Law in Culture and Society* (Chicago: Aldine Publishing Company, 1969), pp. 69–91; and her *Harmony Ideology: Justice and Control in a Zapotec Mountain Village* (Stanford: Stanford University Press, 1990), p. 131.

[5] See Laura Nader's "Styles of Court Procedure," pp. 88–89; also see Max Gluckman's *Politics, Law and Ritual in Tribal Society* (Chicago: Aldine Publishing Company, 1965) for an excellent example of the opposite structuralist argument.

of adjudication could take place quite informally, some negotiations occur in a relatively formal manner in accordance with pre-established norms and procedures.[6]

In general terms, the Court Model represents a rule-driven process in which the consequences of a proposed resolution do not necessarily accommodate the interests of the litigants. Accordingly, preserving relationships between opposing parties is not a concern for the adjudicators, and for this reason, resolutions usually involve zero-sum results for the parties. In contrast, the Bargain Model is "utilitarian" in the sense that its goal is to maximize the combined interests of the opposing parties and, therefore, the community. Negotiation and mutual compromise are expected to take place in the process of resolution where third-party mediators are optional. The main concern of such a resolution process is the "restoration of the social relations to a former condition of harmony, where conflict was absent"[7] and "to reestablish a state of balance in the community in which people at least feel they are neither threats to, nor threatened by others."[8] In this context, resolution means reconciliation and involves minimizing the sense of injustice and outrage felt by the parties by bringing out the real causes of the conflict, rather than merely dealing with its judicial consequences. In this sense, the bargain model aims to clean up the "social mess" at the heart of the dispute in order to resolve the conflict rather than focusing strictly on its judicial aspects.[9]

With the exception of Haim Gerber, no scholar of Islamic law (including ethnographers interested in judicial practice) acknowledges ties to the literature that produced these models. Nonetheless, these models approximate two approaches that have been implicitly or explicitly adopted by different scholars to characterize the operations and orientations of the Islamic courts. In what follows, I will present a synopsis of the existing viewpoints on the practice of law and

---

[6] Phillip Gulliver, "Process and Decision," in Phillip H. Gulliver ed. *Cross-Examinations; Essays in Memory of Max Gluckman* (Leiden: E.J. Brill, 1978), p. 37.

[7] Nader, *Harmony Ideology*, p. 121.

[8] Nader, "Styles of Court Procedure," p. 72.

[9] There are no guarantees in this process, and the processes of resolution might not assure social harmony. Indeed, Elizabeth Colson argues that despite the effort to restore good relationships among the disputants, some parties could remain as hostile as ever, and disputes could continue to erupt among them. See Elizabeth Colson, "The Contentiousness of Disputes" in Pat Caplan ed., *Understanding Disputes: The Politics of Argument* (Oxford Providence: Berg Publishers, 1995), pp. 69–70.

forms of dispute resolution in modern and pre-modern Muslim communities and compare my observations in Çankırı and Kastamonu court records and Western accounts of Ottoman justice with these characterizations.

Lawrence Rosen is among the best-known representatives of Geertz's interpretive anthropology in Islamic studies, and his contributions to legal anthropology are based on extensive research in modern-day Morocco. One of Rosen's most relevant findings to this chapter is that, within the reciprocity-oriented, moralistic context of modern Moroccan society, the predominant goal of law is not simply to resolve differences, but to put people back into a position in which they can, with the least adverse implications for the social order, continue to negotiate their own arrangements with one another.[10] Consistent with the premises of the Bargain Model, the resolutions produced by Moroccan courts depend on the types of the disputes, the characters of those involved in the case, the nature of the relationships between the disputants, and local values and traditions. In this sense, justice is nothing more than a "regulated reciprocity" among freely contracting members of the community. And because the conditions of reciprocity depend on the social relations and the cultural and historical contexts in which the disputants are living, administration of justice reflects a relational and contextual character.

If the main function of the court is the regulation of reciprocity among members of the community, as Rosen argues, then mediation and arbitration are the primary means to achieve it. Indeed, Rosen claims that in most cases the role of the judge in Morocco is limited to mediation and arbitration between the litigants,[11] and he is not alone in this characterization. Mohammad Fadel also argues that "[Islamic] courts gain their basic legitimacy from the perception that they are a neutral third party, somewhat akin to a mediator."[12] Fadel observes:

[10] Lawrence Rosen, *The Anthropology of Justice: Law as Culture in Islamic Society* (Cambridge: Cambridge University Press, 1989); idem, *Bargaining for Reality: The Construction of Social Relations in a Muslim Community* (Chicago: University of Chicago Press, 1984).

[11] He even suggests that this situation is characteristic of Islamic legal culture in general. Rosen, *The Anthropology of Justice*, p. 43.

[12] Fadel, p. 60.

> The basic legitimacy of triadic structures of conflict resolution was a result of the belief of both parties to the dispute that the third party, whose help was sought in reaching a solution to the conflict, was neutral and thus, fair. However, this logic of two seeking the help of one to resolve a dispute breaks down precisely at the moment when judgment is rendered. The loser is likely to perceive himself as a victim of two against one. The coercive element inherent in any judgment inevitably threatens the legitimacy of the process. . . . *One of the most important means used to prevent the breakdown of the triad into two against one situation is the use of mediation*. . . . [T]he judge needs to garner the consent of the parties in each step of the proceedings to the furthest possible extent so that it appears that his decision was consensual, emerging as result of the freely given consent of both parties.[13]

Other researchers—especially those whose understandings of judicial practice are based on first-hand observations of actual court processes—have confirmed the validity of these assertions. Scholars like Richard Antoun and Aharon Layish, for example, have found evidence in legal judgments of an "ideological commitment" to reconciliation and compromise. These scholars demonstrate that in modern Jordan and Palestine, the judges tend not to apply the law when the dispute can be settled by agreement between the parties.[14]

How can we characterize "ideological commitments" in the Ottoman courts?[15] Haim Gerber insists that the highly bureaucratized Ottoman

---

[13] Ibid., pp. 56–57. Emphasis added. *Pace* Rosen, Fadel argues that structural—rather than cultural—factors necessitate a judge's mediation. He quotes from Martin Shapiro: "It might once have been argued that the emphasis on mediation in oriental courts was wholly or largely a result of Confucianism or the like, so that the oriental judge as a mediator was a peculiar and culturally determined phenomenon. Structural rather than cultural factors, however, seem to be at the root of the matter. Even where law and courts are accorded a high level of legitimacy, true adversary proceedings culminating in dichotomous verdicts are an optional mode of conflict resolution only for parties who in the future need have no relations or only arm's length relations with one another. For those who must maintain close economic or social relations, proceedings according to prototype of courts are unlikely to be satisfactory." Ibid., pp. 56–57, fn. 50.

[14] See Richard Antoun, "The Islamic Court, the Islamic Judge, and the Accommodation of Traditions: A Jordanian Case Study," *International Journal of Middle East Studies*, vol. 12 (1980), pp. 455–467; idem, "Litigant Strategies in an Islamic Court in Jordan," in Daisy H. Dwyer ed., *Law and Islam in the Middle East* (New York: Bergin & Garvey Publishers, 1990); Aharon Layish, *Women and Islamic Law in a Non-Muslim State* (New Jersey: Transaction Books, 1975). Also see Anna Würth, "A Sanaʿa Court: The Family and the Ability to Negotiate," *Islamic Law and Society*, no. 2, vol. 3 (1995) for the impact of social change on litigation and negotiation patterns in the Islamic court. The term "ideological commitment" is Antoun's.

[15] I am aware that this is a teleological question. Antoun acknowledges that ideo-

state produced a uniform set of adjudicative procedures within its domains.[16] Accordingly, rather than seeking social harmony or regulating reciprocity, the Ottoman *kadı*s were obliged to enforce the regulations that had been sanctioned by the state. Indeed, Gerber maintains that legalistic and rule-driven orientation was an important characteristic of the Ottoman legal system.[17]

Although Gerber may be the most vocal supporter of this line of thinking among those who study Ottoman court records, he is not alone. Arguably, by locating the basis of the courts' judicial operations solely within the judicial frameworks established by the sharia and imperial orders and regulations and, therefore, by implicitly ignoring the extra-judicial ties between the provincial courts and the local community, the majority of the *sicil* scholars—especially Turkish-speaking ones—have contributed to this orientation.[18] In their studies these scholars seem to disregard the possibility that the courts' objectives of maintaining social and neighborly relations in a particular setting and of facilitating the community's political and ideological self-reproduction affected how they resolved judicial contentions. Very much like Gerber, if not as explicitly, they insist on the exclusively legalistic nature of the Ottoman courts.

Admittedly, the contents of the Çankırı and Kastamonu records seem to support this characterization of the courts. Consider the following example:

logical variations among the judges have frequently occurred even within the same district and among members of the same legal school in modern Jordan; see his "The Islamic Court," p. 464. Given the vast geographical boundaries of the Ottoman Empire, its long time-span, and the ethnic and religious plurality of its subjects, it would be naïve to expect such a coherent set of ideological commitments in the courts. This fact, however, should not undermine the relevance of the question itself, and I am interested in the directions this question takes us rather than any simplistic answers to it.

[16] Gerber, *State, Society and Law*, pp. 15–18.

[17] See Richard C. Repp, *The Mufti of Istanbul: A Study in the Development of the Ottoman Learned Hierarchy* (London: Ithaca Press, 1986) and Imber, *Ebu's-Su'ud*, for two complementary accounts of this "rationalization" in the Ottoman legal system. However, Repp's and Imber's conclusions are not derived from the Ottoman court records.

[18] See, most notably, Jennings, "*Kadı*, Court, and Legal Procedure" and "Limitations of the Judicial Powers of Qadi." The leading example of such an orientation among Turkish scholars is Ahmet Akgündüz, *Mukayeseli İslam ve Osmanlı*. Also see Bayındır, op. cit., Kemal Çiçek, and Abdullah Saydam, *Kıbrıs'tan Kafkasya'ya Osmanlı Dünyasında Siyaset, Adalet ve Raiyyet* (Trabzon: Derya Kitabevi, 1998).

In Rebiʿülahir 1097/March 1686, Havva bint Abdullah sued the heirs of the late Derviş, claiming that they were refusing to surrender her share from Derviş's inheritance. She claimed that Derviş was her father, that he had impregnated her mother when she was his concubine (*cariye*). According to Havva's statement, Derviş had publicly announced before his death that he was Havva's father. The heirs denied that Derviş was Havva's father and said that he had not made such a statement publicly. When the court asked Havva to substantiate her allegations, she could not produce any evidence. Consequently, the court decided in favor of the defendants.[19]

In the next entry the same parties continue arguing about a separate but related issue. This time Havva claimed that while she was still a minor, her father's mother (that is, Derviş's mother), Ayşe bint Mehmed, had bequeathed her some jewelry. Havva complained that the defendants refused to transfer this jewelry to her after Ayşe's death. In response, the defendants denied both the claim that Havva was related to Ayşe and the claim that Ayşe had bequeathed any jewelry to Havva before she died. Again, Havva could not substantiate her allegations, and the court decided against her.[20]

This example indicates that separate processes of adjudication were initiated to resolve disagreements on different issues even when both the litigants and the real cause of contention remained the same.[21] It is noteworthy that the courts were more interested in checking the accuracy of the claims made in the court and determining their legal consequences than they were in dealing with the substantive issues behind these claims. Indeed, in no instance in the *sicil*s does "cleaning up the social mess" appear to be an objective of the court.

The next example is even more interesting:

In Cemaziyelevvel 1069/February 1659, a case was brought to the *na'ib* of Çankırı, Mevlana Şaban Efendi, for legal settlement while he was passing through the village of Törlü. A certain Süleyman,

[19] KCR, vol. 3, 126–49.

[20] KCR, vol. 3, 127–50. Both of these entries were recorded in Rebiʿülahir of 1097 (March 1686) although there might be seven to ten days' difference between them. The first registry is dated "evahir-i Rebiʿülahir" (late Rebiʿülahir), and the second one is dated "evasıt-ı Rebiʿülahir" (mid-Rebiʿülahir). It is probable that the dates in the entries do not indicate when the cases were concluded. There is evidence that the dates of the actual conclusion of a case in the court and the transcription of its account in the *sicil*s could be quite different. The names of the witnesses are identical in both of these entries, which might possibly indicate that both of these cases were indeed heard or resolved in the same day.

an inhabitant of the village, accompanied his wife, Ayşe, and his sister-in-law, Emine, to the presence of the *na'ib* and declared that Emine had been living in his house under his guardianship for five or six years. However, because she could not get along (*hüsn-i zindegane(si) olmayub . . .*) with her sister Ayşe recently, he asked the *na'ib* to appoint the women's brother, Mustafa, as her new guardian and to allow Emine to move into Mustafa's house. Süleyman also asked the *na'ib* to witness and notarize his sister-in-law's statement that she did not have any complaints against him and, in fact, she felt grateful to him (*benden raziye ve şakire olduğun dahi tahrir edüb yedine hüccet-i şerʿiyye verilmesin taleb ederim dedikte . . .*). When she was asked for her statement, Emine announced that she indeed had no complaints against Süleyman and that she was grateful to him. Yet, she also stated that her sister, Ayşe, had been harassing her by falsely claiming that Emine had been behaving improperly and interacting with Süleyman in ways against the law. (*. . . lakin mezbur Süleyman'ın zevcesi Ayşe kızkarındaşım olup bana zevci Süleyman ile hilaf-ı şerʿi muʿamele ve muʿaşeret eder deyu su'-i halime müteʿallik bazı kelimat eder*). Emine asked the *na'ib* to punish Ayşe for spreading false allegations. After Ayşe denied Emine's accusations, the *na'ib* asked Emine to prove her claims. Emine could not produce any evidence, and the *na'ib* acquitted Ayşe after making her take an oath to legally verify her prior testimony that she did not harass Emine or spread any allegations against her.[22]

One of the most interesting points regarding this case is its vagueness in terms of the nature of the real problem among Süleyman, Ayşe, and Emine. Although it is obvious that there was some sort of conflict between the sisters, the nature of this conflict is not stated clearly. Possibly, Emine's report of Ayşe's accusations referred to specific actions of sexual transgression although the entry is extremely, and perhaps deliberately, vague about this point. More important, perhaps, is the fact that we get no indication from the entry that the *na'ib* was interested in the relationships among the parties and

[21] In another example we find a man suing two brothers individually—that is, in separate hearings—for usurping his house and land (in this particular case the dates of the registries as well as the witnesses are identical); see KCR, vol. 5, 133–284 and 133–285. It should be noted, however, that this is not something observed frequently in the *sicils*. The general practice in these kinds of cases is to summon the defendants to the court and adjudicate them all together.

[22] ÇCR, vol. 2, 8–21.

the real source of the conflict: There is no evidence that the *na'ib* attempted to discover why the sisters were unable to get along, nor did he try to question Süleyman regarding the accusations that Emine had reported.

Fortunately, another entry answers at least some of these questions. According to this second entry, Emine came to the court of Çankırı a couple of days after the initial proceeding that had taken place in her village, and claimed that Süleyman had previously had intercourse with her and taken her virginity (. . . *mezbur Süleyman beni tasarruf edüb bikrim izale eylemiştir*). She asked that the court question him and that the requirements of the law be carried out. After Süleyman denied these claims, the court asked Emine to substantiate her allegations. Once again, Emine could not produce any evidence, and consequently, the court acquitted Süleyman after making him take an oath that he had not had intercourse with Emine.[23]

It is possible that Emine did have a sexual relationship with Süleyman and her previous conflict with Ayşe was a consequence of this situation. It is not clear whether or not this relationship was consensual, but if it was, it is also probable that Emine accused Süleyman in the court because he was trying to wash his hands of her, presumably as a result of his wife's pressures. A couple of factors might also have played a role in Emine's decision to turn against Süleyman after the first trial. Upon being removed from Süleyman's house, she might have planned to force him to marry her by publicizing the nature of their relationship.[24] Or perhaps she felt more comfortable confronting Süleyman in Çankırı rather than in front of the inhabitants of her village, where the first trial had taken place.

There are many unanswered questions regarding this case. More important for the concerns of this chapter is the fact that Emine had to approach the court of Çankırı because she was not satisfied with the result of the first hearing. She was not satisfied because *na'ib* Mevlana Şaban Efendi had not resolved the dispute in a manner that would have appeased all parties involved. This kind of a resolution would have necessitated an investigation of the relation-

[23] ÇCR, vol. 2, 9–23.

[24] This would have necessitated that Süleyman divorce Ayşe since according to law a man could not marry a sister of his wife while he was still married to the latter. See Akgündüz, *Mukayeseli İslam ve Osmanlı*, pp. 153–154; Ünal, pp. 154–156; Art, p. 39.

ships among the parties to determine the underlying sources of the conflict. It is clear from these two entries that the legally acknowledged procedures were strictly followed; yet this was hardly adequate for the litigants' conciliation.[25]

These examples do lead the researcher to think that the Ottoman judicial practice conforms to the main premises of the Court Model. However, before characterizing the practice of law in Ottoman courts as a single-mindedly rule-imposed process, it is necessary to take into consideration the fact that certain qualities of the Bargain Model are also identifiable in the operations of the Ottoman courts—even if they are not evident in the court records. For example, and as demonstrated earlier, although legal functionaries (*kadı*, *na'ib*, *katib*, *müfti*, etc.) played important roles in judicial processes, so did many other people who cannot be considered legal experts (such as *a'yan* and military-administrative authorities). Also, and more important, there is evidence that the *kadı*s did not limit themselves to adjudication; they also acted as mediators and arbitrators on various occasions and forced opposing parties to settle their differences amicably. In the case of Hans Ulrich Krafft (chapter six), the objective of the *kadı*'s intervention was not to establish guilt of one party by applying a set of highly regarded norms, or to reach an either/or decision between sides. Instead, and in conformity with the functions of the third parties in the Bargain Model, the *kadı* forced the disputants to reach a compromise with each other. The agreement enacted at the end of this process was based on a utilitarian rationality, which was oriented to maximize everybody's (including the *kadı*'s) interests.

It is true that the court records are usually silent about the identities of those individuals who, while not members of the court, played important roles in the processes of dispute resolution. Nor do these documents display the mediative roles that the *kadı*s and other court functionaries played in their courts. Indeed, what we know about these issues is not based on information in the *sicil*s, but on our observations in other sources (mainly Western accounts of Ottoman justice), which should remind us that what we find in the court records may not always be an accurate representation of the reality. As Najwa al-Qattan insists, court records streamline "unique

[25] See Starr, *Dispute and Settlement*, pp. 256–279, for a similar assessment of court operations in modern-day Turkey.

events of human interaction into formularies" and, therefore, almost certainly discriminate against selective aspects of the processes that took place in the court.[26]

At the same time, it should be emphasized that the court records cannot affirm or deny the possibility that *kadı*s and other members of the court participated in negotiations or that people outside the court played active roles in the proceedings. Silence is not denial; it is likely, for example, that at least some of the amicable settlements in the court records are the products of—and, therefore, muted witnesses to—those processes in which *kadı*s took upon themselves meditative roles. It is unfortunate that the records of these settlements do not inform us about the actual resolution processes, but only about their results.

It is doubtful that either the Court Model or the Bargain Model can accurately portray the ways the Ottoman courts operated, which means that those depictions of Islamic judicial practice that correspond to these models also fail to represent the court processes. For one thing, it would be safer to assume that the processes of dispute resolution in Ottoman courts combined certain characteristics of both models, even when they resembled one model more than the other. For example, the process that Krafft got involved in, which approximates the Bargain Model more than the Court Model, was nevertheless over-determined by the judicial norms and limits of the legal system. Although, in this case, the *kadı* did not have the option of enforcing a resolution through adjudication, he, nevertheless, threatened the Jewish creditors with using his judicial authority to transfer the case to Istanbul, where the Jews would have been alienated from their social networks in Tripoli and the German might have obtained the support of more powerful allies. Likewise, and despite what we *generally* observe in the court records, adjudications in Ottoman courts might have also occasionally exhibited qualities that can be associated with the Bargain Model. Leslie Peirce, for example, claims that in the Antep court in the sixteenth century, the processes of adjudication, although faithful to the established norms, procedures, and regulations as described by Gerber and others, were also shaped by the *kadı*'s concern to appease all the involved parties when and if possible.[27]

---

[26] Al-Qattan, pp. 141–142.
[27] Peirce, p. 324.

More important perhaps, is that a number of scholars have recently demonstrated that "legal pluralism,"—the co-existence of different sites and modes of dispute resolution in a particular social setting—is a reality in many pre-modern, as well as modern, societies.[28] Indeed, chapter nine has argued that many Ottomans were hesitant to bring certain kinds of disputes to the court, and they presumably resolved them in different arenas. There are reasons to assume that a similar kind of "plurality" also characterized the operations of the Ottoman courts. Krafft's case has already demonstrated that when adjudication was not possible, the *kadı* could easily appropriate a different mode of dispute resolution. Traces of such an operational flexibility are also evident in the court records of Çankırı and Kastamonu: It seems probable that the courts took upon themselves a mediative role in the disputes between related parties and pushed them to settle their disputes amicably: This may be why in 57 of the 140 (41 per cent) amicable settlements in the *sicil*s, as far as I can determine, the disputants are related to each other. This ratio is only 16 per cent (80 of the 515 cases) in adjudications. It is also possible that some disputes were more appropriate than others to be resolved through negotiations. Whereas only about 5 per cent of the amicable settlements (7 of 140 cases) were related to disputes that involved some form of violence (murder, rape, bodily injury, etc.), as many as 22 per cent of the adjudications (111 of 515) concerned those disputes that involved violence.

These observations suggest that when the dispute in question took place between related parties, the courts frequently encouraged the parties to settle their differences through negotiations. The same may also have been true when the dispute was deemed not significant enough to compromise the neighborly ties. As Gulliver suggests, encouraging disputants to negotiate settlements must have been one

[28] See, for example, Sally Engle Merry, "Legal Pluralism," *Law and Society Review*, vol. 22, no. 5 (1988), pp. 869–896; Masaji Chiba, "Three Dichotomies of Law in Pluralism," in *Legal Pluralism: Toward a General Theory Through Japanese Legal Culture* (Tokyo: Tokai University Press, 1989), pp. 171–180; Sally Falk Moore, "Law and Social Change: The Semi-Autonomous Social Field as an Appropriate Subject of Study," *Law and Society Review*, vol. 7, no. 4 (1973), pp. 719–749; Leopold Pospisil, "The Structure of a Society and Its Multiple Legal Systems," in Phillip Gulliver ed., *Cross Examinations: Essays in Memory of Max Gluckman* (Leiden: E.J. Brill, 1978); John Comaroff and Simon Roberts, *Rules and Processes: The Cultural Logic of Dispute in an African Context* (Chicago: University of Chicago Press, 1981).

way for the courts to protect communal and kinship ties from breaking down:[29]

> In disputes within multiplex relationships the outcome can of course be decided by an adjudicator, who may, perhaps, try to ensure that careful account is taken of the complexity of the reasons and issues. Yet under adjudication, the disputants and those intimately associated with them, do not necessarily have the opportunities that are available in negotiations to work through that multiplexity and its implications, to learn about their own and each other's interests, expectations and emotions, and to make their adjustments accordingly. Thus negotiators with their associates can arrive at a mutually acceptable accommodation both of the immediate issues and of their ongoing relationships. This is probably more effective than an imposed outcome, however careful, tolerant and empathetic the adjudicator might be.[30]

On the other hand, when disputes involved physical violence and, therefore, in most cases, had already disrupted communal or familial relations, or when the disputants were strangers and therefore had no relationship between them to be compromised, the courts may have had no objections against adjudication.

Obviously, further research is necessary to adequately demonstrate that the Ottoman courts utilized different modes of dispute resolution. And even more research is required to find out how different kinds of disputes were handled by the courts; my findings are impressionistic. Yet, should we be surprised to discover, someday, that the operations of the Ottoman courts were indeed flexible? In other words, how does this flexibility correspond to what we know about Islamic law?

Characterizing "Islamic Law"

At present, not many students of Islamic law seem to be interested in producing a general characterization of this judicial system from

[29] Of course, this does not mean that the preference between settling a dispute through negotiation or adjudication was solely based on the court's discretion; indeed, I cannot deny the possibility that the high rate of amicable settlements among related parties was a consequence of the disputants' own willingness for reconciliation. Nor does it mean that the *kadı* and other members of the court always pushed for negotiation and amicable settlement in such disputes; the *sicil*s contain numerous cases of adjudication that relate to disputes between related parties.

[30] Gulliver, "Process and Decision," p. 43.

a comparative perspective. There are understandable reasons to avoid such a taxonomic attempt: Racial and stagist biases of earlier characterizations are, at least partially, responsible for our aversion to classifying and compartmentalizing. Also, living in the age of post-structural criticism, many of us share a tendency to focus on the particular at the expense of the general; reductionism, unlike the inability to see the big picture, has turned into an offense that we want to avoid at all costs.[31]

Lawrence Rosen is one of the few who makes comparisons among different legal systems and characterizes them in relation to each other. The fact that he is particularly interested in representing the "logic" of Islamic law makes his work relevant to this study.[32] What follows is an overview of what he calls the "Islamic legal regime," and an assessment of whether his observations correspond with how Ottoman court processes are characterized in this book.

Rosen insists that Islamic law's place in the power structure of the society and the way it relates to the local culture distinguish it from civil and reciprocity-based legal regimes.[33] According to Rosen, Islamic law, like Anglo-American law, is a common law system because:

---

[31] In a recent book, Hayden White shares this sensitivity:

"I understand, I think; the desire—after decades of 'star wars' on a grand scale—to abandon theory and get back to the text, back to what Wittgenstein called 'the rough ground,' back to personal experience and attention to the phenomena of everyday life; these cries go up regularly after every era of efforts to envision the whole, whether of culture, society of civilization, history, or being in general. And in such postmodernist times it is understandable why people of goodwill, wanting to do justice to particularities of existence, should turn against totalizing systems of thought which privilege the whole and ignore the parts of life which are to be sacrificed to it. The reaction is in my view, healthy and morally justified.

But it is a mistake to think that theoretical thinking itself is the cause of the ills that an atheoretical or antitheoretical mode of reflection can set right. And this is because that very distinction between a theoretical mode of thought and whatever is conceived to be an alternative to it (empiricism, facts, particularity, the humble, the abject, or the practical) is itself founded on a theoretical or more precisely, a metatheoretical point of view. To think that one can think outside or without theory is a delusion."

See Hayden White, *Figural Realism: Studies in the Mimesis Effect* (Baltimore and London: The Johns Hopkins University Press, 1999), pp. vii–viii.

[32] See especially Lawrence Rosen, "Common Law, Common Culture, Commonsense: An Introduction to Arab Legal Reasoning," *POLAR: Political and Legal Anthropology Review*, no. 2, vol. 19 (1996), pp. 27–32; idem, *The Justice of Islam*, pp. 38–68. The latter study is a significantly longer and more developed version of the former article.

[33] Ibid., p. 46.

1) It disperses social power, and, therefore, reflects the local power relations in its operations, while still retaining ultimate power at the apex.[34] Despite the organizational variations among different Islamic regimes, they all press the issues and disputes down to local venues. The importance of local experts and witnesses in the practice of law, and the lack of appellate structures, according to Rosen, are indications of this power dispersion.[35]

2) It allows "local cultural conceptualizations and information to fill up much of the content of the law through indirectly administered mechanisms of incorporation."[36] Rosen argues that "local custom *is* Islamic law unless it violates Quranic prescriptions."[37] Islamic law acknowledges the importance of social and cultural ideals, and it has thus far been capable of incorporating "constantly moving cultural concepts"[38] into its makeup.[39]

Rosen has been criticized for his tendency to make overly general and a-historical statements in his earlier work.[40] Nevertheless, what is known about the operations of the Ottoman courts is generally consistent with his depiction of Islamic law. In terms of their ability to disperse power at the local level, I have demonstrated that the courts of Çankırı and Kastamonu both tended to reflect the socioeconomic balance among different social groups and, at the

[34] Ibid., p. 48.

[35] Ibid., p. 50.

[36] Ibid., p. 48.

[37] Ibid., p. 53. Emphasis as in the original.

[38] Ibid., pp. 51–53.

[39] In civil law systems, which are generally associated with continental European nations, their former colonies, and those nations that appropriated the codes or regulatory systems of eighteenth- and nineteenth-century European nation-states, power is not dispersed, but concentrated in the hands of the state. Also, Rosen believes that civil law systems are amalgamative and absorptive in regard to the culture: "Culture is subject to reception by the legal system, which receives it . . . reluctantly, if at all. Thus a sharp distinction can be made conceptually between law and custom, the latter having no force unless marked as part of the former, thereby losing its separable identity." Ibid., pp. 55–56.

The reciprocity-based legal systems (such as Hindu and Buddhist law), on the other hand, support social conventions and allow social processes, rather than law, to resolve social tensions. At the same time, legal institutions do not propose a moral order separate from the ideals of larger cosmological order; the processes of dispute resolution merely articulate cultural concepts inscribed in conventional behavior. Ibid., pp. 59–61.

[40] See Martha Mundy, "Between the Oral and the Written," *History Workshop*, vol. 31 (1991), pp. 184–192 and al-Qattan, pp. 88–148 for two comprehensive critiques of Rosen's work.

same time, to enforce the will of the community upon particular individuals. From a cultural perspective, it is clear that the Ottoman courts frequently justified their decisions by referring to local customs and traditions. Abraham Marcus, for example, claims that the courts of Aleppo enforced local customs because they "provided some legislative expression to local interests."[41] Gerber's findings in the *sicils* of Bursa and al-Qattan's analysis of Damascene court records confirm the validity of this observation, as do my findings in the *sicils* of Çankırı and Kastamonu.[42] In this sense the Ottoman legal system did indeed incorporate specific cultural traits and enforced them when appropriate or necessary.

In addition to these correspondences, and if I turn back to my question at the end of the previous section, what makes Rosen's characterization of Islamic law attractive is its compatibility with the seemingly contradictory nature of legal practice in the Ottoman Empire: To put it briefly, according to Rosen what separates Islamic law from many other legal regimes is its ability to retain an identifiable form while accommodating predominant social and cultural pressures.[43] In other words, Islamic law has an ability to exist as an independent ontological entity in spite of its tendency to respond to various social, political, and cultural pressures in practice.[44]

---

[41] Abraham Marcus, *The Middle East on the Eve of Modernity: Aleppo in the Eighteenth Century* (New York: Columbia University Press, 1989), pp. 104–105.

[42] Gerber, "Sharia, Kanun and Custom," p. 145; al-Qattan, pp. 63–76. Also see KCR, vol. 39, 39–64, for an example from the Kastamonu *sicils*. This particular entry reports a dispute between goat-hair spinners and rope makers. The goat-hair spinners claimed in court that the rope makers were supposed to sell their products in the market only two days of the week according to ancient laws and customs (*kanun-u kadim ve örf-ü kavim*), but they had been coming to the market and selling their products every day. At the end of the litigation, the court ordered the rope-makers to act in accordance with the ancient rules and the existing customs. There are other examples of similar situations in the *sicils* of Çankırı and Kastamonu.

[43] Ibid., pp. 49–50.

[44] One cannot help noticing a tension between Rosen's earlier and later contributions. "Islamic justice" defined as a regulated reciprocity does not sound compatible with an understanding that identifies Islamic law as a distinct ontological entity. Indeed, in his previous work, Rosen does not seem to be particularly interested in the processes of adjudication; instead, mediative and conciliatory processes occupy the center of his attention. Consequently, the court's ability to utilize alternative modes of dispute resolution, although consistent with Rosen's depiction of Islamic law as a common law system, is not something that Rosen bore in mind when he was characterizing the ways Moroccan courts functioned in his earlier studies.

If my impression of the Ottoman courts' operational flexibility is indeed accurate, this characterization of Islamic law would be consistent with what our sources reveal: On the one hand, the court records of Çankırı and Kastamonu demonstrate the uniformity and temporal consistency of the legal processes in the Ottoman courts. According to *sicils*, pre-established and well-known judicial rules and procedures generally set the frameworks within which disputes were tackled and resolved. At the same time, the court's ability to bend and stretch these frameworks—as we saw in the case of Krafft and as Peirce demonstrates in her work—and even to choose between alternative modes of dispute resolution in different contexts, must also have given the Ottoman courts some capacity to respond to the extra-judicial pressures and to control the sociopolitical impact of their own operations.

It should be acknowledged that taxonomies have a limited ability to characterize the particular. Rosen's description of Islamic law is no exception to this rule, as it can provide only a partial understanding of legal practices in a particular setting and of the exact roles that specific courts played in the processes of dispute resolution. And although Islamic courts, in general, might have been concerned about the social and cultural—as well as legal—impacts of their operations, it is also true that the Ottoman courts had certain distinguishing particularities, shaped by the historical contexts in which they operated. The unique role courts played in the Ottoman administrative structure, their intermediary position between the center and the local, the nature of the relationships that existed between the court officials and other provincial authorities, and the existence of alternative sites for dispute resolution at the local level, must all have complicated the ways in which these courts administered justice.

Furthermore, Rosen's characterization of Islamic law fails fully to satisfy our curiosity about many issues related to the processes of dispute resolution. For example, this characterization does not help us to understand the ways the litigants utilized the courts, what litigation strategies the litigants commonly employed, and how the community perceived the courts and their operations. As I have tried to demonstrate in this book, these questions can only be answered historically—that is, with reference to those circumstances (including, but not limited to, the power balance between the litigants, the nature of their contentions, their ability to play the legal game successfully) that actually existed in a particular time and a particular place.

That is why we need more studies that pay attention to the historical contexts in Ottoman legal history. It seems plausible that we will become increasingly hesitant about making generalizations about "Ottoman courts" as more and more such studies appear. There are already a number of legitimate reasons to be hesitant: Gerber, for example, recognizes certain important distinctions in the ways particular courts practiced law in different parts of the Ottoman Empire.[45] I have also shown in a previous chapter that the functions and responsibilities of the courts in Çankırı and Kastamonu were quite different from each other in the seventeenth and the eighteenth centuries. In this sense, al-Qattan is of course right to assert that scholarly attempts at generalization undermine the "interplay between structure and history," that is, between the legal regime and the historical context in which this regime operated.[46]

Nevertheless, we also have to acknowledge that the emphasis on the interplay between structure/doctrine and history/practice sanctions the very taxonomic attempts that al-Qattan criticizes in her work as legitimate efforts of academic interest. If we agree with her that "it is the dialectical interplay between [the doctrine and the practice] that accounts for the authority that legal practice procures," how can we disregard those scholarly endeavors that seek to formulate doctrinal representations (even to criticize or discard them)? In this sense, taxonomic approaches to Islamic law are necessary. We need them because it is the tension that these attempts generate when they meet with our observations of the particular that seduces many of us intellectually, and that makes us believe that our observations are original and important. And it is this tension that encourages us to pursue our (historical) studies further.

---

[45] Haim Gerber, *Islamic Law and Culture*, p. 44.
[46] Al-Qattan, p. 135.

EPILOGUE

We still do not know much about the social, political, and judicial functions of the Ottoman courts, or about the exact nature of the relationship that existed between them and the communities in which they operated. In this book, I have attempted to come up with some new questions regarding the practice of law and the processes of dispute resolution in the Ottoman Empire and suggest various techniques of analysis that may help us to better interpret what we observe in the court records and other sources. Nevertheless, I do not claim here to have developed a definitive analysis of the judicial operations of the Ottoman courts in Anatolia or of their socio-political impact upon the provincial society. Such an objective could only be achieved through a long-term collaboration of those scholars who specialize in different regions and periods.

Admittedly, many of my conclusions are tentative. Notwithstanding their great historical value and still largely unexplored potential, the court records were not produced to serve as historical sources. While they provide information about how litigants brought their disputes to the courts and how these disputes were resolved in these sites, court records also hide many important details of these processes. For this reason, this book can be characterizes as a product of negotiation with the court records: It takes what they offer and tries to make sense of this information with the help of other sources available to us—namely, the Western accounts of Ottoman administration of justice. The result is not a systematic or comprehensive investigation of judicial and administrative processes that took place in the courts, but a selective and speculative representation of bygone experiences: Many important questions about the processes of litigation and dispute resolution remain untouched in this book, and a number of those that are being investigated remain in need of further elaboration.

This being said, I should also emphasize that attempting to make sense of the court records is an exciting process. This is not only because they contain layers of information, as evidenced by the fact that "case-study-based" investigative approaches occasionally produce different results than the "holistic" ones, but also that every collection of court records seem to produce a unique, if partial, characterization of the "historical," which may explain why those historians who study different collections of court records disagree frequently about the practice of Islamic law in the Ottoman Empire. Although the original function of the court records is to classify the past events and realities, and to reduce them to their judicial-administrative common denominators, they cannot help reflecting, at least to some degree, the color and variety of life: These documents are filled with surprises, contradictions, and unexpected encounters.

So, what have we learned from our sources regarding provincial courts, their judicial-administrative operations, and the processes that took place in their arenas? One thing that I proposed early is that dramatic variations could exist among individual courts in terms of their functions and responsibilities. Indeed, my sources indicate that there was a significant difference in notarial and administrative workloads between the Çankırı and Kastamonu courts relative to the magnitude of their judicial operations. There is no way to be sure about the reasons for this disparity, but my observations suggest that the people of Çankırı and Kastamonu utilized their courts very differently, which is, of course, a consequence of the multifunctional character of the Ottoman courts. Even in the matter of legal contentions, litigants could choose to have local courts resolve their differences with their opponents or demand the courts to direct their cases to the provincial and imperial centers. Local conditions and the balance of power between the disputants must have played a role in this choice.

Another important argument of this book is that the operations of the provincial courts reflected the social, economic, and political balance of power among different classes in their localities. In addition to those individuals who initiated court proceedings, the rich and the socially prominent parties usually won the cases in the court. Furthermore, we also observed that court usage in Çankırı and Kastamonu was financially burdensome, which made it relatively difficult for those at the lower echelons of the society to utilize the courts frequently. These findings indicate that local courts did not exist in a social vacuum, but assumed the socioeconomic and political characteristics of their environments. They were very much part of the provincial order, and their operations, in general, contributed to its maintenance.

My examinations of individual cases both corroborate and modify these conclusions. On the one hand, there is evidence that the court officials were susceptible to external pressures: The allegations of bribery, coercion, and corruption are too numerous in both court records and the Western accounts to ignore, and it is only natural to assume that it was the wealthy and influential parties who benefited most from these "irregularities." On the other hand, we should resist the temptation to depict the court operations in simplistic terms. Indeed, I demonstrated that there existed legal mechanisms through which weaker parties could overcome the odds against their more powerful opponents. Social networks, communal solidarity among the common people, and an insider's knowledge of law, which seems to be shared by a significant portion of the provincial society, gave some leverage to the weak.

It should also be emphasized that the courts were generally careful not to overstep the legitimate boundaries of the judicial system even when they reinforced the existing inequalities and hierarchies within the provincial society with their decisions and operations. This situation may be explained by a number of reasons: First of all, and as has been pointed out by many historians, it was to the interest of the central government that provincial courts functioned relatively fairly. In order to maintain its basis of political legitimacy, the center made an effort to monitor the operations of the court officials, and it punished who broke the rules too obviously. Furthermore, and following the insights of Pierre Bourdieu, we may suppose that the court officials tried to maintain some sense of self-importance and professional identity by observing the rules of the legal game and forcing their clients to do so as well.[1]

It is probable that the "alternative sites of dispute resolution," further compelled the provincial courts to maintain the image that their operations functioned within the limits of the legal system. The litigants' ability to choose between taking their disputes to their courts or, for example, to local military-administrative authorities, must have

[1] Although, according to Bourdieu, the "juridical field" tends to function in close relation with the existing patterns of domination, it does not simply "consecrate" the established order. Since legal practices are firmly shaped by the established legal codes, judicial traditions, and self-perceptions of the legal professionals, these practices cannot be reduced to actual relations of power within the society. See Pierre Bourdieu, "The Force of Law: Toward a Sociology of the Juridical Field," *The Hastings Law Journal*, vol. 38 (1987), pp. 805–853.

contributed to their independence and forced the courts, which were under constant pressure for funding and for clients, to generate a sense of fairness by observing the well-known procedures of litigation and adjudication. At the same time, and it is important to acknowledge this point in order to avoid seductive idealizations, the concern for communal appeal did not always guarantee justice: The need for local support and legitimacy also occasionally forced the courts to acknowledge and enforce the will of the community over those who were deemed "undesirable," to the extent of ignoring their rights.

Finally, and on a different note, the last chapter showed that there is no easy way to characterize the "ideological commitments" of the Ottoman courts. Although the court records attribute a rule-oriented character to judicial processes, I have also maintained that the courts had the ability to appropriate more socially conciliatory modes of dispute management, when this was deemed necessary. This flexibility is consistent with my claim in this book that the Ottoman courts were responsive to social, political, and cultural pressures in their localities.

APPENDIX

WHERE DID THE COURT CLIENTS COME FROM AND WHY?

It might be interesting to track where the out-of-town clients came from to utilize the court services. The maps in this section reveal those villages and districts around Çankırı and Kastamonu where these clients were identified as residing in the court records. These maps also give us some idea about the distance between these locations and the two towns and about how long the clients had to travel in order to get to the courts. The approximate distance between the clients' villages or districts and the town centers can be calculated with the help of the circles superimposed on the maps. The innermost circles indicate the five-kilometer marks from the town centers. The radii of the subsequent circles are equivalent to ten, fifteen, twenty, and twenty-five kilometers respectively, and they denote two, three, four, and five hours of walking distance to the town centers. Here, I am assuming that an adult can walk approximately five kilometers per hour and there is evidence for the accuracy of this assumption in the court records: For example, ÇCR, vol. 6, 53–92 identifies Korgun, located seventeen or eighteen kilometers northwest of Çankırı according to modern maps, as being four hours' walking distance from the town.

It seems that the out-of-town clientele did not employ the courts of Çankırı and Kastamonu too frequently. As indicated in the second chapter, the district of Çankırı contained about seventy-five villages during the late seventeenth and early eighteenth centuries. In the court records of Çankırı, however, there are only about thirty different villages from which people came to utilize the courts. The situation is less drastic for Kastamonu: between 1684 and 1694, people from fifty different villages came to town to utilize the court services. This number is forty-five villages for the period between 1735 and 1743.[1] Since the district of Kastamonu had about seventy-five

[1] Not all of these villages could be identified on maps A.1, A.2, and A.3.

villages at the turn of the eighteenth century, we can suppose that the court of Kastamonu was probably more popular than the court of Çankırı among out-of-town clients.

Yet, even in Kastamonu, most (75 per cent) villages are named only once in the court records. And there are only ten villages from which people came to the court of Kastamonu three or more times. This information suggests that even the inhabitants of close-by villages frequently preferred to resolve their disputes and arrange their contractual dealings without the intermediacy of the courts.

The maps indicate that many of the out-of-town clients came from locations of "close proximity:"[2] In maps A.1 and A.3, such locations constitute the majority of the observations. Nevertheless, it is also clear that quite a few clients came from more distant places. In fact, we observe in the first four registers of Kastamonu (see map A.2) that between 1684 and 1694 the number of clients who came from distant locations is greater than the number of clients from "close proximity" locations. In particular situations, these people traveled quite long distances—as much as fifty kilometers in certain cases.

If we attempt to identify the reasons that brought people from various distances to Çankırı and Kastamonu, we can make some interesting observations. It seems that when people traveled long distances (over twenty-five kilometers, which would oblige them to spend at least a night in the town), they usually brought criminal disputes (claims of robbery, rape, physical assault, and murder) or contractual arrangements pertaining to criminal matters (amicable settlements among the parties who were involved in criminal disputes, contracts related to blood-money payments, etc.). The relatively few non-criminal cases brought from distant locations involve disagreements on taxation between the inhabitants of a particular locality and their military-administrative officials as well as communal disputes in relation to public matters (such as contentions over the boundaries between neighboring villages, disputes over water rights, etc.). Still fewer disputes involve disagreements over the ownership and usufruct rights of sizable estates. Somewhat more frequent

[2] In the context of this discussion, I define a location of "close proximity" as somewhere that was located within a walking distance of four hours or less. I assume that clients from such locations might have had the opportunity to do their traveling, finish their court activities, and return to their houses in one day.

are contentions over prebendal revenues among the members of the military.

Clients living in close proximity to the towns, however, tended to use the courts very differently: They usually sought assistance for private, non-criminal matters. Hence, it can be concluded that when court use necessitated the investment of a significant amount of time and money, it was usually criminal disputes and contentions related to the interests of the general public that were brought to the court.

It is true that the proximity of the clients' residences to the town centers must have influenced their tendency to use the courts: The maps demonstrate that almost all of those locations where the clients most frequently came from were located fewer than twenty kilometers away from the town centers. Nevertheless, it should also be emphasized that other factors must have played a role in the decision to go to the court. It is apparent in the maps that those places the clients came from were not necessarily the closest locations to town centers. Korgun in map 1, for example, was about seventeen or eighteen kilometers away from Çankırı. Clients from the villages of Has and Kavak had to walk for more than two hours to reach Kastamonu (see map A.3). Also, the finding that there are no clients, or a very few number of them, from much closer locations suggests that the nature of disputes in these places and the ways in which alternative dispute resolution mechanisms operated must also have influenced in the decisions of the individuals who had the option of going to the court.

Finally, it is interesting that we find a number of clients in the records of Çankırı and Kastamonu who came from other districts (*kazas*) even though there were courts in their own districts. For example, Köprülü and Kapaklı were among the villages of the district of Kurşunlu, which was also very close to them (see map A.1). Likewise, Ünür was a village of Toht (see map A.1); Boğdam, Tobrak, and Huruçviran were villages of Araç; Virancik was a village of Taşköprü (see map A.2); Bazergan was a village of Daday (see map A.3), etc.[3] On many occasions we find clients in the courts of Çankırı and Kastamonu who came from the centers (not villages) of other districts. At this point, it is not clear why these people preferred the

[3] Again, not all such places for which we have information could be identified on our maps.

courts in Çankırı and Kastamonu over the courts in their own districts. It is possible that some of them came to Çankırı and Kastamonu because their opponents lived in or somewhere close to these towns, and it was easier for them to arrange for their opponents to be summoned to the court there. However, there is also evidence that many individuals who came to Çankırı and Kastamonu from other districts brought their disputes with people of their own villages or districts. This finding indicates that choosing a court had something to do with the subjective judgments and calculations of the clients, the nature of personal connections they had with court officials in different locations, and the reputations of the courts.

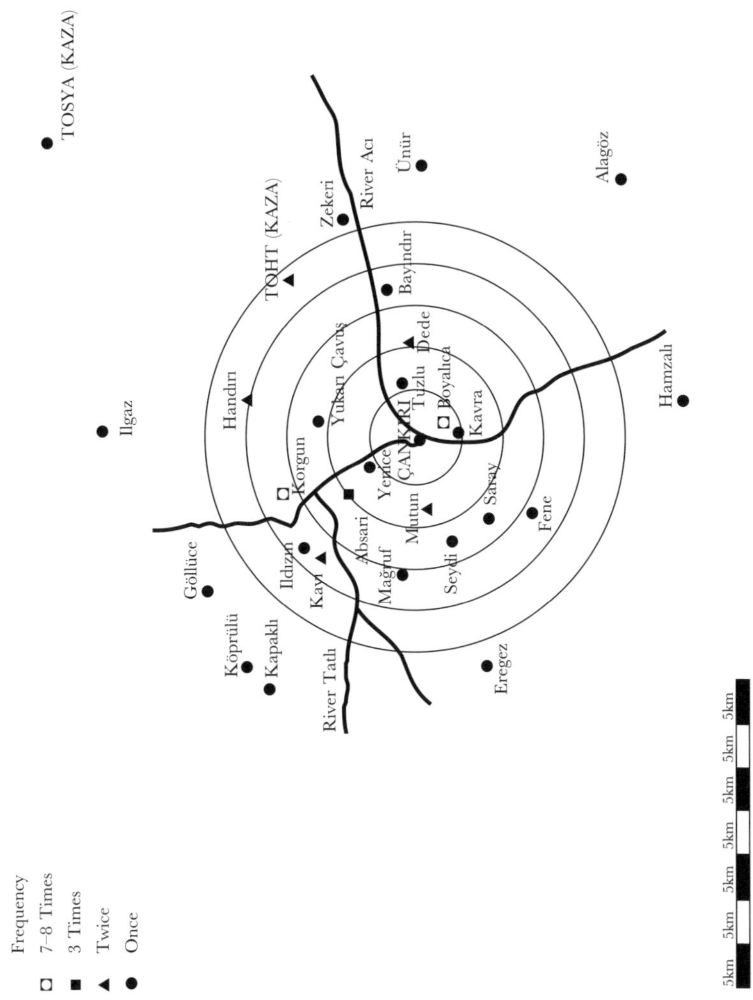

Map A.1: Home Locations of Out-of-Town Clients in Çankırı (1652–1741)

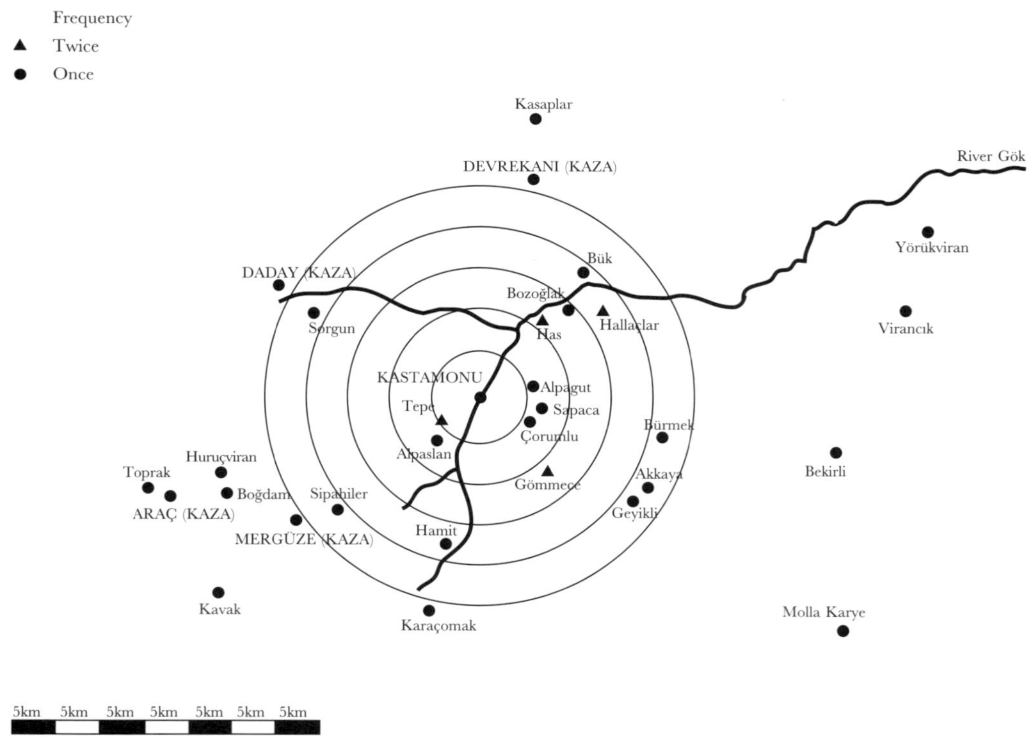

Map A.2: Home Locations of Out-of-Town Clients in Kastamonu (1684–1694)

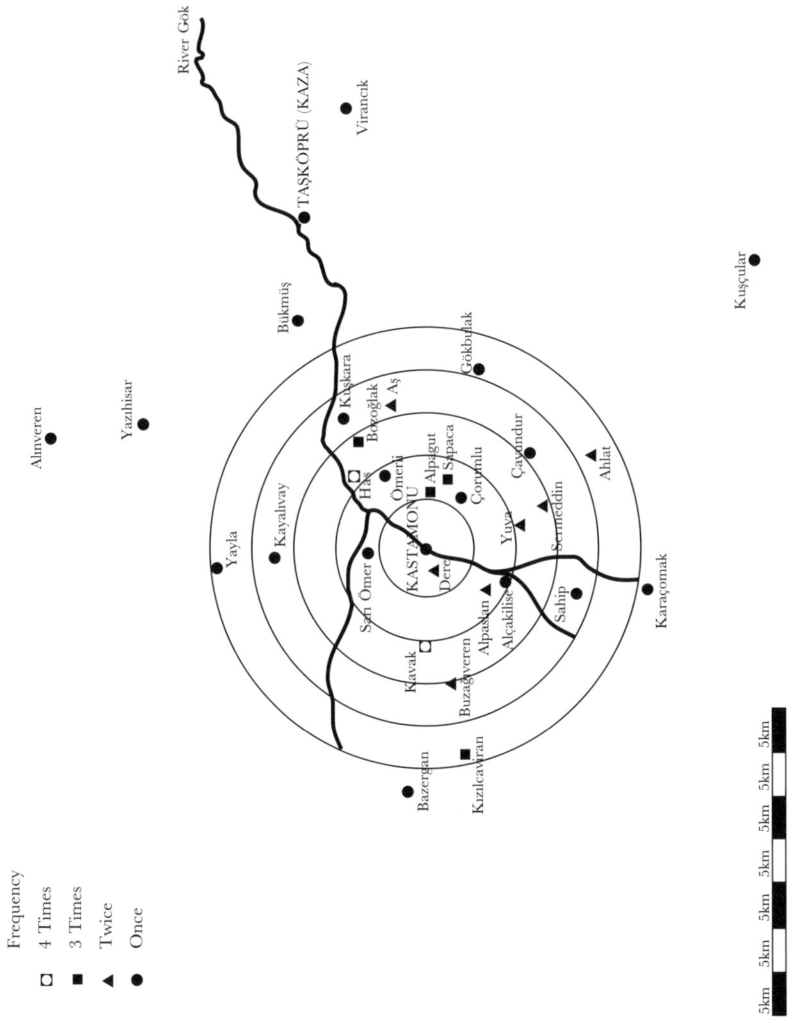

Map A.3: Home Locations of Out-of-Town Clients in Kastamonu (1735–1743)

BIBLIOGRAPHY

Primary Sources

Court Records

Çankırı Court Records (ÇCR): Volumes 1, 2, 3, 4, 5, 6, 7, 8, 9, 10, 11, 12, 13.
Kastamonu Court Records (KCR): Volumes 1, 3, 4, 5, 12, 19, 34, 35, 36, 37, 38, 39.

Prime Ministry Archive Documents

Cevdet Adliye (CA): 96, 121, 188, 192, 196, 197, 251, 272, 294, 306, 512, 533, 564, 591, 646, 762, 824, 902, 934, 1003, 1006, 1014, 1020, 1038, 1052, 1091, 1130, 1164, 1305, 1375, 1414, 1509, 1524, 1534, 1572, 1574, 1585, 1601, 1636, 1648, 1674, 1696, 1775, 1781, 1832, 1842, 1921, 1945, 1981, 2067, 2072, 2095, 2127, 2133, 2236, 2293, 2307, 2309, 2311, 2394, 2409, 2421, 2429, 2466, 2467, 2516, 2606, 2665, 2670, 2711, 2759, 2771, 2783, 2808, 2809, 2948, 2968, 2978, 3051, 3097, 3130, 3144, 3154, 3185, 3222, 3318, 3319, 3444, 3483, 3539, 3634, 3715, 3796, 3797, 3809, 3842, 3840, 3858, 3876, 3891, 3904, 3949, 3951, 3960, 4004, 4025, 4026, 4079, 4080, 4082, 4095, 4111, 4216, 4384, 4393, 4419, 4439, 4458, 4466, 4473, 4475, 4486, 4495, 4525, 4547, 4564, 4582, 4629, 4634, 4654, 4657, 4658, 4715, 4729, 4733, 4735, 4756, 4805, 4808, 4822, 4828, 4832, 4840, 4849, 4851, 4852, 4864, 4901, 5002, 5040, 5072, 5177, 5277, 5312, 5320, 5341, 5476, 5551, 5616, 5663, 5709, 5752, 5805, 5873, 5882, 6007, 6057, 6065, 6080, 6116, 6154, 6163, 6194, 6196, 6197, 6198, 6240, 6268, 6330.
Cevdet Dahiliye (CD): 254, 570, 852, 1062, 1284, 1322, 1345, 1863, 1954, 2701, 3112, 3365, 3573, 3607, 3674, 3675, 3795, 3888, 3916, 4230, 4657, 4714, 4751, 4952, 4881, 5220, 5269, 5883, 6039, 7204, 7272, 9132, 97151, 11809, 12048, 12151, 12569, 12620, 12903, 13019, 13210, 13570, 13707, 14091, 14095, 14150, 14157, 14164, 14280, 14386, 14806, 15142, 15317, 15505, 15653, 15672, 16118, 16539, 16582, 16829.
Cevdet Zabtiye (CZ): 15, 17, 29, 128, 129, 202, 214, 222, 247, 247, 427, 690, 756, 774, 1041, 1179, 1305, 1418, 1478, 1904, 1933, 1941, 1195, 2009, 2156, 2474, 2495, 2517, 2545, 2601, 2622, 2661, 2808, 2850, 2890, 2913, 2933, 3055, 3290, 3291, 3330, 3369, 3546, 3550, 3614, 3737, 3972, 4070, 4172, 4174, 4227, 4237, 4259, 4273, 4307, 4344, 4370, 4400, 4457.

Fiscal Surveys (Tapu-Tahrir Defterleri)

Çankırı: Fiscal Register (*Tapu Defteri*) 81.
Kastamonu: Fiscal Registers (*Tapu Defterleri*) 143, 176, 200.

Contemporary Western Accounts

G.F. Abbott, *Under the Turk in Constantinople. A Record of Sir John Finch's Embassy 1674–1681* (London: Macmillan, 1920).
Ogier Ghislain de Busbecq, *The Turkish Letters of Ogier Ghiselin de Busbecq, Imperial Ambassador at Constantinople, 1554–1562*, translated by Edward Seymour Forster (Oxford: Clarendon Press, 1968).

A.L. Castellan, *Turkey, Being a Description of the Manners, Customs, Dresses, and Other Peculiarities Characteristic of the Inhabitants of the Turkish Empire*, translated by Fr. Shoberl (Philadelphia: H. Cowperthwait, 1829).

William Eton, *A Survey of the Turkish Empire*... 3rd edition (London: T. Cadell & W. Daves, 1801).

Hans Ulrich Krafft, *Türklerin Elinde Bir Alman Tacir*, trans. Turgut Akpınar (Istanbul: İletişim, 1997).

Mouradgea Ignatius D'Ohsson, *Tableau général de l'empire othoman, divisé en deux parties, dont l'une comprend la législation mahométane; l'autre, l'histoire de l'empire othoman*, 7 volumes (Paris: De l'imprimerie de monsieur [Firmin Didot], 1788).

Sir James Porter, *Observations on Religion, Law, Government and Manners of the Turks*, 2nd edition (London: J. Nourse, 1771).

Report on the Manuscripts of Allan George Finch, Esq., Burley-on-the-Hill, Rutland, vol. 1 Historical Manuscripts Commission (London: His Majesty's Stationary Office, 1913).

Sir Thomas Roe, *The Negotiations of Sir Thomas Roe, in his Ebassy to the Ottoman Porte, from the year 1621 to 1628*... (London: Printed by S. Richardson at the expense of the Society for the Encouragement of Learning, 1740).

Baron Francois de Tott, *Memoirs of Baron de Tott; Containing the State of the Turkish Empire and the Crimea During the Late War with Russia*... (London: G.G.J.[?] and J. Robinson, 1785).

John Sanderson, *The Travels of John Sanderson in the Levant, 1584–1602*, edited by William Foster (London: Printed for the Hakluyt Society, 1931).

Secondary Sources

Richard Abel, "A Comparative Theory of Dispute Resolutions in Society," *Law and Society Review*, vol. 8 (1974), pp. 217–347.

Rifaat Abou-El-Haj, *Formation of the Modern State: the Ottoman Empire, Sixteenth to Eighteenth Centuries* (Albany: State University of New York Press, 1991).

Iris Agmon, "Gender and Welfare: The Discourse of the Family and the State in Late Ottoman Shariʿa Court Records," Unpublished Paper, Ben-Gurion University of the Negev (1999).

Mustafa Akdağ, *Türkiye'nin İktisadi ve İctimai Tarihi* (Istanbul: Cem Yayınevi, 1974).

——, *Türk Halkının Dirlik ve Düzenlik Kavgası: Celali İsyanlari* (Ankara: Bilgi Yayınevi, 1975).

Ahmet Akgündüz, *Mukayeseli İslam ve Osmanlı Hukuku Külliyati* (Diyarbakır: Dicle Üniversitesi Hukuk Fakultesi Yayınları, 1986).

——, *İslam Hukukunda Kolelik – Cariyelik Müessesesi ve Osmanlı'da Harem* (Istanbul: Osmanlı Araştırmaları Vakfi Yayınları, 1995).

Şinasi Altundağ, "Osmanlılarda Kadıların Salahiyet ve Vazifeleri Hakkında," *VI. Türk Tarih Kongresi Bildirileri* (Ankara: Türk Tarih Kurumu, 1967), pp. 342–354.

Richard Antoun, "The Islamic Court, the Islamic Judge, and the Accommodation of Traditions: A Jordanian Case Study," *International Journal of Middle East Studies*, vol. 12 (1980), pp. 455–467.

——, "Litigant Strategies in an Islamic Court in Jordan," in Daisy H. Dwyer ed., *Law and Islam in the Middle East* (New York: Bergin & Garvey Publishers, 1990), pp. 35–60.

Gökçen Art, *Şeyhülislam Fetvalarında Kadın ve Cinsellik* (Istanbul: Çiviyazıları, 1996).

Bekir Kemal Ataman, "Ottoman Demographic History (14th–17th Centuries); Some Considerations," *Journal of the Economic and Social History of the Orient*, vol. 35 (1992), pp. 187–198.

Karl Barbir, "The Changing Face of the Ottoman Empire in the Eighteenth Century: Past and Future Scholarship," *Oriente Moderno*, no. 1, vol. 18 (1999), pp. 253–267.

Mikhail Mikhailovic Bakhtin, "Discourse in the Novel," in *The Dialogic Imagination; Four Essays* (Austin: University of Texas Press, 1990), pp. 259–422.

Ömer Lütfi Barkan, "Avarız," *İslam Ansiklopedisi*, vol. 2, pp. 13–19.

——, "Essai sur les données statistiques des registres de recensement dans l'Empire ottoman aux XVe et XVIe siécles," *Journal of the Economic and Social History of the Orient*, vol. 1 (1958), pp. 9–36.

——, "Research on the Ottoman Fiscal Surveys," in M.A. Cook ed., *Studies in the Economic History of the Middle East from the Rise of Islam to the Present Day* (London: Oxford University Press: 1970), pp. 163–171.

Karen Barkey, "The Use of Court Records in the Construction of Village Networks: A Comparative Perspective," *International Journal of Comparative Sociology*, no. 1–2, vol. 32 (1991), pp. 195–216.

——, "Rebellious Alliances: The State and Peasant Unrest in Early Seventeenth-Century France and the Ottoman Empire," *American Sociological Review*, vol. 56 (1991), pp. 699–715.

——, *Bandits and Bureaucrats: the Ottoman Route to State Centralization* (Ithaca, N.Y.: Cornell University Press, 1994).

——, "Networks of Contention: Villages and Regional Structure in the Seventeenth-Century Ottoman Empire," *American Journal of Sociology*, no. 5, vol. 102 (1997), pp. 1345–1382.

J.A. Barnes, "The Politics of Law," in Mary Douglas and Phyllis M. Kaberry (ed.), *Man in Africa* (London: Tavistock Publications, 1969), pp. 99–118.

Tayip Başer, *Dünkü ve Bugünkü Çankırı* (Ankara: İstiklal Matbaası, 1956).

Abdülaziz Bayındır, *İslam Muhakeme Hukuku: Osmanlı Devri Uygulaması* (Istanbul: İslami İlimler Araştırma Vakfi, 1986).

Brandon Beck, *From the Rising of the Sun: English Images of the Ottoman Empire to 1715* (New York: Peter Lang, 1987).

Walter Benjamin, "The Right to Use Force," in *Selected Writings, Volume 1* (Cambridge, Mass.: The Belknap Press of Harvard University Press, 1996), pp. 231–234.

——, "Critique of Violence" in *Selected Writings, Volume 1* (Cambridge, Mass.: The Belknap Press of Harvard University Press, 1996), pp. 236–252.

Kenan Bilici, *Kastamonu'da Türk Devri Mimarisi ve Şehir Dokusunun Gelişimi (18. Yüzyıl Sonuna Kadar)*, Unpublished Ph.D. Dissertation, Ankara Universitesi (1991).

Pierre Bourdieu, *Outline of a Theory of Practice*, trans. Richard Nice (Cambridge: Cambridge University Press, 1977).

——, "The Force of Law: Toward a Sociology of the Juridical Field," *The Hastings Law Journal*, vol. 38 (1987), pp. 805–853.

——, *The Logic of Practice*, trans. Richard Nice (Cambridge: Polity Press, 1990).

René Brunschvig, "ʿAbd," *Encyclopedia of Islam*, 2nd edition, vol. 1, pp. 24–40.

Davis C. Buxbaum, "Some Aspects of Civil Procedure and Practice at the Trial Level in Tanshui and Hsinchu from 1789 to 1895," *Journal of Asian Studies*, no. 2, vol. 30 (1971), pp. 255–279.

Hülya Canbakal, "Legal Practice and Social Hierarchy: The Truth-Bearers of ʿAyntab," presentation given in the workshop *Law and Its Applications in the Ottoman Empire*, Harvard University, 17 April 1998.

Yavuz Cezar, "From Financial Crisis to the Structural Change: The Case of the Ottoman Empire in the Eighteenth Century," *Oriente Moderno*, vol. 18 (1999), pp. 49–54.

Masaji Chiba, "Three Dichotomies of Law in Pluralism," in *Legal Pluralism: Toward a General Theory through Japanese Legal Culture* (Tokyo: Tokai University Press, 1989), pp. 171–180.

James Clifford, *The Predicament of Culture, Twentieth-Century Ethnography, Literature, and Art* (Cambridge: Harvard University Press, 1986).

Amnon Cohen, "Communal Legal Entities in a Muslim Setting, Theory and Practice: The Jewish Community in Sixteenth-Century Jerusalem," *Islamic Law and Society*, no. 1, vol. 3 (1996), pp. 75–87.

Elizabeth Colson, "The Contentiousness of Disputes" in Pat Caplan ed., *Understanding Disputes: The Politics of Argument* (Oxford Providence: Berg Publishers, 1995), pp. 65–82.

John Comaroff and Simon Roberts, *Rules and Processes: The Cultural Logic of Dispute in an African Context* (Chicago: University of Chicago Press, 1981).

Musa Çadırcı, "II. Mahmut Döneminde Mütesellimlik Kurumu," *Ankara Üniversitesi Dil ve Tarih-Coğrafya Fakültesi Dergisi*, vol. XXVIII, nos. 3–4 (1970), pp. 287–96.

"Çankırı," *Yurt Ansiklopedisi*, vol. 3, pp. 1934–2008.

Aslı Çırakman, "From Tyranny to Despotism: The Enlightenment's Unenlightened Image of the Turks," *International Journal of Middle East Studies*, no. 1, vol. 33 (February 2001), pp. 49–68.

Kemal Çiçek, "Osmanlılar Zamanında Kıbrıs'ta Türk Adaleti ve Rumlar," in Kemal Çiçek ve Abdullah Saydam, *Kıbrıs'tan Kafkasya'ya Osmanlı Dünyasında Siyaset, Adalet ve Raiyyet* (Trabzon: Derya Kitabevi, 1998), pp. 67–97.

——, "Osmanlı Devletinde Asayiş ve Emniyet Hizmetleri," in Kemal Çiçek ve Abdullah Saydam, *Kıbrıs'tan Kafkasya'ya Osmanlı Dünyasında Siyaset, Adalet ve Raiyyet* (Trabzon: Derya Kitabevi, 1998), pp. 163–171.

——, "Osmanlı Adliye Teşkilatinda Mahkeme Tercümanları," in Kemal Çiçek ve Abdullah Saydam, *Kıbrıs'tan Kafkasya'ya Osmanlı Dünyasında Siyaset, Adalet ve Raiyyet* (Trabzon: Derya Kitabevi, 1998), pp. 184–195.

Linda Darling, "Review of Rifaat Abou-El-Haj's *Formation of the Modern State*," *International Journal of Middle East Studies*, no. 1, vol. 25 (1993), pp. 118–120.

——, *Revenue-Raising and Legitimacy; Tax Collection and Finance Administration in the Ottoman Empire, 1560–1660* (Leiden: E.J. Brill, 1996).

Daisy H. Dwyer, "Substance and Process: Reappraising the Premises of the Anthropology of Law," *Dialectical Anthropology*, vol. 4 (1979), pp. 309–320.

Dale F. Eickelman, "The Art of Memory: Islamic Knowledge and Its Social Reproduction," *Comparative Studies in Society and History* vol. 20 (1978), pp. 484–516.

Leila Erder and Suraiya Faroqhi, "Population Rise and Fall in Anatolia, 1550–1620," *Middle Eastern Studies*, vol. 15 (1979), pp. 322–345.

Özer Ergenç, *XVI. Yüzyılda Ankara ve Konya* (Ankara: Ankara Enstitüsü Vakfi Yayınları, 1995).

Boğaç Ergene, "On Ottoman Justice: Interpretations in Conflict (1600–1800)," *Islamic Law and Society*, no. 1, vol. 8 (2001), pp. 52–87.

——, "Local Court, Community and Justice in the 17th- and 18th-Century Ottoman Empire," Unpublished Ph.D. Dissertation, Ohio State University (2001).

Kemal Kutgün Eyüpgiller, *Bir Kent Tarihi: Kastamonu* (Istanbul: Eren Yayınları, 1999).

Mohammad Fadel, "Adjudication in the Maliki Madhhab: A Study of Legal Process in Medieval Islamic Law," Unpublished Ph.D. Dissertation, University of Chicago (1995).

Suraiya Faroqhi, "Ankara Çevresindeki Arazi Mülkiyetinin ya da İnsan-Toprak İlişkilerinin Değişimi," in Erdal Yavuz and Ümit Nevzat Uğurel (eds.), *Tarih İçinde Ankara: Eylül 1981 Seminer Bildirileri* (Ankara: ODTÜ Mimarlık Fakültesi Basım İşliği, 1984), pp. 61–88.

——, *Towns and Townsmen of Ottoman Anatolia; Trade, Crafts and Food Production in an Urban Setting, 1520–1650* (Cambridge, London, New York: Cambridge University Press, 1984).

——, "Civilian Society and Political Power in the Ottoman Empire: A Report on Research in Collective Biography (1480–1830)," *International Journal of Middle East Studies*, vol. 17 (1985), pp. 109–117.

——, "Town Officials, Timar-Holders, and Taxation: The Late Sixteenth-Century Crisis as Seen from Çorum," *Turcica*, vol. 18 (1986), pp. 53–82.
——, "Political Activity among Ottoman Taxpayers and the Problem of Sultanic Legitimation (1570–1650)," *Journal of the Economic and Social History of the Orient*, vol. 35 (1992), pp. 1–39.
Clifford Geertz, *Local Knowledge: Further Essays in Interpretative Anthropology* (New York: Basic Books, 1983).
Haim Gerber, "*Sharia, Kanun* and Custom in the Ottoman Law: The Court Records of 17th-Century Bursa," *International Journal of Turkish Studies*, vol. 2 (1981), pp. 131–147.
——, *Economy and Society in an Ottoman City: Bursa, 1600–1700* (Jerusalem: The Hebrew University of Jerusalem, 1988).
——, *State, Society and Law in Islam: Ottoman Law in Comparative Perspective* (Albany: State University of New York Press, 1994).
——, *Islamic Law and Culture 1600–1840* (Leiden: E.J. Brill, 1999).
Eyal Ginio, "The Administration of Criminal Justice in Ottoman Selanik (Salonica) during the Eighteenth Century," *Turcica*, vol. 30 (1998), pp. 185–209.
Max Gluckman, *Politics, Law and Ritual in Tribal Society* (Chicago: Aldine Publishing Company, 1965).
Jack Goody, *Interface between the Written and the Oral* (Cambridge: Cambridge University Press, 1987).
——, *The Power of the Written Tradition* (Washington and London: Smithsonian Institution Press, 2000).
Murray Gordon, *Slavery in the Arab World* (New York: New Amsterdam Press, 1989).
Rossitsa Gradeva, "Orthodox Christians in the Kadı Courts: The Practice of the Sofia Sheriat Court, Seventeenth Century," *Islamic Law and Society*, no. 1, vol. 4 (1997), pp. 37–69.
——, "The Activities of a Kadı Court in Eighteenth-Century Rumeli: The Case of Hacıoğlu Pazarcık," *Oriente Moderno*, no. 1, vol. 18 (1999), pp. 177–190.
Phillip Gulliver, "Process and Decision," in P.H. Gulliver ed., *Cross-Examinations; Essays in Memory of Max Gluckman* (Leiden: E.J. Brill, 1978).
——, *Disputes and Negotiations: A Cross-Cultural Perspective* (New York: Academic Press, 1979).
Ahmet Refik Gür, "Osmanlı İmparatorluğunda Kadılık Müessesesi," Unpublished Ph.D. Dissertation, Istanbul University (1971).
Nelly Hanna, "The Administration of Courts in Ottoman Cairo," in *The State and Its Servants* (Cairo: The American University in Cairo Press, 1995), pp. 44–59.
Jane Hathaway, "The role of the Kızlar Ağası in 17th–18th Century Ottoman Egypt," *Studia Islamica*, vol. 75 (1992), pp. 141–158.
——, *The Politics of Households in Ottoman Egypt: The Rise of the Qazdaglis* (Cambridge, New York: Cambridge University Press, 1997).
Uriel Heyd, "Some Aspects of the Ottoman Fetva," *Bulletin of the Oriental and African Studies*, vol. 32 (1969), pp. 35–56.
——, *Studies in Ottoman Criminal Law*, edited by V.L. Ménage (Oxford: Clarendon Press, 1973).
Colin Heywood, "Kastamonu," *Encyclopedia of Islam*, 2nd edition, vol. 4, pp. 737–739.
Susan F. Hirsch, *Pronouncing and Persevering; Gender and the Discourses of Disputing in an African Islamic Court* (Chicago: The University of Chicago Press, 1998).
Douglas Howard, "The Ottoman *Timar* System and Its Transformation, 1563–1656," Unpublished Ph.D. Dissertation, Indiana University (1987).
Philip Huang, *Civil Justice in China; Representation and Practice in the Qing* (Stanford: Stanford University Press, 1996).
Sally Humpreys, "Law as Discourse," *History and Anthropology*, vol. 1 (1985), pp. 241–264.

Svetlana Ivanova, "Muslim and Christian Women before the *Kadı* Court in Eighteenth Century Rumeli: Marriage Problems," *Oriente Moderno*, no. 1, vol. 18 (1999), pp. 161–176.

Colin Imber, *Ebu's-Su'ud; The Islamic Legal Tradition* (Stanford: Stanford University Press, 1997).

Halil İnalcik, "Mahkama," *Encyclopedia of Islam 2nd edition.*

——, "Bursa'nın XV. Asır Sanayi ve Ticaret Tarihine Dair Vesikalar," *Belleten*, XXIV/93 (1960), pp. 45–102.

——, "The Ruznamçe Registers of the Kadıasker of Rumeli as Preserved in the Istanbul Müftülük Archives," *Turcica*, vol. 20 (1988), pp. 251–275.

——, "Şikayet Hakkı: 'Arz-ı Hal ve 'Arz-ı Mahzar'lar," *Osmanlı Araştırmaları*, vol. 7–8 (1988), pp. 33–45.

Huri İslamoğlu-Inan, *State and Peasant in the Ottoman Empire: Agrarian Power Relations and Regional Economic Development in Ottoman Anatolia during the Sixteenth Century* (Leiden: E.J. Brill, 1994).

Ronald Jennings, "The Office of Vekil (Wakil) in 17th Century Ottoman Sharia Courts," *Studia Islamica*, vol. 42 (1975), pp. 147–169.

Ronald C. Jennings, "*Kadı*, Court, and Legal Procedure in 17th C. Ottoman Kayseri," *Studia Islamica*, vol. 48 (1978), pp. 133–172.

——, "Limitations of the Judicial Powers of Qadi in 17th C. Ottoman Kayseri," *Studia Islamica*, vol. 50 (1979), pp. 151–184.

Baber Johansen, "Casuistry: Between Legal Concept and Social Praxis," *Islamic Law and Society*, no. 2, vol. 2 (1995), pp. 135–156.

——, "Signs as Evidence: The Doctrine of Ibn Taymiyya (1263–1328) and Ibn Qayyim al-Jawziyya (d. 1351) on Proof," *Islamic Law and Society* vol. 9 (2002), pp. 168–193.

Gyula Kaldy-Nagy, "Kadı," *EI*², vol. 4, pp. 373–375.

Mohammad Hashim Kamali, "Appellate Review and Judicial Independence in Islamic Law" in Chibli Mallat ed., *Islam and Public Law: Classical and Contemporary Studies* (Boston: Graham & Trotman Press, 1993), pp. 49–84.

Ahmet Kankal, *Tapu Tahrir Defterlerine Göre 16. Yüzyılda Çankırı Sancağı*, Unpublished Ph.D. Dissertation, Ankara University (1993).

"Kastamonu," *Yurt Ansiklopedisi*, vols. 6–7, pp. 4568–4669.

Hacı Şeyhoğlu Ahmet Kemal, *Çankırı Tarihi* (Çankırı: Çankırı Vilayet Matbaası, 1930).

Adeeb Khalid, *The Politics of Muslim Cultural Reform; Jadidism in Central Asia* (Berkeley: University of California Press, 1998).

Metin Kunt, *The Sultan's Servants; the Provincial Transformation of Ottoman Provincial Government, 1550–1650* (New York: Columbia University Press, 1983).

Aharon Layish, *Women and Islamic Law in a Non-Muslim State* (New Jersey: Transaction Books, 1975).

Bernard Lewis, *Race and Slavery in the Middle East; An Historical Enquiry* (Oxford: Oxford University Press, 1990).

Matthew Lippman, Sean McConville and Mordechai Yerushalmi, *Islamic Criminal Law and Procedure: An Introduction* (New York: Praeger, 1988).

Melissa Macauley, *Social Power and Legal Culture; Litigation Masters in Late Imperial China* (Stanford: Stanford University Press, 1998).

Florencia Mallon, "The Promise and Dilemma of Subaltern Studies: Perspectives from Latin American History," *American Historical Review*, no. 5, vol. 99 (1994), pp. 1491–1515.

Abraham Marcus, *Middle East on the Eve of Modernity: Aleppo in the Eighteenth Century* (New York: Columbia University Press, 1989).

M. Shairul Mashreque and M. Ruhul Amin, "A Study of Traditional Adjudication in Rural Bangladesh," *The Eastern Anthropologist*, no. 2, vol. 48 (1995), pp. 177–184.

Lynn Mather and Barbara Yngvesson, "Language, Audience, and the Transformation of Disputes," *Law and Society Review*, no. 3–4, vol. 15 (1980–81), pp. 775–821.

Bruce McGowan, *Economic Life in Ottoman Europe; Taxation, Trade and the Struggle for Land, 1600–1800* (Cambridge: Cambridge University Press, 1981).

Sally E. Merry, "Going to Court: Strategies of Dispute Management in an American Urban Neighborhood," *Law and Society Review*, 13 (1979), pp. 891–926.

Sally Engle Merry, "Legal Pluralism," *Law and Society Review*, vol. 22, no. 5 (1988), pp. 869–896.

——, "Courts as Performances: Domestic Violence Hearings in a Hawai'i Family Court," in Mindie Lazarus-Black and Susan F. Hirsch (eds.), *Contested States; Law Hegemony and Resistance* (London and N.Y.: Routledge, 1994), pp. 35–58.

Brinkley Messick, "Literacy and the Law: Documents and Document Specialists in Yemen," in Daisy H. Dwyer (ed.), *Law and Islam in the Middle East* (New York: Bergin & Garvey Publishers, 1990), pp. 61–76.

——, *The Calligraphic State; Textual Domination and History in a Muslim Society* (Berkeley: University of California Press, 1993).

İsmail Metin, *Alevilerde Halk Mahkemeleri* (Istanbul: Alev Yayınevi, 1995).

Anton Minkov, "Ottoman *Tapu* Title Deeds in the Eighteenth and Nineteenth Centuries: Origin, Typology and Diplomatics," *Islamic Law and Society*, no. 1, vol. 7 (2000), pp. 65–101.

Sally Falk Moore, "Law and Social Change: The Semi-Autonomous Social Field as an Appropriate Subject of Study," *Law and Society Review*, vol. 7, no. 4 (1973), pp. 719–749.

——, *Law as Process; An Anthropological Approach* (London: Routledge & Kegan Paul, 1978).

J.H. Mordtmann, "Çankırı," *Encyclopedia of Islam*, 2nd edition, vol. 2, pp. 13–14.

Vera Moutafchieva, *Agrarian Relations in the Ottoman Empire in the 15th and 16th Centuries* (New York: Columbia University Press, 1988).

Ahmet Mumcu, *Osmanlı Devletinde Siyaseten Katl* (Ankara: Birey ve Toplum Yayınları, 1973).

——, *Osmanlı Devletinde Rüşvet (Özellikle Adli Rüşvet)* (Ankara: İnkilap Kitabevi, 1985).

Martha Mundy, "Between the Oral and the Written," *History Workshop*, vol. 31 (1991), pp. 184–192.

Mahmut Mutman, "Yasa, Şiddet ve Adalet," *Birikim*, vol. 93–94 (1997), pp. 67–77.

Laura Nader, "Choices in Legal Procedure: Shia Moslem and Mexican Zapotec," *American Anthropologist*, no. 2, vol. 67 (1965), pp. 394–400.

——, "Styles of Court Procedure: To Make the Balance," in Laura Nader ed., *Law in Culture and Society* (Chicago: Aldine Publishing Company, 1969), pp. 69–91.

——, *Harmony Ideology: Justice and Control in a Zapotec Mountain Village* (Stanford: Stanford University Press, 1990).

Yuzo Nagata, *Tarihte Ayanlar: Karaosmanoğulları Üzerine Bir İnceleme* (Ankara: Türk Tarih Kurumu Basımevi, 1997).

Galal H. El-Nahal, *The Judicial Administration of Ottoman Egypt in the Seventeenth Century* (Minneapolis & Chicago: Bibliotheca Islamica, 1979).

İbnürrefik Ahmet Nuri, *Şer'iye Mahkemesinde: Bir Perde Komedi* (Ankara: Hakimiyeti Milliye Matbaası, 1933).

İlber Ortaylı, "Some Observations on the Institution of Qadi in the Ottoman Empire," *Bulgarian Historical Review*, no. 10, vol. 1 (1982), pp. 57–67.

——, *Hukuk ve İdare Adamı Olarak Osmanlı Devletinde Kadı* (Ankara: Turhan Kitabevi, 1994).

Baki Öz, *Aleviliğe İftiralara Cevaplar* (Istanbul: Can Yayınları, 1996).

Rıfat Özdemir, *XIX. Yüzyılın İlk Yarısında Ankara (Fiziki, Demografik, İdari ve Sosyo-Ekonomik Yapısı), 1785–1846* (Ankara: Kültür Bakanlığı Yayınları, 1998).

Mehmet Zeki Pakalın, *Osmanlı Tarih Deyimleri Sözlüğü*, 3 volumes (Istanbul: Milli Eğitim Basımevi, 1972).

Şevket Pamuk, "The Price Revolution in the Ottoman Empire Reconsidered," *International Journal of Middle East Studies*, no. 1, vol. 33 (February 2001), pp. 69–89.

——, *A Monetary History of the Ottoman Empire* (Cambridge: Cambridge University Press, 2000).
Leslie Peirce, "Le dilemme de Fatma: crime sexuel et culture juridique dans une cour ottomane au début des temps modernes," *Annales: Histoire, Sciences Sociales*, vol. 53, no. 2 (1998), pp. 291–318.
——, *Making Justice: Women, Law, and Morality in an Ottoman Court* (Berkeley: University of California Press, forthcoming).
Rudolph Peters, "Islamic and Secular Criminal Law in Nineteenth Century Egypt: The Role and Function of the Qadi," *Islamic Law and Society*, no. 1, vol. 4 (1997), pp. 70–90.
Leopold Pospisil, "The Structure of a Society and Its Multiple Legal Systems," in Phillip Gulliver ed., *Cross Examinations: Essays in Memory of Max Gluckman* (Leiden: E.J. Brill, 1978).
Najwa Al-Qattan, "Dhimmis in the Muslim Court: Documenting Justice in Ottoman Damascus 1775–1860," Unpublished Ph.D. Dissertation, Harvard University (1996).
Abdul-Karim Rafeq, "The Syrian *ʿUlama*, Ottoman Law and Islamic *Sharīʿa*," *Turcica*, vol. 26 (1994), pp. 9–29.
Richard C. Repp, *The Mufti of Istanbul: A Study in the Development of the Ottoman Learned Hierarchy* (London: Ithaca Press, 1986).
Lawrence Rosen, *Bargaining for Reality: The Construction of Social Relations in a Muslim Community* (Chicago: University of Chicago Press, 1984).
——, *The Anthropology of Justice: Law as Culture in Islamic Society* (Cambridge: Cambridge University Press, 1989).
——, "Law and Custom in the Popular Legal Culture of North Africa," *Islamic Law and Society*, no. 2, vol. 2 (1995), pp. 194–208.
——, "Common Law, Common Culture, Commonsense: An Introduction to Arab Legal Reasoning," *POLAR: Political and Legal Anthropology Review*, no. 2, vol. 19 (1996), pp. 27–32.
——, *The Justice of Islam; Comparative Perspectives on Islamic Law and Society* (Oxford, New York: Oxford University Press, 2000).
John Rothenberger, "The Social Dynamics of Dispute Settlement," in Laura Nader and Harry F. Todd (eds.), *The Disputing Process: Law in Ten Societies* (New York: Columbia University Press), pp. 152–180.
Clarence Dana Rouillard, *The Turk in French History, Thought and Literature (1520–1660)* (Paris: Bouvin, 1938).
Deena R. Sadat, "Urban Notables in the Ottoman Empire: The Ayan," Unpublished Ph.D. Dissertation, Rutgers University (1969).
——, "Rumeli Ayanları: The Eighteenth Century," *Journal of Modern History*, no. 3, vol. 44 (1972), pp. 346–363.
——, "Ayan and Ağa: The Transformation of the Bektashi Corps in the Eighteenth Century," *Muslim World*, no. 3, vol. 63 (1973), pp. 206–219.
Yushau Sadiq, "Application of the Islamic Law in Nigeria: A Case Study," *Hamdard Islamicus*, no. 2, vol. 17 (1992), pp. 55–76.
Ariel Salzmann, "An Ancien Regime Revisited: 'Privatization' and Political Economy in the Eighteenth-Century Ottoman Empire," *Politics and Society*, no. 4, vol. 21 (1993), pp. 393–423.
Yvonne J. Seng, "Standing at the gates of Justice: Women in the Law Courts of Early-Sixteenth-Century Üsküdar," in Mindie Lazarus-Black and Susan F. Hirsch (eds.), *Contested States; Law, Hegemony and Resistance* (London and N.Y.: Routledge, 1994), pp. 184–206.
Ezel Kural Shaw and Colin J. Heywood, *English Continental Views of the Ottoman Empire 1500–1800* (Los Angeles: University of California Press, 1972).
Amy Singer, *Palestinian Peasants and Ottoman Officials: Rural Administration around Sixteenth-Century Jerusalem* (Cambridge, New York: Cambridge University Press, 1994).

A(?) Smirnov, "Understanding Justice in an Islamic Context: Some Points of Contrast with Western Theories," *Philosophy East & West*, no. 3, vol. 46 (1996), pp. 337–350.
Tarık Mümtaz Sözengil, *Tarih Boyunca Alevilik* (Istanbul: Çözüm Yayıncılık, 1991).
June Starr, *Dispute and Settlement in Rural Turkey: An Ethnography of Law* (Leiden: E.J. Brill, 1978).
Cemal Şener, *Alevi Törenleri* (Istanbul: Anadolu Matbaası, 1991).
Işık Tamdoğan-Abel, "L'écrit comme échec de l'oral? L'oralité des engagements et des règlements à travers les registres de cadis d'Adana au XVIIIe siècle," *Revue du Monde Musulman et de la Méditerranée*, vol. 75–76 (1995), pp. 155–165.
"Tevki'i Abdurrahman Paşa Kanunnamesi," *Milli Tetebbu'lar Mecmu'ası*, no. 3 (1331/1913), pp. 497–544.
Harry F. Todd "Status Disputing in a Bavarian Village," *Ethnologia Europaea*, no. 1, vol. 10 (1977/78), pp. 58–75.
Judith Tucker, *In the House of the Law; Gender and Islamic Law in Ottoman Syria and Palestine* (Berkeley: University of California Press, 1998).
Osman Turan, *Selçuklular Zamanında Türkiye; Alp Arslan'dan Osman Gazi'ye (1071–1318)* (Istanbul: Turan Neşriyat Yurdu, 1971).
Victor Turner, "Process, System, and Symbol: A New Anthropological Synthesis," *Daedalus*, no. 3, vol. 106 (1977), pp. 61–80.
Ömer Türkoğlu, *Salnamelerde Çankırı; Kastamonu Vilayeti Salnemelerinde Çankırı (Kengiri) Sancağı (1869–1903)* (Çankırı: Çankırı Valiliği Yayınları, 1999).
İsmail Hakkı Uzunçarşılı, "Naip," *İslam Ansiklopedisi*, vol. 9, pp. 50–52.
——, *Osmanlı Devletinin İlmiye Teşkilatı* (Ankara: Türk Tarih Kurumu Basımevi, 1965).
——, *Kastamonu Meşahiri* (Ankara: Kastamonu Eğitim Yüksekokulu Yayınları, 1990).
Asife Ünal, *Yahudilik'te, Hıristiyanlık'ta ve İslam'da Evlilik* (Ankara: T.C. Kültür Bakanlığı Yayınları, 1993).
Gilles Veinstein, "İnalcık's Views on the Ottoman Eighteenth Century and the Fiscal Problem," *Oriente Moderno*, no. 1, vol. 18, pp. 1–10.
Jeanette A. Wakin, *The Function of Documents in Islamic Law* (Albany: State University of New York Press, 1972).
Anna Würth, "A Sana'a Court: The Family and the Ability to Negotiate," *Islamic Law and Society*, no. 2, vol. 3 (1995), pp. 320–340.
Hayden White, *Figural Realism: Studies in the Mimesis Effect* (Baltimore and London: The Johns Hopkins University Press, 1999).
Talat Mümtaz Yaman, *Kastamonu Tarihi I (XVinci Asrın Sonlarına Kadar)* (Kastamonu: Ahmed İhsan Matbaası Ltd., 1935).
Hıdır Yıldırım, *Alevi Din ve Ahlak Kültürü* (Istanbul: Yıldırım Yayıncılık, 1999).
Barbara Yngvesson, "Legal Ideology and Community Justice in the Clerk's Office," *Legal Studies Forum*, vol. 9 (1985), pp. 71–89.
——, "Making Law at the Doorway: The Clerk, the Court and the Construction of Community in a New England Town," *Law and Society Review*, vol. 22 (1988), pp. 409–448.
Yaşar Yücel, "XVIII. Yüzyılda Mütesellimlik Müessesesi," *Ankara Üniversitesi Dil ve Tarih-Coğrafya Fakültesi Dergisi*, nos. 3–4, vol. XXVIII (1970), pp. 369–85.
——, *XIII–XV. Yüzyıllar Kuzey-Batı Anadolu Tarihi; Çoban-Oğulları Çandar-Oğulları Beylikleri* (Ankara: Türk Tarih Kurumu, 1980).
Dror Ze'evi, "The Use of Ottoman Shari'a Court Records as a Source for Middle Eastern Social History: A Reappraisal," *Islamic Law and Society*, no. 1, vol. 5 (1998), pp. 35–56.
Farhat J. Ziadeh, "Integrity (*'Adalah*) in Classical Islamic Law," in Nicholas Heer ed. *Islamic Law and Jurisprudence* (Seattle: University of Washington Press, 1990), pp. 73–93.
Madeline Zilfi, *The Politics of Piety: The Ottoman Ulema in the Post Classical Age (1600–1800)* (Minneapolis: Bibliotheca Islamica, 1988).

INDEX

STUDIES IN ISLAMIC LAW AND SOCIETY

Edited by

RUUD PETERS and BERNARD WEISS

ISSN 1384–1130

1. Jackson, S.A. *Islamic Law and the State.* The Constitutional Jurisprudence of Shihāb al-Dīn al-Qarāfī. 1996. ISBN 90 04 10458 5
2. Saeed, A. *Islamic Banking and Interest.* A Study of the Prohibition of Riba and its Contemporary Interpretation. 1996. ISBN 90 04 10565 4
3. Shaham, R. *Family and the Courts in Modern Egypt.* A Study Based on Decisions by the Sharīʿa Courts 1990-1955. 1997. ISBN 90 04 10742 8
4. Melchert, C. *The Formation of the Sunni Schools of Law, 9th-10th Centuries C.E.* 1997. ISBN 90 04 10952 8
5. Khalilieh, H.S. *Islamic Maritime Law.* An Introduction. 1998. ISBN 90 04 10955 2
6. Hoexter, M. *Endowments, Rulers and Community.* Waqf al Ḥaramayn in Ottoman Algiers. 1998. ISBN 90 04 10964 1
7. Johansen, B. *Contingency in a Sacred Law.* Legal and Ethical Norms in the Muslim *Fiqh.* 1999. ISBN 90 04 10603 0
8. Vogel, F. *Islamic Law in the Modern World.* The Legal System of Saudi Arabia. ISBN 90 04 11062 3 *(In preparation)*
9. Gerber, H. *Islamic Law and Culture 1600-1840.* 1999. ISBN 90 04 11939 3
10. Müller, C. *Gerichtspraxis im Stadtstaat Córdoba.* Zum Recht der Gesellschaft in einer mālikitisch-islamischen Rechtstradition des 5./11. Jahrhunderts. 1999. ISBN 90 04 11354 1
11. Leeuwen, R. van. *Waqfs and Urban Structures.* The Case of Ottoman Damascus. 1999. ISBN 90 04 112995
12. Gleave, R. *Inevitable Doubt.* Two Theories of Shīʿī Jurisprudence. 2000. ISBN 90 04 115951

13. Donaldson, W.J. *Sharecropping in the Yemen.* A study in Islamic Theory, Custom and Pragmatism. 2000. ISBN 90 04 11490 4

14. Brockopp, J.E. *Early Mālikī Law.* Ibn ʿAbd al-Ḥakam and his Major Compendium of Jurisprudence. 2000. ISBN 90 04 11628 1

15. Weiss, B.G. (ed.) *Studies in Islamic Legal Theory.* 2001. ISBN 90 04 12066 1

16. Layish, A. and G.R. Warburg. *The Reinstatement of Islamic Law in Sudan under Numayrī.* An Evaluation of a Legal Experiment in the Light of Its Historical Context, Methodology, and Repercussions. 2002. ISBN 90 04 12104 8

17. Ergene, B.A. *Local Court, Provincial Society and Justice in the Ottoman Empire.* Legal Practice and Dispute Resolution in Çankırı and Kastamonu (1652-1744). 2003. ISBN 90 04 12609 0